Handed Down

The Catholic Faith of the Early Christians

JAMES L. PAPANDREA

Handed Down

The Catholic Faith of the
Early Christians

Published by Catholic Answers, Inc.
2020 Gillespie Way
El Cajon, California 92020
1-888-291-8000 orders
619-387-0042 fax
catholic.com

Printed in the United States of America

Cover design by Devin Schadt
Interior design by Sherry Russell

978-1-941663-53-0 hardcover
978-1-941663-54-7 paperback
978-1-941663-55-4 Kindle
978-1-941663-56-1 ePub

*This book is dedicated to the memory of
Innocence G. Vetrano (1922-2012),
and to three generations of the Vetrano family:
living witnesses to God's love and hospitality.*

Contents

Preface

St. Peter wrote to the early followers of Jesus, "Always be ready to give an explanation to anyone who asks you for a reason for your hope" (1 Pet. 3:15). However, many Catholics are not prepared for that conversation, and sometimes they even end up reinforcing myths and mistaken assumptions about Catholicism. By highlighting the consistency between the earliest Christians and the Catholic Church of today, by demonstrating that Catholicism is both rational and ancient, this book will help prepare you to answer the questions posed by your non-Catholic friends and relatives, and to defend and share your Catholic faith.

In the very next verse, of course, Peter adds, "but do it with gentleness and reverence, keeping your conscience clear." So this book is not "ammunition" to be used against fellow Christians. It is not meant to fuel the fire of mistrust, or create more distance between us and our "separated brethren." Rather, it is meant to draw us together into conversation, in the spirit of unity that Christ intended for his universal Church. It is more like food for the journey, as we walk alongside our non-Catholic brothers and sisters.

—*James L. Papandrea*

Introduction

Who Are the Church Fathers, and Why Do They Matter?

All Christians accept that God is active within creation, within and throughout human history. We believe that God's greatest and most significant act in history is the Incarnation—in the conception, birth, life, ministry, death, and resurrection of Jesus Christ. In the person of Jesus, the Divine entered history—and entered humanity—by becoming one of us. For Christians, then, *history matters*. Ours is not a religion based on mythical events that happened in some hazy "time before time," or on the top of Mount Olympus; ours is a religion based on recorded historical events, in which God has revealed to humanity something about himself—definitively in the person of Jesus Christ.

We further believe that Jesus founded a fellowship that he called his Church, and that the men and women who were his first followers, and whom he chose to succeed him in the mission of his Church, were real people who laid the foundation for our religion on their faith in him and his teachings.[1] Any religion is, by definition, conservative. In other words, it "conserves," or preserves, a tradition by handing it on from one generation to the next. Even the apostle Paul admitted that he had received something from the other apostles who had been eyewitnesses of Jesus' ministry.[2] Therefore, Christianity is a *faith tradition* that was founded by Jesus and the apostles, and the mission of the Church is to faithfully hand on what was started by them, in terms of both its teaching and ministry.[3] We may talk about to what extent the Church has succeeded in that mission (it is still a human institution, after all), but we cannot ignore the foundation of our Faith and still call ourselves Christians.

Furthermore, we cannot ignore Jesus' promise that the Church would never completely fail in its mission. In response to Peter's confession of faith in him, Jesus said: "Blessed are you, Simon, son of Jonah. For flesh and blood has not revealed this to you, but my heavenly Father. And so I say to you, you are Peter, and on this rock I will build my church, and the gates of the netherworld shall not prevail against it" (Matt. 16:17–18).[4] In other words, if the Church fails in its mission to faithfully and correctly preserve and pass on the Tradition that Jesus and the apostles founded, then the Church is no longer the Church and hell wins. But Jesus has promised that this will not happen. Could he fail to keep his promise? We say no, and we believe that the Holy Spirit has been active throughout the entire history of the Church to make sure that the gates of hell do not prevail against it.

THE FIRST STEWARDS OF TRADITION

The author of the letter to the Hebrews wrote, "Therefore since we are surrounded by so great a cloud of witnesses, let us rid ourselves of every burden and sin that clings to us and persevere in running the race that lies before us, while keeping our eyes fixed on Jesus, the leader and perfecter of faith" (Heb. 12:1–2). "Cloud of witnesses" is a way of talking about the "communion of saints," which includes all Christians who have ever lived. It means that in a way, all those who went before us in the Faith— indeed all those who participated in handing on the Faith to us—are cheering us on in this marathon that is the Christian journey. They are our ancestors in the Faith—all those who lived (and many who died) to give it to us.

Of course, most of those people didn't write books or documents that we can read today, or leave any other tangible legacy. But some did. And the earliest of these we call the Fathers of the Church.

The Fathers were not simply theologians speculating in ancient ivory towers. They were pastors, preachers, and teachers, often more concerned with instructing and guiding the people of their churches than writing for fellow scholars.[5] In fact, when it came to teaching the laity, they were usually more interested in how to *live* as a Christian than how to *think* as a Christian. Of course, they did write books on theology—a lot of them—and we are blessed by that gift because in those books they interpret and help us understand the meaning of God's revelation, especially in Scripture.

The successors of the apostles are the bishops of the Church, and many of the first bishops were handpicked by the apostles themselves.[6] But not all the Church Fathers were bishops. Some were lay catechists and theologians. Others were priests, but not bishops. These theologians supported the work of the bishops and submitted their own work to the bishops for the Church's official affirmation. (On the other hand, not all bishops can be considered Fathers of the Church, since some of them deviated from the apostolic Tradition and became heretics, teaching alternative theologies that led the laity astray and caused division within the Church.) Together these Fathers of the Church—the early bishops, along with other theologians—passed the faith-tradition from one generation to the next.

We can see this beginning with Peter himself, in the last chapter of the Gospel of John. There, as Peter is reconciled to Jesus after denying him, Jesus tells him to feed and tend his sheep (John 21:15–17).[7] Clearly, it was Jesus' intention that Peter and the other disciples take over for him when he was gone, and continue what he started. Furthermore, after Jesus gave Peter his new name in the verses quoted above, he went on to say, "I will give you the keys to the kingdom of heaven. Whatever you bind on earth shall be bound in heaven; and whatever you loose on earth shall be loosed in heaven" (Matt. 16:19). This concept of the *keys* comes from the Old Testament. In Isaiah, chapter 22, we read of the "key of the house of David"—a reference to the authority of the king's steward, who ran the royal household when the king was away, and even acted as the king's representative with the king's authority. When a king died and the throne

was vacant, the royal steward kept the lights on, so to speak, and
functioned as a kind of viceroy. If the steward died before a new
king was crowned, the keys—that is, the authority of the office—were passed on to a successor, and the office continued until the throne was no longer vacant. In the Church, the apostles
(and then their successors, the bishops), are the stewards of the
kingdom on earth until the King returns.[8]

Therefore the early Fathers of the Church are those who received what was handed on to them from Jesus and the apostles,
and faithfully transmitted it to the Christians of their day—and
through their writings, to the Christians of future generations. We
will meet several of these writers as we explore the beliefs and
practices of Catholicism, and we will see how what they taught has
been preserved in the Catholic Church down to the present day.

What Did the Church Fathers Say About Themselves?

Each of the chapters in this book will have a section on what the
Fathers of the Church taught about a given subject. But before
we can get to that, we have to ask: what did they teach about
their own authority? The most relevant teaching for our purposes here is a concept called *apostolic succession*. I've already in-
troduced it to you, in a way: the first bishops of the Church were
the successors of the apostles, and they carried on the apostles'
ministry and teachings. This assumes that through the commissioning, consecration, and ordination of Church leaders,
the anointing of the Holy Spirit was also passed down to the
next generation. Furthermore, apostolic succession affirms that
Christian truths were accurately transmitted within the Church,
so that the teachings of any Church authority at any time could
be traced back in an unbroken chain to the apostles, and through
them to Jesus himself. You knew you could trust the teachings
of your bishop because he would have gotten his teachings from
his predecessor, and so on, going all the way back to Christ.

To be sure, as we have already noted, some bishops did deviate from what they had received, and to that extent they are

considered heretics. But that's the point. When they were faithful to the Tradition, their teachings were trustworthy. So this is not to claim that there was never dissent or disagreement in the early Church—indeed there was, and it was precisely this disagreement that led to the discussion of theological concepts, and eventually to authoritative decisions about how to understand the person and work of Jesus Christ, and how to interpret Scripture. Eventually the debates led to councils of bishops, the successors of the apostles gathering to clarify the correct interpretations of Jesus' intentions for the Church and of the apostolic writings. These conclusions of the early Church Fathers and the councils of bishops were confirmed as the dogmas of Christianity—the theological positions that were consistent with the conclusions of the previous generations, going all the way back to the apostles.

Let's meet just a few of the early Church Fathers, and see what they said about apostolic authority and succession.

St. Clement, Bishop of Rome (writing c. A.D. 93)

As the fourth bishop of Rome, Clement wrote a letter to the church in the city of Corinth, Greece. We know this letter as *First Clement*, though we have no other certain letters from this bishop. What is remarkable about this letter is that Clement writes with authority over the Christians in another city where he was not the bishop. His authority comes from his assumption that he holds an office in which he is the successor of Peter, the leader of the apostles. And even though the Church in Corinth could claim that its own apostolic succession goes back to the apostle Paul, Clement's letter presumes that Peter's authority is greater. We will examine the role of the bishop of Rome (the pope) in the chapter on the papacy, but for now, here is what Clement says about succession:

> The apostles have preached the gospel to us from the Lord Jesus Christ; Jesus Christ has done so from God. Christ

therefore was sent forth by God, and the apostles by Christ.
Both these appointments, then, were made in an orderly
way, according to the will of God . . . And thus preaching
through countries and cities, they appointed the first-fruits
of their labors, having first proved them by the Spirit, to be
bishops and deacons of those who should afterwards believe
. . . they appointed those already mentioned, and afterwards
gave instructions, that when these should fall asleep, other
approved men should succeed them in their ministry.[9]

Therefore it is right for us, having studied so many and
such great examples, to bow the neck and, adopting the attitude of obedience, to submit to those who are the leaders of
our souls . . . For you will give us great joy and gladness if you
obey what we have written through the Holy Spirit.[10]

Notice how in these passages Clement claims the authority of
an apostle for himself, and even implies that this affords him a
kind of inspiration. This assumes that the anointing of the Holy
Spirit is on him by virtue of his office, and thus the audience of
his letter should listen to him as though it were Peter himself
who sent it. Here we have an indication of one of the early successors of the apostles writing with apostolic authority.

St. Ignatius, Bishop of Antioch (c. A.D. 108)

As bishop of Antioch in Syria, Ignatius was concerned that some
people in his region were teaching a view of Christ that was
not consistent with Scripture. They were trying to attract faithful Christians away from the Church and were having separate,
unauthorized meetings. To deal with this, Ignatius wrote of the
role of the bishop—the office of the Church that was charged
with maintaining the Church's unity by clarifying its doctrine
and enforcing its discipline. In other words, Ignatius knew that
without the authority of the bishops, and the limitation of one
bishop per city, the Church would face division. He called himself "a man set on unity," and to that end he wrote:

I have this advice: Be eager to do everything in godly harmony, the bishop presiding in the place of God, and the priests in the place of the council of the apostles and the deacons, who are especially dear to me, since they have been entrusted with the ministry of Jesus Christ . . . Let there be nothing among you that is capable of dividing you, but be united with the bishop . . . Therefore as the Lord did nothing without the Father, either by himself or through the apostles (for he was united with him), so you must not do anything without the bishop and the priests. Do not attempt to convince yourselves that anything done apart from the others is right, but, gathering together, let there be one prayer, one petition, one mind, one hope.[11]

Let everyone respect the deacons as Jesus Christ, just as they should respect the bishop, who is a model of the Father, and the priests as God's council and as the band of the apostles. Without these, no group can be called a church.[12]

For all those who belong to God and Jesus Christ are with the bishop, and all those who repent and enter into the unity of the Church will belong to God, so that they may be living in accordance with Jesus Christ. Do not be misled, my brothers and sisters: if any follow a schismatic [someone who causes division in the Church] they will not inherit the kingdom of God. If any hold to heretical views, they disassociate themselves from the passion. Take care, therefore, to participate in the one Eucharist (for there is one flesh of our Lord Jesus Christ, and one cup that leads to unity through his blood; there is one altar, just as there is one bishop, together with the council of priests and the deacons, my fellow servants), in order that whatever you do, you do in accordance with God.[13]

For Ignatius, the importance of the office of bishop was not for the sake of control, but for the sake of unity. He knew that the very integrity of the Christian religion was at stake, since it was not even a century old and already threatening to fall into factions. If there were more than one bishop per city, and if they should disagree, Ignatius knew that they would then be forcing every Christian in that city to choose between them—a choice the average lay person was not prepared to make. Therefore, unity requires a singular bishop as leader of a region. And the authority of that bishop must be granted to him by a previous recognized authority, otherwise he has no right to speak for the Church or lead the Christian people.

Ignatius is the first author we know of to use the word *catholic* to describe the Church.[14] As you may know, the term originally meant something like "universal," as in *the universal Church*. However, even at this early stage, Ignatius is using it to distinguish the Church whose leaders are in succession from the apostles from those who would claim to speak for Jesus but have a different interpretation of his person and teachings. For Ignatius, "catholic" means the one, unified, worldwide Church that stands within the Tradition of the apostles and whose leaders are the successors of the apostles. Those who stand apart from those bishops and their apostolic teachings are, by definition, not "catholic."

St. Irenaeus, Bishop of Lyons (c. A.D. 185)

Bishop Irenaeus wrote a document that we refer to as *Against Heresies*, in which he described the beliefs of the Gnostics: a pagan-influenced sect on the fringes of the Church.[15] Since these Gnostics disagreed with the Christian bishops and teachers on the nature of Christ and his salvation, it is understandable that the subject of authority would come up. How was Irenaeus to reassure his flock that the received tradition was the correct interpretation of Jesus Christ, and not the teachings of the Gnostics? Writing about the belief in one God, as opposed to many, Irenaeus argued that such a belief was evident in creation. But moreover:

> The universal Church . . . through the whole world, has received this Tradition from the apostles.[16]

It is within the power of all, therefore, in every church, who may wish to see the truth, to contemplate clearly the

Tradition of the apostles manifested throughout the whole world; and we are in a position to reckon up those who were by the apostles instituted bishops in the churches, and the succession of these men to our own times, those who neither taught nor knew of anything like what these [Gnostics] rave about. For if the apostles had known hidden mysteries, which they were in the habit of imparting to "the perfect" apart and privately from the rest, they would have delivered them especially to those to whom they were also committing the churches themselves. For they were desirous that these men should be very perfect and blameless in all things, whom also they were leaving behind as their successors, delivering up their own place of government to these men; which men, if they discharged their functions honestly, would be a great boon, but if they should fall away, the direst calamity. Since, however, it would be very tedious, in such a volume as this, to reckon up the successions of all the churches, we do put to confusion all those who, in whatever manner, whether by an evil self-pleasing, by vainglory, or by blindness and perverse opinion, assemble in unauthorized meetings, by indicating that Tradition derived from the apostles, of the very great, the very ancient, and universally known Church founded and organized at Rome by the two most glorious apostles, Peter and Paul; as also the faith preached to men, which comes down to our time by means of the successions of the bishops.[17]

Here Irenaeus is responding to the Gnostics' claim that they have "secret knowledge"—teachings of Jesus that the bishops don't know about. Irenaeus proves that this cannot be true with the doctrine of apostolic succession. He argues that anything Jesus taught would have been passed down from the apostles to the bishops, of which Irenaeus was one. In effect, he was saying, "If there was secret knowledge, I would know about it, because I'm a bishop, and the bishops are the successors of the apostles." In fact, Irenaeus tells us that he was a student of the bishop Polycarp of Smyrna, who "always taught the things which he had learned from the apostles, and which the Church has handed down, and which alone are true."[18] Later in *Against Heresies*, Irenaeus has more to say about apostolic succession:

> Suppose there arise a dispute relative to some important question among us, should we not have recourse to the most ancient churches with which the apostles held constant intercourse, and learn from them what is certain and clear in regard to the present question? For how should it be if the apostles themselves had not left us writings? Would it not be necessary, to follow the course of the Tradition which they handed down to those to whom they did commit the churches?[19]

Here Irenaeus is writing only a century after the time of the apostles, and he is still concerned to know the teachings of "the most ancient churches," since he assumes that such teaching is the most trustworthy.

Tertullian,[20] *lay teacher of Carthage (c. A.D. 210)*

Tertullian was a North African who may have traveled to Rome, and who may have at one time been an ordained priest. However, he writes as a lay teacher—and as one of the most important theologians of the early Church—and he follows Irenaeus's lead in assuming that the most trustworthy teachings are the ones that originated with Jesus and the apostles and were handed down through the generations by the bishops of the Church. Tertullian knows that any such teaching must have roots in Scripture; however, the problem is that people can disagree on the interpretation of Scripture, even when they are reading the same passages. So he argues that only those in the line of apostolic succession have the right to interpret the scriptures:

> But even if a discussion from the scriptures should not turn out in such a way as to place both sides on a par, the natural order of things would require that this point should be first

proposed, which is now the only one which we must dis-
cuss: With whom lies that very faith to which the scriptures
belong? From what and through whom, and when, and to
whom, has been handed down that rule, by which men become Christians? For wherever it shall be manifest that the
true Christian rule and faith shall be, there will likewise be
the true scriptures and expositions thereof . . . [the apostles]
then in like manner founded churches in every city, from
which all the other churches, one after another, derived the
Tradition of the Faith, and the seeds of doctrine, and are every
day deriving them, that they may become churches. Indeed,
it is on this account only that they will be able to deem themselves apostolic, as being the offspring of apostolic churches
. . . Therefore the churches, although they are so many and
so great, comprise but the one primitive church, (founded)
by the apostles, from which they all (spring). In this way all
are primitive, and all are apostolic, whilst they are all proved
to be one, in (unbroken) unity . . . If, then, these things are
so, it is in the same degree manifest that all doctrine which
agrees with the apostolic churches—those molds and original
sources of the Faith—must be reckoned for truth, as undoubtedly containing that which the churches received from the
apostles, the apostles from Christ, Christ from God.[21]

Tertullian goes on to affirm that the Holy Spirit guarantees the
correct interpretation of Scripture within the Church, in fulfillment of Jesus' promise that the gates of hell will not prevail against
it.[22] He further argues that those who are not in succession from
the apostles have no right to interpret the scriptures, since they do
not have the benefit of the Church's teaching and interpretations
from the time of the apostles to their own day. They have broken
the chain, as it were, and are attempting to teach without the benefit of having had a teacher. In a sense, since the apostles are the
authors of Scripture (that is, the New Testament), therefore they
are the owners of Scripture, and they have willed Scripture to their
successors. No one else, says Tertullian, has any claim to them.[23]

~

Apostolic succession is based on the reality that religious truth must be preserved over time—it has a source, and must be handed on from that source in order for it to be faithfully transmitted to future generations. For Christians, our source is Jesus Christ. He handed on divine truth to his apostles, and they handed it on to the next generation of Christians who did not know Jesus personally. One of the ways that they handed on Jesus' teachings was by writing the New Testament, and that will be the subject of the next chapter. But that is not the only way that the apostles taught. They also directly taught their own disciples, who then became their chosen successors and the first bishops. These, in turn, taught the next generation of Church leaders, and so on. What this means is that we are connected to Jesus and the apostles through the Fathers of the Church. Let me say that again: It is the Fathers of the Church who connect our faith to that of the apostles and to Jesus.

Therefore, the Church Fathers are in a way the protectors and guarantors of truth. They matter because without them, disagreements over the interpretation of Scripture would escalate to division—a reality that has plagued the Protestant world since the Reformation. So the unity of the Church is not something we can think of in terms of the present day only. The unity of the Church also requires unity with its history—we must be connected to our collective past in order to be connected to each other, and to be part of the communion of saints, that "great cloud of witnesses."

Featured Father

Clement of Rome: Slave and Bishop

The historical record of the early years of Christianity in Rome has some gaps in it. We know that the apostles Paul and Peter were martyred in Rome in the mid-sixties of the first century, and their tombs are there to this day. We also know that Clement was bishop of Rome when he wrote his letter to the Corinthians in the early nineties. But the thirty years in between are somewhat hazy. Official lists of the bishops of Rome (the popes) list Peter as the first, then someone named Linus, and then someone named Anacletus (or Cletus). Fourth on the list is Clement. However, some sources say that Clement was the third bishop of Rome, either conflating Linus and Anacletus into one person, or implying that Anacletus is actually the same as Bishop Anicetus, who lived in the second century. Other sources seem to imply that Clement was the second bishop of Rome, right after Peter. Some of these sources even say that Clement was ordained by Peter himself, and that Clement became bishop when Peter died, in the sixties.

Most likely, Clement became bishop of Rome in the year A.D. 88 (more than twenty years after the death of Peter), and held that office until he was sent into exile in 97. He probably knew both Peter and Paul during their time in Rome, and he is considered one of Peter's disciples, which is probably the reason why some said he was ordained by Peter. In fact, Paul mentions a Clement in his letter to the Philippians (4:3), though we cannot know if he is referring to the Clement who would later become bishop.

According to tradition, Clement was once a slave in the household of a Roman senator named Flavius Clemens, who was a cousin of the emperor Domitian and a Christian. As the story goes, the emperor had Flavius Clemens executed for his faith, which resulted in the liberation of his slaves. Clement, newly freed, took the name of his master (which is why we call him Clement—we don't know what his birth name was). The interesting thing is that the execution of Flavius Clemens did not take place until about A.D. 95, which would mean that for the first seven years of his episcopate, Clement was still a slave. This is entirely plausible, since slaves in the Roman world often had the freedom to come and go from their household, especially if that household was Christian. This is further evidence that the leadership of the early Church was not based on power or wealth, but on discipleship, succession, and a concern for unity. Even a slave could be bishop, as long as he was in succession from the apostles.

Eventually Clement himself, as bishop of Rome, was targeted by the authorities, and the emperor Trajan had him arrested and exiled to hard labor in the mines, in a remote location on the coast of the Black Sea. There he continued to preach the gospel, which resulted in many conversions to the Faith, including both fellow prisoners and their guards, and ultimately led to his own execution. As the story goes, he was tied to an anchor and thrown into the sea.

Legend has it that eight centuries later, St. Cyril had a dream in which he was told where to find the bones of Clement. Sailing to an island, he found Clement's bones, still tied to the anchor. He brought Clement's remains back to Rome, but died on the trip, so both Clement and Cyril were buried (along with Ignatius of Antioch) under the Roman church named after Clement: San Clemente.

1

Scripture and Tradition

In the musical *Fiddler on the Roof*, the main character Tevye sings passionately about "tradition!" as everything changes around him. He feels as though the rug is being pulled out from under him, since for him, tradition is stability—it is the foundation of his very life. As we saw in the last chapter, it's also an important part of any religion. Religious tradition provides a foundation for life by handing on from past generations the very things that give life stability, and sometimes the *only* things that give life stability in a world of constant change and confusion. For Catholicism, a big part of the tradition is that tradition itself is a source of authority for life and faith. As Catholics, we are accountable to the Tradition that handed down our Faith.

Isn't the Bible All We Need?

Yet the Catholic Church is often accused of making too much of tradition, or of adding unnecessary traditions that have changed or obscured the "original" biblical Christianity. But the Western world has been taught an oversimplified story of the Protestant Reformation that presents it as a return to some pristine original version of Christianity—like stripping the barnacles off the hull of a ship, leaving a cleaner, faster, safer ship. This Protestant view is often characterized by the Latin phrase *sola scriptura*, which means, "Scripture alone." The assumption is that everything a Christian needs to worship God faithfully, is to be found in the Old and New Testaments. The Catholic view, on the other hand, is that there is more to it: specifically, that the Holy Spirit is continually active in the Church in a way that helps us interpret and understand Scripture—through the Fathers of the Church and through the Church's Tradition.

So we come to the question of Scripture and Tradition. Protestants will sometimes go so far as to condemn the very concept of tradition, based on such Gospel passages as Matthew 15:3, 15:6, 15:9, and Mark 7:8. In all of these, Jesus criticizes the Pharisees for abandoning the word of God in favor of "human tradition." The logic here is that Scripture is revelation from God, but whatever is not in Scripture is a product of human speculation and therefore inferior to, or even opposed to Scripture. It certainly is true that Jesus was critical of the Pharisees for the way they majored on the minors, using the letter of the law to exempt them from the spirit of the law—which is to show love and compassion to God's people. But it is not true that Jesus was saying that all tradition is opposed to God's revelation. Jesus himself instituted traditions, including the Lord's Supper, so clearly he was not opposed to all tradition.

Paul is also brought into the debate, citing Colossians 2:8 where he says, "See to it that no one makes a prey of you by philosophy and empty deceit, according to human tradition, according to the elemental spirits of the universe, and not according to Christ." But Paul could not be opposed to all tradition either, since he speaks of tradition in positive ways in 2 Thessalonians 2:15, 1 Corinthians 11:23, Ephesians 2:19–20, and 2 Timothy 2:2. In fact, in 1 Corinthians 15, Paul admits that the very gospel that he preached was (before it was written down) a tradition that he received and handed on. He even knew of a saying of Jesus that never got included in the Gospels: in Acts 20:35, Paul quotes Jesus as saying, "It is more blessed to give than to receive." How did Paul know about that saying of Jesus? Because he received tradition handed on to him from the other apostles.

So Paul's point in warning the Colossians of "an empty deceit according to human tradition" was to prevent them from abandoning the Faith and going back to their *pagan* tradition—that is, superstition, "according to the elemental spirits of the universe," and to warn them against combining their old pagan beliefs with Christianity, which would water down the Faith.[24]

DID THE CATHOLIC CHURCH ADD TO THE BIBLE?

We need to be clear that Catholics do believe that the Old and New Testaments are the inspired word of God. We have this in common with our Evangelical Protestant brothers and sisters. The Second Vatican Council document *Dei Verbum* (*The Word of God*) says that "we must acknowledge that the books of Scripture firmly, faithfully, and without error, teach that truth which God, for the sake of our salvation, wished to see confided to the sacred Scriptures."[25] And about the Gospels in particular, it says that they "faithfully hand on what Jesus, the Son of God, while he lived among men, really did and taught for their eternal salvation . . . always in such a fashion that they have told us the honest truth about Jesus."[26] The document goes on to affirm that, "the study of the sacred page should be the very soul of sacred theology."[27]

If all that is true, the questioning goes, then why did the Catholic Church add to the Bible? The short answer to that question is that the Church did not really add to the Bible. In fact, the Catholic Church determined what would be in the Bible as it evaluated the earliest documents and discerned which ones were truly inspired Scripture and which were not. But even in doing so, the Church never meant to imply that the Bible was to be the exclusive and exhaustive source for the Christian life. In other words, the Bible is our primary written guide for our faith, but it could not say everything, as the apostle John admits at the end of his Gospel (21:24–25).

Remember that Church teaching is based on apostolic succession, which was the way that the Church determined correct teaching even before the New Testament was compiled. But even when the New Testament came together, there were already traditions that were not fully explained in the Bible, and were *older* than the Christian Bible, that the Church considered established and essential to the Faith. To cite just one example, there was the emergence of the clergy offices as part of the apostolic succession (remember Ignatius of Antioch, and how he understood authority to be essential for unity).

The key point here is that in some important ways, the Tradition of the Church is older than the New Testament. And in most cases, the traditions that the Protestant Reformers later removed were not "barnacles" that were added to the ship of the Church late in its journey, but were in fact part of its rigging from the beginning.

But didn't the Catholic Church add more books to the Bible? After all, Protestant Bibles have seven fewer books than Catholic Bibles. Again, the answer is no. The Church did not add to the Bible; the Reformation subtracted from it. (That is, from the Old Testament—the New Testament is exactly the same for all Christians: Catholic, Protestant, and Orthodox.) Remember that the New Testament did not exist yet during Jesus' ministry. The Bible at that time, the Bible of Jesus and the apostles, was the same as the Catholic Old Testament, including the so-called deuterocanonical (or apocryphal) books such as Maccabees, Wisdom, Sirach, and Tobit, that Protestant Bibles omit. These books had been written in Greek, not Hebrew, and were included in the Greek translation of the Old Testament called the *Septuagint* (abbreviated LXX). And this is the Bible that Jesus and the apostles read—in fact Jesus himself quoted from or referred to the books of Tobit, Sirach, and others on several occasions.[28]

However, when St. Jerome translated the Old Testament into Latin around the turn of the fifth century, he wanted to translate it directly from Hebrew, and so he followed the rabbis of his day by favoring the books originally written in Hebrew. Centuries later, Protestant Reformers would follow Jerome's lead and exclude from their Old Testament those books that originally had been written in Greek, rather than Hebrew. But the Catholic Church kept these documents as part of its Old Testament, in part because Jesus himself quoted from this body of writings.

After the ministry of Jesus, the apostles continued his mission, and part of their own ministry included writing the letters and Gospels which would become our New Testament. But they did not set out to write the Bible, per se, or even to add to it. They wrote as circumstances required, and it was up to the successors of the apostles to discern which of the earliest writings would become part of the Christian scriptures. How did they make the decision about whether to include a particular document? It had a lot to do with the authorship of any given document, but the process was one of growing consensus over time, and in fact there was no single point of decision, no specific council that ruled which books would be in the New Testament.[29]

The important thing to remember here is that there was a Tradition before there was a New Testament, which even Protestant scholars admit.[30] In fact, some of this pre-New Testament Tradition found its way into the New Testament, in the form of quotations of confessions of faith, doctrinal formulas, and even hymns.[31] Keep in mind that it was the early Church Fathers themselves, and especially the bishops as the successors of the apostles, who decided which books would make it into the New Testament. In other words, the Tradition of the Church (preserved through apostolic succession) came before our Christian Bible, and in fact gave us our Christian Bible. Another way to say this is that the Bible comes from the Church, not the other way around. The Church came before the Bible, and the Church decided what books would be in the Bible—any document that is in our New Testament is in there precisely because it was part of the received *Tradition* of the Church, a *Tradition* that comes from Jesus and the apostles, handed down by apostolic succession.

Therefore, the New Testament is part of the Tradition, and so we cannot separate Scripture from Tradition, as if they are two separate things, let alone two opposing things. In fact one could say that Scripture is a subset of the Church's Tradition. The Tradition is broader than Scripture, and includes Scripture. *yes!*

WHAT IS TRADITION?

But surely not every little tradition adopted by the Church throughout history has been retained, even by the Catholics, right? Didn't Catholics once have to abstain from meat on Fridays all year long, but now only during Lent? Isn't it hypocritical for the Catholics to keep some traditions and change others? To answer this, we need to define what we mean by tradition. In fact, the truth is that all Christians change some traditions over time. The real question is how to know what parts of the tradition are so important that they cannot be changed, and what parts are bound to a particular time or place so that they could be changed at a different time or in a different place.

Some people find it helpful to make a distinction between traditions (with a lower case "t") and Tradition (with a capital "T"). The traditions (small "t") are those that could be changed, such as fasting rituals, or whether the Mass must be conducted in Latin. These traditions are distinguished from Tradition (capital "T"), which is essential to the Faith—in fact some parts of this Tradition are what make the Christian faith *Christian*, such as the doctrine of the Trinity. Of course this still leaves the question of how to distinguish between "traditions" and "Tradition," and of who has the authority to make changes. We will turn to this important question below.

Tradition, in the singular, capital "T" sense (also called Sacred Tradition), comprises a body of teachings that originated with Jesus and the apostles and has been fleshed out and explained by the successors of the apostles, the bishops, and the other early Church Fathers. It includes oral teachings passed down by apostolic succession, as well as liturgical elements, creeds, and the decisions of councils of bishops. All of these things pre-date the standardization of the New Testament canon, but this Tradition also includes the process of the creation of the Christian Bible, and of course the Bible itself.

Once the documents that make up our New Testament were written, and even while the Church was still coming to a consensus on which documents should be considered part of Scripture, the early Church Fathers were interpreting the Tradition (including the scriptures) and explaining it to their fellow Christians. They were, after all, pastors and teachers, and their concern was faithfully to teach the Christian people how to live, and what to believe, as members of the Body of Christ. The

Church Fathers believed that the Holy Spirit was still working in the Church in their day, to help them with their task.[32] And when they held council meetings to make important decisions, they believed that the Holy Spirit was guiding those proceedings. Therefore, Tradition is the record of the teachings of the apostles, and of the Church Fathers' explanation of apostolic teachings in their theology and pastoral application.

The Second Vatican Council affirmed this:

Thus the apostolic preaching, which is expressed in a special way in the inspired books, was to be preserved in a continuous line of succession until the end of time. Hence the apostles, in handing on what they themselves had received, warn the faithful to maintain the traditions which they had learned either by word of mouth or by letter . . . In this way the Church, in her doctrine, life, and worship, perpetuates and transmits to every generation all that she herself is, all that she believes.[33]

Tradition is based on apostolic succession, which preserves and protects it. As an explanation of apostolic teaching, Tradition provides the Church with an authoritative interpretation of Scripture. So Tradition is what preserves and transmits both Scripture and its interpretation.

But this does not mean that Tradition is static. In fact, since the Holy Spirit is still working in and through the Church, our understanding of apostolic teaching grows over time. The above quotation from Vatican II goes on to say, "The Tradition that comes from the apostles makes progress in the Church, with the help of the Holy Spirit. There is a growth in insight into the realities and words that are being passed on . . . Thus, as the centuries go by, the Church is always advancing towards the plenitude of divine truth."[34] However, although later teachings can build on, and further clarify, the established Tradition, they cannot contradict the conclusions of the apostles and Fathers.[35] In fact, the early Church Fathers themselves pointed to an Old Testament rule against moving the property boundary markers set up by the ancestors[36] as a precedent for their assumption that previous Tradition could not be changed. The Tradition established by previous generations of the Church marks the boundaries of correct doctrine, and those boundaries cannot be moved. Within those boundaries, however, over time Tradition can become more clearly explained and richly understood.[37]

Therefore, Tradition is consistent with Scripture. It could never contradict it, because Scripture was written from Tradition, and Tradition interprets Scripture. This does not mean that the Church Fathers were infallible, or that everything they wrote must be included in the Church's unchangeable Tradition; however, as the *Catechism* says, "the sayings of the holy Fathers are a witness to the life-giving presence of this tradition, showing how its riches are poured out in the practice and life of the Church, in her belief and prayer."[38]

This brings us back to the question of how we as Christians are to know or determine which aspects of Tradition are essential to the Faith, and which are the changeable traditions that "can be retained, modified, or even abandoned under the guidance of the Church's magisterium."[39] The term *magisterium* refers to the teaching authority of the Church, as expressed in its bishops, who are in succession from the apostles. In other words, the authority to decide what traditions may be changed, and how they may be changed, is in the bishops, and is based on the Tradition itself, preserved and handed down through apostolic succession. Vatican II clarifies, "Yet this magisterium is not superior to the Word of God, but is its servant."[40]

And so we see that the same authority that determined which books should be in the Bible is the one that determines which traditions we should keep: that is, the Magisterium of the Church, with its bishops in direct and unbroken succession from the apostles. As St. Paul himself wrote, it is the Church (and not Scripture) that is "the pillar and foundation of truth" (1 Tim 3:15).

The Question of Interpretation

But how do we know that the Church Fathers interpreted Scripture correctly? That's a fair question. As just about any Bible-reading Christian can attest, it is not uncommon for two Christians to arrive at different interpretations of the same passage. For example, even among the Protestant denominations, Calvinists and Wesleyans do not agree on how to interpret Paul's reference to "predestination" in Romans 8. And of course many of the passages cited in this book will be interpreted differently by Protestants than by Catholics. Human nature being what it is, our interpretations tend to fall in line with the theological or denominational presuppositions that we held before coming to the text.

In any case, it is obvious to anyone who has studied Scripture that two people can be looking at the same passage, and get radically different interpretations from it. This demonstrates that the meaning (let alone the application) of a biblical passage is not always self-evident, and yet it can't be denied that both sides of an argument are being "biblical." Both sides are reading the same Bible, indeed the same passages, and yet they are coming to different conclusions. So how do we know who is right? Catholics believe that the better interpretation is the one that is most consistent with Tradition, and the burden of proof is on the one who would deviate from the received interpretation.

Now, it must be said that it's always possible that both sides can be right in a way. Catholics do not believe that there is always only one possible interpretation of a biblical passage. However, in those cases where two or more interpretations are mutually exclusive—they cannot both be right—then the question has to be settled in the same way it might be settled in a court of law: with precedent. Just as lawyers cite previous cases to see how the law was applied in the past, the Church looks to the early Fathers to see how the passages in question have been interpreted in the past. Interpretations are judged based on the Tradition—the conclusions of previous generations which become the foundation for the present case.[41]

Since the Protestant Reformation, there have been two competing ways to look at the interpretation of Scripture. I present them here in a simplified form.

The Catholic approach is that there may be multiple meanings in any given passage, but that there is a Tradition to give us the parameters (or boundary markers) within which to understand the text, and the teaching authority of the Church to guide us in our interpretation. The Church Fathers of the past and the Church leaders of the present give us the checks and balances to keep us from an interpretation that might lead us astray. We take into consideration not only the passage in question, but the whole witness of Scripture, as well as the overarching narrative of salvation history—and that narrative includes taking into account the way that the early Christians interpreted the passage we are reading.[42]

On the other hand, the Protestant Reformation gave the Western world a different way of reading Scripture. For the first time in history, it was suggested that there is only one right way to read a passage but that there was no central authority to help readers figure out what that one right interpretation was. Furthermore, many interpreters operated as though there was no historical tradition of interpretation, either. It was claimed that the meaning of Scripture would always be on the surface, accessible even to the untrained, without doing the work of study and without accountability to any authority.

To be fair, many of the Reformers did read the Church Fathers, and did take their writings into account. But in their zeal to reject papal authority and put the Bible in the hands of the people, they individualized the interpretation of Scripture in a way that goes against Scripture itself. As St. Peter wrote, "there is no prophecy of Scripture that is a matter of personal interpretation" (2 Pet. 1:20). Nevertheless, this individualization of interpretation has found a welcome home in the Christianity of Western culture, especially in the context of American individualism, which affirms a personal permission to know better than those who came before.

Thus the Catholic way of interpretation is communal, and connectional—that is, it's meant to be done within the Body of Christ, with all the checks and balances that come from the Church's Tradition, and from the Church's leaders in succession from the apostles. As the saying goes, there is no "my" in the Our Father.

During the time of the early Church Fathers, an important tipping point was the controversy over a heretic named Arius, and the resulting councils of Nicaea and Constantinople in the fourth century.[43] It's not necessary to know all the details of the debates at these two councils in order to understand the big picture of their implications for the Church. Suffice it to say that the debate came down to a matter of interpretation, with both of the major parties reading the same Bible, and even the same passages.

Arius, and those who agreed with him, were taking passages such as Colossians 1:15 (which refers to Jesus Christ as "the first-born of all creation") as though the meaning was plain, and concluded that the Son of God was a created being (that is, not fully divine). The majority of bishops, on the other hand, knew that there was more to it than that, and that the whole witness of Scripture (for example, John 1:1–3) *and Tradition* demanded that those words in Colossians should be taken to mean not that Christ was created, but that he was the *agent* of creation. In the Eastern part of the Roman Empire, there was a real danger that the Church could split over this issue.

But who was right? Both sides were being biblical. In fact it could be argued (and was argued at the time) that the Arians were being *more* biblical than their opponents, since they did not take into account Tradition when coming to their conclusions about how to interpret the scriptures. The Arians were operating on the principle of *sola scriptura*. As it turned out, the Church declared Arianism a heresy, but that could not have been done without an appeal to Tradition. In fact, the creed produced at the Council of Nicaea included a word that is not in the Bible: *consubstantial*. The meaning of this word includes the doctrine that the divine nature of Jesus Christ is the same divine "substance" as God the Father, and that the divine nature of Jesus Christ is therefore equally eternal as the Father. (If that were not the case, the Father would not always have been a Father, and the Trinity would not always have been a Trinity.) The point for our purposes is to demonstrate the fact that orthodoxy (cor-

rect doctrine) could not be defined, or the unity of the Church
maintained, by appealing to passages (or even words) from the
Bible only. Scripture alone was not enough.

The truth is that there has never been a sense that only words
found in the Bible can be used to explain what the Church believes. In the end, Arianism could not be refuted with biblical
language alone precisely because that language is open to differ-
ing interpretations. The Arians could interpret it their way, and
even find their own prooftexts for their interpretation. This goes
on to this day, in fact, with the modern version of Arianism: the
Jehovah's Witnesses. Their understanding of Christ is the result
of an interpretation of Scripture cut off from Tradition. It could
even be said that *all* heresy is the result of interpreting Scripture without some authority outside of the Bible to provide the
checks and balances against incorrect interpretation.

The Council of Nicaea in the year 325 was the first worldwide
(or *ecumenical*) council of the Church. The creed produced there
was expanded at the second ecumenical council, the Council of
Constantinople in 381. The result is the statement of faith that
we know as the Nicene Creed. The creed is biblical, but it is also
an interpretation of the Bible, summarizing the teachings of the
New Testament much as the Ten Commandments summarize
the Old Testament. But if the creed is true and correct in what
it teaches about Christianity (and all Christians, Catholic and
Protestant, agree that it is—even those who do not use it), this
proves that Scripture alone is not enough. In fact Scripture alone
often leads to heresy, as it did with the Arians, and as it continues
to do with the Jehovah's Witnesses and similar groups. As history demonstrates, a strict adherence to *sola scriptura* can lead to
a rejection of the doctrine of the Trinity.

What Did the Fathers Say
About Scripture and Tradition?

I want to reiterate that the Church Fathers are not considered
infallible, and that their writings are not considered the inspired

word of God. Individual Church Fathers could (and did) make mistakes, and some of their proposed teachings were later corrected or even rejected.[44] But when they came to consensus on something, and especially when that consensus was confirmed by a council of bishops, then their teaching makes up a part of our Tradition.

At this point, we can look at a few of the Fathers and what they had to say about the interdependence of Scripture and Tradition, and later we can look at how they applied the concept to particular issues. We begin with a letter by an anonymous Father, written to a Roman pagan named Diognetus. As part of his explanation of the Christian Church and its faith, the author writes:

> [H]aving been a disciple of the apostles, I am become a teacher of the gentiles. I minister the things delivered to me to those that are disciples worthy of the truth . . . and the Faith of the Gospels is established, and the Tradition of the apostles is preserved, and the grace of the Church exults.[45]

The point of including this passage from an unknown author is to demonstrate how the earliest Christians understood the content of their teaching to be the Tradition that was handed down to them. It is based on the Gospel story, but it was passed on orally, through the Church's catechesis, before there was a New Testament.

St. Irenaeus, Bishop of Lyons (c. A.D. 185)

Similarly, Irenaeus, the second-century bishop of Lyons, wrote:

> [T]he Church, having received this preaching and this Faith, although scattered throughout the whole world . . . carefully preserves it. She also believes these points [of doctrine] just as if she had but one soul, and one and the same heart, and she proclaims them, and teaches them, and hands them down, with perfect harmony, as if she possessed only one mouth.

For, although the languages of the world are dissimilar, yet
the import of the Tradition is one and the same. For the
churches which have been planted in Germany do not believe
or hand down anything different, nor do those in Spain, nor
those in Gaul, nor those in the East, nor those in Egypt, nor
those in Libya, nor those which have been established in the
central regions of the world. But as the sun, that creature of
God, is one and the same throughout the whole world, so also
the preaching of the truth shines everywhere, and enlightens
all men that are willing to come to a knowledge of the truth.

Nor will any one of the rulers in the churches, however
highly gifted he may be in point of eloquence, teach doctrines different from these . . . nor, on the other hand, will he
who is deficient in power of expression inflict injury on the
Tradition. For the Faith being ever one and the same, neither
does one who is able at great length to discourse regarding
it, make any addition to it, nor does one who can say but
little diminish it. It does not follow because men are endowed
with greater and less degrees of intelligence, that they should
therefore change the subject-matter [of the Faith] itself.[46]

Note that Irenaeus, who preached the importance of Scripture over against human philosophy, and who had great influence over the Church's eventual consensus on the books of the
New Testament, here speaks of the doctrine of the Church in
terms of Tradition.

Tertullian, lay teacher of Carthage (c. 200)

At the turn of the third century, Tertullian wrote, "Notice that
Jesus said, 'Your faith has saved you,' not your skill in the scriptures."[47] Tertullian and other early Christian teachers and leaders were complaining that heretics were using Scripture to their
advantage. They cited the scriptures to support their teachings,
but they were picking and choosing which passages to emphasize and which to ignore, based on their theological agenda. For

the Church Fathers, what prevented the misuse of Scripture was the received Tradition, which they often referred to as the "rule of faith." And the most concrete expression of the "rule of faith" was the Church's creeds.

St. Cyril, bishop of Jerusalem (c. 350)

As bishop of Jerusalem, Cyril was responsible for the content of the creed that Jerusalem Christians would say as their statement of faith and as part of their baptism ritual. About that creed, Cyril preached:

> But in learning the Faith and in professing it, acquire and keep that only, which is now delivered to you by the Church, and which has been built up strongly out of all the scriptures. For since all cannot read the scriptures, some being hindered as to the knowledge of them by want of learning, and others by a want of leisure, in order that the soul may not perish from ignorance, we comprise the whole doctrine of the Faith in a few lines . . . For the articles of the Faith were not composed as seemed good to men; but the most important points collected out of all the scriptures make up one complete teaching of the Faith.[48]

Notice that Cyril affirms that the creeds were meant to be summaries of Scripture, explained by means of the Church's Tradition.

St. Augustine, bishop of Hippo (c. 400)

Augustine, arguably the most famous of the Church Fathers, preached a sermon in which he shows that he agreed with what Cyril was saying. He proclaimed, "For whatever you hear in the creed is contained in the inspired books of holy Scripture."[49] But he was talking about the Nicene Creed, and as we have already noted, that creed contained a word not in Scripture. So how could Augustine say this? It was because he understood the connection between Scripture and the creed—that the creeds were faithfully based on Scripture and faithfully interpreted it.

Augustine also wrote, in his *On Christian Doctrine*:

> If, when attention is given to the passage, it shall appear to be uncertain in what way it ought to be punctuated or pronounced, let the reader consult the rule of faith which he has gathered from the plainer passages of Scripture and from the authority of the Church.[50]

Augustine was writing about interpretation, and how one has to consider the context and comparison with other passages when attempting to understand a text. His point here is that in interpretation (which includes how a passage "ought to be punctuated"), one also consults the "rule of faith," which is the Church's Tradition. This rule of faith comes from Scripture, and includes the creeds, which are "gathered from the plainer passages of Scripture."

St. Vincent, bishop of Lérins (c. 434)

Vincent, the fifth-century bishop in Gaul, wrote this famous passage, which became the traditional approach to defining orthodoxy for the early and medieval Church:

> [W]hether I or anyone else should wish to detect the frauds and avoid the snares of heretics as they rise, and to continue sound and complete in the Catholic faith, we must, the Lord helping, fortify our own belief in two ways; first, by the authority of the Divine Law, and then, by the Tradition of the Catholic Church.
>
> But here someone perhaps will ask, "Since the canon of Scripture is complete, and sufficient of itself for everything, and more than sufficient, what need is there to join with it the authority of the Church's interpretation?" For this rea-

son—because, owing to the depth of holy Scripture, all do not accept it in one and the same sense, but one understands its words in one way, another in another; so that it seems to be capable of as many interpretations as there are interpreters . . .

Moreover, in the Catholic Church itself, all possible care must be taken, that we hold that faith which has been believed everywhere, always, by all. For that is truly and in the strictest sense Catholic, which, as the name itself and the reason of the thing declare, comprehends all universally. This rule we shall observe if we follow universality, antiquity, consent. We shall follow universality if we confess that one faith to be true, which the whole Church throughout the world confesses; antiquity, if we in no wise depart from those interpretations which it is manifest were notoriously held by our holy ancestors and Fathers; consent, in like manner, if in antiquity itself we adhere to the consentient definitions and determinations of all, or at the least of almost all priests and doctors.

This text is part of what is often referred to as the "Vincentian rule," or the "Vincentian canon." The principle is that the most trustworthy teaching is that which has been taught as a consensus—as Vincent says, "everywhere, always, and by all." Of course there was disagreement within the early Church, so technically it is not really the case that the established doctrine was believed by absolutely everyone. So what is to be done when one or more teachers deviate from the Tradition? Vincent goes on:

What then will a Catholic Christian do, if a small portion of the Church have cut itself off from the communion of the universal faith? What, surely, but prefer the soundness of the whole body to the unsoundness of a pestilent and corrupt member? What, if some novel contagion seek to infect not merely an insignificant portion of the Church, but the whole? Then it will be his care to cleave to antiquity, which at this day cannot possibly be seduced by any fraud of novelty. But what, if in antiquity itself there be found error on the part of

two or three men, or at any rate of a city or even of a province?
Then it will be his care by all means, to prefer the decrees,
if such there be, of an ancient General Council to the rash-
ness and ignorance of a few. But what, if some error should
spring up on which no such decree is found to bear? Then
he must collate and consult and interrogate the opinions of
the ancients, of those, namely, who, though living in various times and places, yet continuing in the communion and
faith of the one Catholic Church, stand forth acknowledged
and approved authorities: and whatsoever he shall ascertain to
have been held, written, taught, not by one or two of these
only, but by all, equally, with one consent, openly, frequently,
persistently, that he must understand that he himself also is to
believe without any doubt or hesitation.[51]

The point is that the majority of Church leaders and teachers
came to a consensus about what was the best interpretation of
Scripture—just as they came to a consensus about which documents should be considered Scripture. This consensus is not
simply a case of majority rule—though it did work that way in
the councils. The bishops voted on their conclusions, which prevented any one powerful person from controlling the outcome.
But even more important, the same Holy Spirit who inspired the
writings of the sacred texts also guided the process of consensus,
which was hammered out in councils and which stood the test
of time in liturgy and catechesis.

St. Gregory the Great, bishop of Rome (c. 600)

Pope Gregory I wrote many letters to other bishops around the
world. In one of his letters, he made this comment about the
relationship of the New Testament and the first four ecumenical
(worldwide) councils of bishops:

Since with the heart man believes unto righteousness, and
with the mouth confession is made unto salvation, I confess

that I receive and revere, as the four books of the gospel so also the four councils: to wit, the Nicene, in which the perverse doctrine of Arius is overthrown; the Constantinopolitan also, in which the error of Eunomius and Macedonius is refuted; further, the first Ephesine, in which the impiety of Nestorius is condemned; and the Chalcedonian, in which the pravity of Eutyches and Dioscorus is reprobated. These with full devotion I embrace, and adhere to with most entire approval; since on them, as on a four-square stone, rises the structure of the holy Faith.[52]

Gregory's point is that the faith of the Church is built on the foundation of Tradition, here epitomized in the decisions of the first four ecumenical councils (Nicaea, Constantinople, Ephesus, and Chalcedon) as four cornerstones of the Church's foundation. He compares them to the four Gospels in a way that implies they are equal in authority.

A Test Case: Is Purgatory Biblical?

A questioner might press the point: interpretation of what Scripture says is one thing, but what about teaching as doctrine things that aren't even *mentioned* in Scripture, like purgatory?

This is a fair question, but to answer it, we have to begin by questioning the question itself. Remember that the word "Trinity" is not in the Bible, and yet, all Christians would agree that the doctrine of the Trinity is in fact taught in Scripture (anyone who does not agree with this is not properly called a Christian). In the same way, other doctrines may not be named in Scripture by the names that we call them—in fact some of the fancy doctrinal terms come up much later in the Church's history—but that does not mean that the concepts are not found in Scripture. In most such cases, the Church maintains that the doctrines are in fact *taught* in the Bible, and so they are "biblical." And the few that are not explicitly supported by Scripture are at least not contradicted by it.

It comes down to how one uses the Bible. Such an extreme version of *sola scriptura* would insist that everything not commanded in the Bible is prohibited. But this will lead to a kind of legalism that would prevent us from ever using microwave ovens or electric guitars. On the other hand, the Catholic Church (and indeed most Christians) would say that what is not prohibited by Scripture may be allowed, depending on what Tradition says on the subject. In some cases, the question may not be, *Does the Bible teach this?* but rather, *Does the Bible prohibit this?* We will apply this to some of the other controversial doctrines and practices in later chapters, but for now we will take one example: the doctrine of purgatory.

The concept of purgatory is often cited as a classic example of a Catholic doctrine that is not in the Bible. But actually, that's not true. There are several Scripture passages that, taken together, give evidence of the reality of purgatory. But to look at this, we may first need to set aside an erroneous notion of what we think purgatory is. It is not a punishment for sins, nor is it a loophole providing an escape from hell; rather it is a purification, after death, of whatever remains of sin.[53] The word *purgatory* itself suggests a "purging," or purification.

In the Old Testament, there are many laws about circumstances that could make a person "unclean." The consequence of being "unclean" was that the person was not fit to approach the presence of God in the temple. Although we as Christians do not follow all of these laws, there remains a great truth in the idea that one must be prepared—in a state of holiness—to approach the presence of God. If it was true for entering the temple of God on earth, how much more is it true when it comes to entering the presence of God in eternity? Even when we die justified in Christ, before we can "see the face of God," we must be purified—the process of sanctification being completed, so that we can be holy enough to enter the realm of God.

In Scripture, the image of fire can mean at least two things. It can mean destruction, and so sometimes Jesus uses the image of fire to speak of damnation.[54] But the other prominent meaning is purification. This is the "refiner's fire" of the prophets.[55] As we are told several times in the Old Testament, just as fire is used to purify gold and silver in a crucible, so God's people will be purified.[56] And it is clear that the apostle Paul believed this, since he refers to it in his first letter to the Corinthians:

> For no other foundation can anyone lay than that which is laid, which is Jesus Christ. Now if any one builds on the foundation with gold, silver, precious stones, wood, hay, straw—each man's work will become manifest; for the Day will disclose it, because it will be revealed with fire, and the fire will test what sort of work each one has done. If the work which any man has built on the foundation survives, he will receive a reward. If any man's work is burned up, he will suffer loss, though he himself will be saved, but only as through fire (3:11–15).

Paul is not talking about physical fire; rather he is using the image of fire to represent purification. In the end, anyone whose works are imperfect can only be saved by going through the purification. Note that this does not imply that a person's salvation could be earned by works. In fact, the concept of purgatory presumes that we all must assume that our works will be judged imperfect, so that those who are being saved by the merit of Christ need to be purified to prepare them to enter eternal life. In their writings, both Peter and John also implied that they believed in the necessity of a purification after a person's death.[57] Traditionally, the Church has taught that the only people who did not need purification after their death (apart from Jesus, of course, as well as Mary, and we'll talk about her in a later chapter) were the martyrs, because it was always believed that when people die for their faith in Christ, they are, in a sense, baptized in their own blood, and therefore purified by their sacrifice.[58]

A good way to think of purgatory is as the completion of sanctification after one's death. Since death is not the end of one's Christian journey, the Church has always taught that we may pray for those who have passed on, as their journey continues.

This is reflected in an Old Testament story that shows us that the Hebrew people believed it was appropriate to pray for the souls of the dead.[59] The Jewish tradition of *Kaddish*, the mourner's prayer, as well as the early Christian tradition of praying for the peaceful repose of the souls in purgatory, is based on this ancient belief. In Christianity, since it was assumed that there is a span of time between a person's death and the final resurrection at the end of the age, the Church also began including petitions for the souls of the dead in Masses, and even accepting alms as an act of intercession for the dead. Christians, especially those in mourning, have throughout the centuries taken comfort in the belief that their intercession could support those who have passed on, as they continue the journey through purification.[60]

Now let's take a look at what some of the early Fathers said about purgatory, to demonstrate how they interpreted the relevant biblical passages, especially 1 Corinthians 3:15.

What Did the Church Fathers Say About Purgatory?

From a time even before the earliest surviving quotes from the Church Fathers on this subject, we know that the belief in purgatory existed among the grassroots of the faithful. A second-century document known as *The Acts of Paul*, which contains the story of "The Acts of Paul and Thecla," mentions the practice of prayer for the dead in such a way as to imply a belief in purgatory—and it does this as though its readers should not be surprised by it. Although this document is not authoritative for the Church, it does show that as early as the second century, a writer could take it for granted that Christians believed that it was beneficial to pray for the souls of the dead, which also tells us that they believed in purgatory. Another famous document, the *Martyrdom of Perpetua and Felicitas*, is actually the diary of an early third-century martyr, Perpetua, executed for her faith as public entertainment in an arena in North Africa in the year 203. In this story, as well, it is assumed that those who have died can benefit from the intercession of the living.

Tertullian (c. 200)

Writing of the obligation a widow owes to her deceased husband, Tertullian said:

> [S]he prays for his soul, and requests refreshment for him meanwhile, and fellowship (with him) in the first resurrection; and she offers (her sacrifice) on the anniversaries of his falling asleep. For, unless she does these deeds, she has in the true sense divorced him . . . But if we believe the resurrection of the dead, of course we shall be bound to them with whom we are destined to rise, to render an account the one of the other.[61]

Tertullian's main point aside, we can see that he believes—and assumes his audience believes—that it is appropriate and consistent with Church teaching and tradition to pray for the souls of the dead, and offer Masses (referred to as *the sacrifice*) for them on the anniversaries of their deaths. In other documents, Tertullian also mentions offerings for the dead, and when he was arguing against reincarnation and the transmigration of souls, he affirmed the Christian belief in resurrection, which for him implied that there would be consequences for sin after death but before the final judgment.[62]

St. Cyprian, bishop of Carthage (c. 250)

Cyprian was the bishop of Carthage, in North Africa, during one of the worst and most devastating persecutions the early Church faced at the hands of the Roman Empire. In a letter, he explains the difference between those who are forgiven for their sins by the Church and those who die as martyrs:

> It is one thing to stand for pardon, another thing to attain to glory: it is one thing, when cast into prison, not to go out thence until one has paid the uttermost farthing; another thing at once to receive the wages of faith and courage. It is one thing, tortured by long suffering for sins, to be cleansed and long purged

by fire; another to have purged all sins by suffering. It is one thing, in fine, to be in suspense till the sentence of God at the day of judgment; another to be at once crowned by the Lord.[63]

Cyprian asserts that those who die as martyrs have no need of the purification of purgatory,[64] for they "have purged all sins by suffering," and "at once receive the wages of faith and courage," which is, "to be at once crowned by the Lord." On the other hand, those who do not die as martyrs suffer a different kind of torture, that is, they suffer grief for their sins. They are "tortured by long suffering for sins, to be cleansed and long purged by fire . . ." This is clearly a reference to purgatory.

Lactantius, lay teacher of North Africa (c. 300)

Similarly, Lactantius wrote that it was possible for a person to reach a point of sanctification in this life which would exempt him from purgatory, but that this was not likely, since for most of us our sins outweigh our goodness. "But when he shall have judged the righteous, he will also try them with fire. Then they whose sins shall exceed either in weight or in number, shall be scorched by the fire and burnt."[65]

It would be a mistake to read this as physical fire. Lactantius seems to have understood the fire as "real," in a way, but he described it as a kind of spiritual fire that would purify souls.

St. Cyril, bishop of Jerusalem (c. 350)

In his *Catechetical Lectures*, Cyril preached about the practice of prayer "on behalf also of the holy Fathers and bishops who have fallen asleep before us, and in a word of all who in past years have fallen asleep among us, believing that it will be a very great benefit to the souls for whom the supplication is put up."[66]

As we can see, the belief in purgatory was widespread in the early Church, and was considered to be consistent with the teachings of Scripture and the apostles.

St. Gregory, bishop of Nyssa (c. 380)

Bishop Gregory preached a sermon on the dead, in which he combined his understanding of 1 Corinthians 3:15 with 2 Peter 1:4, which says we "may become partakers of the divine nature." But, Gregory wrote, no one is "able to partake of divinity until he has been purged."[67]

It should be clear from our brief study that anti-Catholic legends claiming that the concept of purgatory was invented in the early Middle Ages are untrue. There are many other early Church Fathers that could be quoted here, including Hilary of Poitiers, John Chrysostom, and Gregory the Great, but it will suffice to conclude with Augustine.

St. Augustine, bishop of Hippo (c. 400)

Toward the end of his famous book, *The City of God*, Augustine wrote to clarify that hell and purgatory are two different things. Hell is for the damned, purgatory is for those being saved:

> But temporary punishments are suffered by some in this life only, by others after death, by others both now and then; but all of them before that last and strictest judgment. But of those who suffer temporary punishments after death, all are not doomed to those everlasting pains which are to follow that judgment; for to some, as we have already said, what is not remitted in this world is remitted in the next, that is, they are not punished with the eternal punishment of the world to come.[68]

Although the Church Fathers do use words like "suffering" and "punishment" to describe purgatory, we have to admit that we do not know with any certainty what people experience in this purification after death. What we do know is that it takes place outside of time and physical space, and so we have to keep in mind that concepts such as duration and pain do not apply in the way that they do here in this life. As Pope Benedict XVI wrote in his encyclical *The Hope of Salvation*:

This encounter with him [Jesus Christ], as it burns us, transforms and frees us, allowing us to become truly ourselves. All that we build during our lives can prove to be mere straw, pure bluster, and it collapses. Yet in the pain of this encounter, when the impurity and sickness of our lives become evident to us, there lies salvation. His gaze, the touch of his heart heals us through an undeniably painful transformation "as through fire." But it is a blessed pain, in which the holy power of his love sears through us like a flame, enabling us to become totally ourselves and thus totally of God . . . The pain of love becomes our salvation and our joy. It is clear that we cannot calculate the "duration" of this transforming burning in terms of the chronological measurements of this world. The transforming "moment" of this encounter eludes earthly time-reckoning—it is the heart's time, it is the time of "passage" to communion with God in the Body of Christ.[69]

The early Church Fathers taught—and the Catholic Church continues to teach—that the doctrine of purgatory is biblical because they believed that the Old Testament supported it and the New Testament (especially Paul in 1 Corinthians) assumed it. Furthermore, the people of the Church have consistently believed the doctrine of purgatory, as far as we can tell, from the very beginning of the Church's existence. It is ironic that some of the very people who criticize the hierarchy of the Church are so quick to abandon a doctrine that was strongly supported by the Christian grassroots. So we must take seriously how the early Church Fathers defined what is *biblical*—especially that a doctrine does not have to be *named* in the Bible (with the name we call it) in order to be supported and taught by Scripture. Just as we saw when the Council of Nicaea defined Jesus as *consubstantial* with the Father, the Church does not have to limit itself to words found in the Bible to describe revealed theological truths. If it did, we could not use the word *Trinity*.

What Were the Protestant Reformers Objecting To?

The Protestant Reformation was, in part, a reaction against some medieval interpretations of Scripture that were so allegorical and speculative that they became disconnected from the story of salvation history.[70] The good news was that the Reformers worked hard to focus attention on the historical meaning of the Bible, including an author's intended meaning. The bad news was that sometimes this meant swinging the pendulum to the other extreme, leading to overly literal interpretations (or ignoring the metaphorical in the text), and setting the stage for fundamentalist interpretations of the Old Testament. To be fair, the original Reformers did not intend a superficially literalistic reading of Scripture. In fact, even when they talked about the literal sense of a passage, they really meant the historical meaning, which could include figures of speech, metaphor, and even allegory.[71] But in their arguments with Catholic interpreters, they summarized their own method in the phrase *sola scriptura*, Scripture alone.

Many Protestant scholars today admit that *sola scriptura* was not a concept that the early Christians would have accepted.[72] As we have seen, especially using the doctrine of purgatory as a case study, the Church has never taught that Scripture alone was sufficient—in fact, the Church Fathers would say that to ignore Tradition would lead to bad interpretation of Scripture, and to heresy. Remember that at the Council of Nicaea, the Arians were the *sola scriptura* party.

In response to the Reformers' concept of *sola scriptura*, the Council of Trent (1545–1563) affirmed that God's revelation comes to us through *both* Scripture and Tradition, and the authority of the Church is based on both together. Either one without the other can lead too easily to error. Both are to be accepted as authoritative because if one is using Scripture without the checks and balances of Tradition, it can be made to say almost anything. In fact, this is the medieval problem that the Protestant Reformers were objecting to. It seems ironic that when medieval interpreters were making fanciful interpretations by over-spiritualizing the text of Scripture, the Reformers' solution was to reject the very thing that could rein that in—Tradition.[73]

It is often assumed that Protestants were the first ones to put
the Bible in the hands of the common people, as though the
Catholic Church had been keeping it from them. But it is simply
not true that the Catholic Church wanted to prevent people from
reading the Bible. In fact, the Catholic Church also translated
the Bible into vernacular languages such as English, French, and
Spanish—sometimes before the Reformers did. It was not that
the Church feared people would think for themselves, it was that
the Church feared they would think *by* themselves, without the
benefit of Tradition and Church teaching, and that by doing so
they would be led into heresy.[74]

Finally, the concept of *sola scriptura* is not itself taught in Scripture, and so it is a logical impossibility. Nowhere does the Bible
proclaim itself to be the limit of theological language or even the
only inspired source of revelation. The one biblical passage that
proponents of *sola scriptura* tend to use in support of the concept
is 2 Timothy 3:16–17, which says that all Scripture is inspired
and useful for teaching. Catholics agree that all Scripture is inspired and useful for teaching, but the passage does not say that
only Scripture is inspired and useful. In fact, when Paul wrote
that to Timothy, he was talking about the Old Testament (the
Scripture that Timothy had known from infancy; see v. 15), and
most of the New Testament had not even been written yet. So if
that passage did promote the concept of *sola scriptura*, it would be
saying that only the Old Testament is the rule of faith!

But that would mean Paul was contradicting himself, since he
clearly accepts the idea of passing on Tradition, as we saw above.
And we know that Peter would come to consider Paul's own writings (including 2 Timothy) as Scripture.[75] In other words, to claim
that we can only believe what is taught in Scripture is to rule out
the doctrine of *sola scriptura*, since it simply isn't in the Bible.

∽

The rejection of Tradition is a product of the Protestant Reformation. But one must ask whether this rejection of interpretive
precedent is like a ship's captain ignoring the maps drawn by
those sailors who have gone before him. Without the Tradition,

we would not have the Faith, or the Church. In our age, too, we have to ask ourselves whether we can know better than those who lived closer in time to the events described in Scripture, and who gave us our Tradition. This is the same presumption that gave the world the false dichotomy of science and faith, as though the two were incompatible, and it has also led to the fundamentalist backlash with its anti-intellectualism and skepticism of scholarship. Catholic Tradition is not an either/or dilemma, but a synthesis of faith and reason, tradition and scholarship.

Catholicism recognizes that Scripture and Tradition have always been integral and interdependent. It is just not true to say that the Church downplays the former in favor of the latter. Scripture's place in the Church can be seen not only in Catholic doctrine but in liturgy. Every Catholic Mass begins with the Liturgy of the Word, which includes an Old Testament reading, a Psalm response, and a New Testament reading—and then we stand while the Gospel is read. I daresay that more Scripture is heard in every Catholic Mass than in most evangelical Protestant services, which often have only a short reading of a text, or interspersed prooftexts, as part of a long sermon.[76]

For present-day Catholics as for the Church Fathers, Tradition was the interpretive precedent for Scripture, much as legal precedent is used to interpret laws in court. The Fathers believed and taught that without such a precedent, competing interpretations would obscure the teaching of Scripture and cause division within the Church. In other words, they know that the interpretation of Scripture was not to be done by individuals, but by the Church.[77] As the Protestant scholar D. H. Williams wrote, for the Church Fathers, "Scripture was the authoritative anchor of tradition's content, and tradition stood as the primary interpreter of Scripture."[78]

Likewise, the Second Vatican Council affirmed:

Sacred Tradition and Sacred Scripture, then are bound closely together, and communicate one another. For both of them, flowing out of the same divine well-spring, come together in some fashion to form one thing, and move towards the same

goal . . . Thus it comes about that the Church does not draw
her certainty about all revealed truths from the holy scriptures
alone. Hence, both Scripture and Tradition must be accepted
and honored with equal feelings of devotion and reverence.
Sacred Tradition and Sacred Scripture make up a single sacred
deposit of the Word of God, which is entrusted to the Church.
By adhering to it the entire holy people, united to its pastors,
remains always faithful to the teaching of the apostles.[79]

Scripture and Tradition deserve equal reverence because each
includes and clarifies the other. Tradition precedes and includes
Scripture, and Scripture includes and assumes the earliest Tradition. They are not two separate authorities—not even two parallel authorities—but are together and combined the one deposit
of faith.[80]

Furthermore, if we leave interpretation up to the individual,
we risk having as many interpretations (and perhaps as many
denominations of Christianity) as there are individuals. Without the interpretive checks and balances of Tradition and apostolic authority, the scriptures can be made to say virtually anything. For Catholics, Tradition and the teaching authority of the
Church protect the Church's unity, as well as guide the Church
in its interpretation of Scripture. So, Catholics are encouraged to
read their Bibles.[81] But, taking our lesson from the early Fathers,
we are not encouraged to do so in isolation from the Church
and Tradition. Neither are we to forget that though the Bible is
the written word of God, the living Word is Jesus Christ, and
the primary revelation of God is his person and his works.[82] In
Scripture, then, "the words, for their part, proclaim the works,
and bring to light the mystery they contain. The most intimate
truth which this revelation gives us about God and the salvation
of man shines forth in Christ, who is himself both the mediator
and the sum total of Revelation."[83] After all, *the living* Word, Jesus Christ, is found in both Scriptures and in the Church—in its
sacraments, and especially at the table of the Eucharist, which, as
we will see, is our primary proclamation of the gospel.

Featured Father

Irenaeus of Lyons: Heresy Hunter

Irenaeus was born around A.D. 125, and grew up in the eastern part of the Roman Empire, in the area we refer to as Asia Minor, which is now Turkey. He probably came from the town of Smyrna (modern Izmir), where the bishop was the famous Polycarp, who tradition says was a disciple of the apostle John. This makes Irenaeus only two degrees removed from the apostles. Irenaeus became a student of Polycarp, and was eventually ordained by him, and sent to the West as a missionary to the wild wilderness of the province of Gaul (what we now call France). He was sent to the town of Lyons, to assist the bishop Pothinus.

While he was a priest in Lyons, Irenaeus got wind of a controversy brewing over a group of charismatics who called themselves the New Prophecy (we now call them Montanists). Some people were saying that they were heretics, and others were saying that they were harmless enthusiasts. They came from Asia Minor, and perhaps Irenaeus had some information about them that he thought would be helpful, so he traveled to Rome in the year 177 to join the debate—it seems in fact that he testified in favor of the Montanists, and true to his name (which means "peaceful") he tried to reconcile the opposing factions.

Meanwhile, back in Lyons, the pagan population of the area rose up in violence against the Christians, and many of the faithful were killed. The bodies of the martyred Christians were desecrated, and were left in the streets, denied a proper burial. The incident is recorded in a document called *The Martyrs of Lyons and Viennes*, which some say was written by Irenaeus himself to keep alive the memory of his fallen brothers and sisters.

When Irenaeus returned from Rome, he found that his bishop had been martyred, and that he had been elected his successor. As bishop of Lyons, Irenaeus wrote several works, but only a

couple of them remain for us to read. In these works, Irenaeus
tirelessly worked to expose the pagan roots of the various gnostic
heresies, and to warn his people to stay true to the teachings
of the apostles, as they were handed down through apostolic
succession. The document we usually call *Against Heresies* was
originally titled, *The Detection and Refutation of Knowledge, Falsely
So-Called*. The "false knowledge" is a reference to the Gnostics'
claim that they had secret knowledge from Jesus. Irenaeus argues
against the very idea of secret knowledge with the doctrine of
apostolic succession—in effect saying, "If there was any secret
knowledge, we bishops would know about it!"

Irenaeus was skeptical of philosophy, and wrote that to use
human reason without Scripture and Tradition is to invite heresy. For him, as for the other Church Fathers, what matters is
what one believes about Jesus Christ, because to believe the
wrong things about Christ is to believe in the wrong Christ—
that is, a Christ who does not exist and therefore cannot save.
Unlike the earlier Christian apologists such as Justin Martyr and
Athenagoras, who were basically Christian philosophers, Irenaeus insisted on supporting all of his arguments from Scripture,
interpreted in light of earlier Tradition. In fact, Irenaeus was one
of the first of the Church Fathers to refer to the two parts of the
Bible as the Old and New Testaments.

Irenaeus died around the year 202. Legend says that he died
a martyr, but we have no real evidence that this is so. If he was
martyred, the date of 202 makes sense, since that was the beginning of another wave of persecution by the Roman Empire.
Irenaeus leaves a legacy that not only helps us understand the
earliest expressions of the Christian faith, it also helps us understand the early heresies, since he spent a lot of ink explaining
them in great detail. His document *Against Heresies* is quite long
and involved, but if you want a shorter more accessible introduction to Irenaeus, read his *Demonstration of the Apostolic Preaching*.
Sometimes also called *Proof of the Apostolic Preaching* (or *Teaching*),
this is an excellent summary of all of Christian teaching up to
the end of the second century.

2

Faith and Works

The Catholic Faith is an active faith. It is a faith that is expressed outwardly, a faith that is expressed by *doing* things. It is not a faith that is internal only, as if one could simply believe the right propositions and leave it at that. This being the case, in the first 1,500 years of the Church's existence, Christians found many ways to actively express their faith, over time leading some to wonder if the Church had become too focused on the outward actions of piety. Add to that a measure of medieval misunderstanding, as well as some real problems and abuses in the Church, and by the time of the Protestant Reformation some people believed that the Church was teaching a salvation by works.

The truth is, the Church never taught salvation by works. Just as Scripture and Tradition are not two opposing, or even separate, authorities, faith and works are not two separate expressions of the Christian religion. To the Catholic mind, faith and works are two sides of the same coin; and in fact faith includes works, and would be incomplete without them. In this chapter we will look at what the Church has historically taught, and what the Church Fathers concluded, on the subject of faith and works, and explore the kinds of questions that Protestants ask about it: *Does the Catholic Church over-emphasize works? Isn't faith all we need for salvation? Didn't my baptism wash away all my sins? Is the practice of penance a form of "works-righteousness"?*

Paul vs. James?

Let's begin with what the apostles taught. St. Paul is often called the Apostle to the Gentiles, but the truth is that he probably converted and discipled more Jews than Gentiles. So why is he called the Apostle to the Gentiles? Because when he would come to a town and tell the people of the synagogue about their Messiah, some of the "God-fearers"—Gentile believers on the fringe of the Jewish community—would also want to get baptized. But that raised the question of whether they would need to become Jews first, in order to become Christians. Would they need to follow the whole Law of Moses to follow Christ? And would the men among them need to be circumcised?

Paul's answer was no, but it wasn't long before a group from Jerusalem challenged him on that, and even traveled around preaching a contradictory message in the places he had been.[84] These "Judaizers," as they are sometimes called, argued that in order to be a Christian, a person had to follow the whole Jewish law. Paul answered that the cross of Christ is sufficient for salvation, and if salvation comes through the law, then Christ died for nothing.[85]

So whenever Paul emphasizes faith over against the law, he is defending his understanding of salvation against these Judaizers. But note that he is emphasizing faith over against *the law*, not over against good works. Therefore, his understanding of salvation should not be characterized as a kind of *sola fide* ("by faith alone," as opposed to by works), as though he anticipated the Protestant Reformation. Instead, it is more like *sola cruci* ("by the cross alone" as distinct from by the law).

When proponents of "faith alone" quote Paul, they often cite Ephesians 2:8–9, which says, "For by grace you have been saved through faith, and this is not from you; it is the gift of God; it is not from works, so no one may boast." However, in the very next verse, Paul goes on to say, "For we are his handiwork, created in Christ Jesus for the good works that God has prepared in advance, that we should live in them." So although Paul clearly says that we do not earn our salvation by works, he also makes it clear that there is an expectation that good works should be part of every Christian life.

In the Gospel of Luke, we read of a time when Jesus visited the home of Mary of Bethany and her sister Martha.[86] Mary sat with the other disciples listening to Jesus, while Martha was busy being the hostess. Martha complained to Jesus that Mary was not helping her with the work. Jesus' response indicated that he had a priority in mind—that you have to seek the Lord before you can serve him.[87] But Jesus did not say there was anything wrong with what Martha was doing, because, after all, she was serving the Lord.

The reality is, every one of us has a personality that makes us lean more one way than the other. In other words, some of us are more like Mary, and some of us are more like Martha. Neither one is wrong, but we do need to find a balance. If we go too far in either direction, we might want to ask ourselves how we can bring more balance into our lives by intentionally stretching ourselves in the other direction. In other words, those of us who are Marys need to get out there and do more service. Those of us who are Marthas need to take a step back from our busyness and reflect and pray more.

So in a way, the apostle Paul was writing to the Marthas, with the same message of concern that Jesus had for the original Martha—there is a certain priority of devotional faith over works, in that faith must come first or else the works are meaningless. At the same time, Paul does assume that faith should lead to works.

James, on the other hand, was writing to the Marys. Maybe some people took Paul's words too far (in a way that Paul never intended), and James wrote his letter later to correct that mistake. In fact, James may be arguing against another fringe group within the early Church—the opposite of the Judaizers—who said that salvation was really about enlightenment, just knowing the right things.[88] In his letters, John was responding to these early "gnostics" as well.[89] For James and John, faith must lead to good works, or it calls that faith into question.[90] So when James says, "faith without works is useless," and "faith without works is dead" (Jas. 2:14–20, 26) he means that just believing the right things is not enough. James goes on to say that "a person is justified by works and not by faith alone" (Jas. 2:24). At first this may sound like a direct contradiction of Paul's words in Ephesians 2. But in reality, they are both saying the same thing. Paul is saying that salvation comes by grace through faith, but it comes with the responsibility to do good works. James is saying that if a person claims to believe, but does not love his neighbor, then he doesn't really believe the right things after all. In other words, works are the evidence of real faith.

So we do not believe that Paul and James are at odds. They are responding to different fringe groups (or heresies), and responding to different needs within the Church. Both believed faith was necessary for salvation, and both believed that faith without works is incomplete.[91] In Galatians 5:22–23, Paul writes of the moral character traits that are the "fruit," or product, of the life of faith. So for Paul, good works are the way we "work out [our] salvation with fear and trembling" (Phil. 2:12). And yet, even our own good works are not ours alone—they are the result of the faith in us, and could not be done without it—so anything good we do is the result of God working in us.[92] Finally, it should go without saying that of course both Paul and James were following the lead of Jesus himself, who certainly advocated good works and love of neighbor. In fact, Jesus implied that our salvation might just depend on our willingness to forgive others![93]

So the apostles were certain that we could not earn our salvation. But they were equally certain that anyone who wishes to claim Christ as Lord and savior cannot presume that it is enough to believe in him, as if nothing further needed to be done. The mistake of the Judaizers was to put their trust in their works. At the other extreme, the mistake of the early gnostics was to put their trust in their knowledge. Both were wrong because true faith is not an either/or proposition. It is both/and—both faith *and* works.

We also have to keep in mind that the New Testament documents are not primarily works of apologetics—in other words, they were not written to convert unbelievers, but to support and encourage believers. So the emphasis is not on how one "gets saved," since it is assumed that the audience for the document is already baptized. The emphasis is on how one "acts saved," or how Christians are supposed to behave once they are in relationship with God in Christ.

What Did the Early Church Conclude About Faith and Works?

The issue of faith and works really goes back to the problem of evil. The problem of evil can be expressed as the question: If God is all-powerful and all-good, why is there evil in the world? The question implies that if God could prevent evil, he would—or at least he should. In other words, the existence of evil is said to prove that God either cannot prevent it (and thus he is not all-powerful) or he refuses to (and thus he is not all-good). From the beginning, the Church's answer to the question has been yes, God is all-powerful, and God is good, but God is also loving, and he wants our love in return. And love must be voluntary, or it's not love. In other words, God gave humans free will, so that if we love him, we do it freely. Our free will is part of what it means to be made in the image of God.[94]

From the beginning of the Church, the Fathers wrote that people have free will, and that is what sets us apart from the animals.[95] Furthermore, they said that evil is not part of God's good creation, but is the result of the misuse of free will (that is, sin), and so God is not responsible for evil.[96] God would prefer a world without evil, and theoretically could prevent evil, but God loves humanity enough to let us make our own choices. In fact, the Fathers went so far as to say that without free will, there would be no moral responsibility, and thus no basis for judgment of sinners.[97] For if we did not have free will, then sin and evil could only be blamed on God.

What all this means is that those who do not receive salvation in the end are rejected by God on the basis of their own choices. God, in his omniscience, knows what choices people will make, and on that basis, God may reject someone. But God does not predestine anyone to either salvation or damnation.[98] Until the time of St. Augustine, when this issue will become controversial (we will explore this below), the Church always taught that we are created in God's image, to love God but only if we choose to—and so we were given the gift of free will. And free will means that we are morally accountable to God and responsible for our choices and actions. The Fathers assumed that all human beings have free will, but they also assumed that no one should expect to get through life without making the wrong choices at least some of the time. In other words, we all sin. Of course, that's why Jesus came, gave his life, and founded the Church—to make forgiveness of sins possible. We include the founding of the Church as part of the story of salvation because the Christians believed that it was not simply by a conversion experience, but through the sacrament of baptism, that God's grace and forgiveness comes to us. We will take a more in-depth look at baptism in the next chapter, but for now we have to clarify what the early Christians believed about baptism in order to understand the relationship of faith and works.

Didn't My Baptism Wash Away All My Sins?

St. Peter wrote that baptism "saves you now" (1 Pet. 3:21). The idea that baptism results in salvation is called *baptismal regeneration*. In baptism we are regenerated, or *born again*.[99] This is, in fact, how the early Church Fathers understood the meaning of "born again."[100] Catholics are often criticized for the doctrine of baptismal regeneration, but usually that's because the critics misunderstand the concept. When Protestants think of baptismal regeneration, they sometimes mistakenly combine it with a doctrine of *perseverance*, which says that once a person is saved, he cannot lose his salvation. But the Fathers did not teach this kind of perseverance. To them baptismal regeneration does mean that one receives salvation in baptism—but it does not imply a guarantee that one will not lose that salvation at some time after the baptism. In other words, one can be born again through baptism, but one also needs to remain in Christ in order to live out that salvation to its completion.[101] Irenaeus of Lyons wrote:

We must hold to the rule of the Faith without deviation, and do the commandments of God, believing in God and fearing him as Lord and loving him as Father . . . For such is the state of those who have believed, since in them continually abides the Holy Spirit, who was given by him in baptism, and is retained by the receiver, if he walks in truth and holiness and righteousness and patient endurance.[102]

Notice that Irenaeus said that the Holy Spirit is retained by the receiver, *if he walks in truth and holiness and righteousness and patient endurance.*

Jesus said, "Remain in me, as I remain in you. Just as a branch cannot bear fruit on its own unless it remains on the vine, so neither can you unless you remain in me. I am the vine, you are the branches" (John 15:4–5).[103] And so we must actively remain in Christ—and the Church has always taught that the primary way we remain in Christ and he remains in us is through the sacraments, especially ongoing participation in the Eucharist. But this means that it is possible to fail to remain in Christ, and to abandon him and his Church. If we do not remain in Christ— that is, if after our baptism we reject Christ by the choices we make with our free will—then we can lose our salvation.

Although there are some Protestant denominations that teach baptism as something that "washes away all sins: past, present, and future," this idea did not exist in the Church before the Reformation. The fact is, the Catholic Church has never taught that baptism guarantees salvation, or that baptism washes away the sins we haven't committed yet.[104] What the Church has always taught is that baptism purifies us from the guilt of original sin, and cleanses us of all sins committed up until the time of the baptism itself.[105] But it does not wash away future sins before we commit them—that would be a license to sin freely. So baptism is a clean slate, but not a free ride.

This means that one can lose one's baptismal grace by habitual sin (which is to say, a lifestyle of rejection of Christ by disobeying his commandments), or by committing mortal sins, or by apostasy, teaching heresy, or creating a schism (division in the Church).[106] Post-baptismal sin is a real problem, not to be taken lightly or waived aside as if inconsequential.[107] This brings us to another Protestant concept that was never taught in the Church before the Reformation: the idea that all sins are equal in the eyes of God. Although the Fathers did certainly understand that no sin is too small to worry about, they also taught that some sins are worse than others.[108]

WHAT ARE MORTAL SINS?

In the first letter of John (5:16–17), we read that there are some sins that lead to death, and some that don't. Of course, death here means spiritual death—separation from God, leading to the death of the soul, or damnation. For, logically, if a person doesn't repent of his sins and dies in a state of separation from God, it could result in eternal separation from God. So there are some sins that can lead to the loss of salvation—and remember, it must be this way if free will is truly free, since if we are free to accept Christ, we must also be free to reject him.[109]

The early Christians did not have the traditional list of "seven deadly sins," that was created in the Middle Ages, but defined a mortal sin as anything that breaks one of the Ten Commandments.[110] And even among those deadly sins, they taught that some are worse than others. For example, apostasy (to deny the Faith) has always been considered one of the worst of the mortal sins, because it is the conscious rejection of Christ.[111] Idolatry is a close second, and in fact in many cases apostasy and idolatry go hand in hand, especially in times of persecution.[112] Teaching a heresy is a mortal sin because it leads others astray, and causes them to deny the true Faith.[113] Note, however, that simply to *believe* a heresy is not necessarily a mortal sin, since it may be unintentional. But to knowingly propagate a false doctrine (especially after being corrected by Church authorities) not only leads the faithful astray, but threatens to split the Church. And such a split, or *schism*, would come to be seen by many as the worst sin of all.

After introducing the concept of mortal sin, John then goes on to advise his people not to pray for those who had committed mortal sins. Why would he do this?[114] Probably the answer is that they were considered *excommunicated*. In other words, by their own actions, and by their refusal to repent, they had not only separated themselves from God, but they had also separated themselves from the communion of the Church. Paul himself advocated excommunication as a form of discipline that, it was hoped, would motivate the sinner to repent and seek reconciliation with God by coming back to the Church.[115] So not only does sin separate us from God, but it also separates us from the Body of Christ, the Church. Excommunication means more than being shunned by a community, it means being excluded from the communion of the Eucharist—and being excluded from that sacrament means one no longer "remains in" Christ. Excommunication also meant that one could not receive a Christian burial, because if one died in a state of excommunication, the Fathers assumed that person would not be welcomed into the kingdom of heaven.[116]

The point of all this is to demonstrate the seriousness of post-baptismal sin, especially the mortal sins. The Church Fathers firmly believed that even a baptized ("saved") Christian could use his free will to sin to the point of rejection of Christ and his Church, which would result in the loss of salvation. This is how they read such New Testament passages as Matthew 7:21–23, in which Jesus says, "Not everyone who says to me, 'Lord, Lord,' will enter the kingdom of heaven, but only the one who does the will of my Father in heaven."[117] Of course this raises the question: How does a person, or the Church, deal with the reality of post-baptismal sin? How do we prevent our sins from damning us?

Isn't Faith All We Need for Salvation?

We can see that the Church Fathers did not believe that faith is all one needs for salvation, since they believed that post-baptismal sin was not washed away by baptism, and so could lead to the loss of salvation. To persevere to the end, one had to remain in Christ (Matthew 24:13, John 15:1–10), and remaining in Christ has meant, to the Fathers, remaining in the Body of Christ, the Church. Therefore, the solution to the separation caused by post-baptismal sin was to be reconciled, both to God and to the Church.

The Fathers reasoned that since free will implies moral responsibility, and since we can separate ourselves from God by the choices we make, in order to re-connect with God once we have separated ourselves, we have to actively participate in the solution to the problem. And just as one comes to Christ through the Church and its sacraments, one also comes *back* to Christ through the Church.[118] For example, Ignatius, bishop of Antioch in the early second century, wrote, "For as many as are of God and of Jesus Christ are also with the bishop. And as many as shall, in the exercise of repentance, return into the unity of the Church, these, too, shall belong to God, that they may live according to Jesus Christ."[119]

In other words, in the same way that the Prodigal Son had to repent and confess his sins to his father in order to return to his home, the sinner who has gone astray must also repent and confess in order to return to the Church. But how is the Church to know if the repentance is real and the confession is sincere? The answer is penance—something active that a person does to demonstrate the sincerity of his repentance. Therefore, reconciliation is both internal and external—internal repentance, and outward confession and penance—and so penance becomes the "outward and visible sign" of the internal repentance.[120]

In the early Church, penance usually took the form of prayer and fasting, along with works of charity and almsgiving. But whatever form it took, the Fathers were unanimous in their belief that works of charity helped not only the recipient, but also the one performing them, because they contributed to a person's reconciliation with God, and therefore were part of the remedy for post-baptismal sin.[121] Polycarp, second-century bishop of Smyrna, wrote, "When you are able to do good, do not put it off, because charity delivers one from death."[122] He does not mean that you might save a starving person's life if you give that person food—he means that you might save yourself from the spiritual death of mortal sin. The second-century *Epistle of Barnabas* advises, "Work with your hands for a ransom for your sins."[123] Clement of Alexandria wrote, "Good works are an acceptable prayer to the Lord."[124] Irenaeus of Lyons said that "possessions distributed to the poor do annul former covetousness."[125] In truth, the idea that good works contributed to a Christian's ongoing reconciliation with God was so prevalent among the early Fathers, it would be impossible to cite all of the examples here. Some even went so far as to say that sins could not be forgiven *without* penance.[126]

From the very beginning of the Church's existence, almsgiving was an especially important form of penance. Even before the tradition of private confession to a priest, in which a person might be directed to do penance of the priest's choosing, Christians believed that almsgiving "relieves the burden of sin."[127] Perhaps this is because all sin ultimately comes from self-centeredness, and charitable giving is in a way the opposite of selfishness. Many Fathers believed that charity was better than prayer and fasting, because charity is a selfless act of love that helps others.[128] And so penance is both private (acts of devotion) and communal (acts of charity) because in that way it covers both love of God and love of neighbor. The Fathers read 1 Peter 4:8, "love covers a multitude of sins," and they knew that Peter meant *love* as more than an emotion—love is action.[129]

With regard to almsgiving, the Fathers envisioned a kind of symbiotic relationship between the rich and the poor, in which the ministry of the rich was to share with the poor out of their abundance, and the ministry of the poor was to pray for the souls of the rich.[130] After all, Jesus said it would be easier for a camel to go through the eye of a needle than for a rich person to enter the kingdom of God.[131] Of course, he went on to say that "for God all things are possible." But this passage of Scripture was troubling enough that it prompted Clement of Alexandria to preach a homily called, "Who is the Rich Man that Shall be Saved?" He said that being rich is not a sin in and of itself.[132] In fact, if there were no people with surplus resources, who would give to the poor? The sin, he said, is hoarding one's resources and refusing to share.[133] Therefore, the rich person who is saved is the one who gives to the poor. The Christian is obligated to give to those who are in need, no questions asked.[134] Abundance always comes with the responsibility of stewardship. God's gifts are meant to be given away, and if a person has surplus resources, then God has blessed that person specifically for the purpose of sharing.

Is Penance a Form of "Works-Righteousness"?

In spite of the longstanding tradition of good works (especially giving to the poor) relieving the burden of post-baptismal sin, the Catholic attitude toward penance has often been criticized as a form of "works-righteousness." But does the Church really teach such a concept as "works-righteousness"? The answer is that it depends on what one means by "works-righteousness." If by "works-righteousness" one means a justification by works, as if salvation were earned by doing good works, then the answer is a resounding no. The Catholic Church has never taught such a doctrine.

Penance is not something that non-Christians do to work their way into a relationship with God. Penance is for Christians, who are baptized and already in the Church. It only works for *post*-baptismal sin.[135] In fact, penance assumes salvation, but then contributes to sanctification. Remember that the early Christians did not believe in the doctrine of perseverance as "once saved always saved." When Jesus said, "Whoever perseveres to the end will be saved," he clearly implied that some would not.[136] So in that sense, the Fathers taught that penance contributes to perseverance, but there are no guarantees. For example, Clement of Alexandria said that perseverance in good works leads to eternal life, but that one should not expect salvation to come without struggle or effort.[137]

Jesus said, "Remain in me, as I remain in you" (John 15:4). This means that we have to *do* something to remain in him—*to remain* is not a static state of being, but an active participation in Christ. Remember that the Fathers taught that the way Christians remain in Christ is through the sacraments of the Church: including regular reception of the Eucharist and regular confession of post-baptismal sin, with penance—that is, ongoing participation in good works, which "covers a multitude of sins," to borrow Peter's language (1 Pet. 4:8).[138] Since a Christian can lose his salvation through mortal sin, something must be done to reconcile him to Christ and the Church in order to overcome the self-imposed separation from God. Penance, whether it is also self-imposed or required by clergy, is what we do to demonstrate the sincerity of our repentance and overcome the distance that sin creates between ourselves and God.[139] It also motivates us to resist temptation in the future, since we are held accountable to the Church, and not only to our own conscience. So, just as the water of baptism is an outward sign of an inward faith (the faith of the parents and sponsors, in the case of infant baptism), penance is an outward sign of an inward repentance, which leads to reconciliation with God, perseverance, and ultimately, salvation.[140]

Therefore, good works do not earn salvation, but in a way they do contribute to salvation, by contributing to perseverance. To put it rather bluntly, the Fathers taught that good works do not get you saved, but they can *keep* you saved. This is how they interpreted Paul's words to the Philippians, "work out your salvation with fear and trembling" (Phil. 2:12). The fear and trembling is real, because one can lose salvation. But on the other hand, Paul goes on to say, "For God is the one who, for his good purpose, works in you both to desire and to work" (Phil 2:13). Therefore we can still have confidence that God's grace is at work in us to encourage us toward perseverance, while there is the expectation that we use our free will to cooperate with God's grace through penance and other good works.[141]

So when the Fathers talk about good works, they are not talking about "works-righteousness." Works do not make one righteous—if they could, then the Law of Moses would have been sufficient for eternal life and Jesus would not have had to die on the cross.[142] The Fathers were writing to believers, who (they assumed) were already saved by their baptism and their membership in the Body of Christ, the Church. So they are not talking about earning salvation, but there is a sense in which good works contribute to "keeping" salvation, or act as a preventative against the loss of salvation. So even though works do not make one righteous, they are a big part of what it means to be righteous.

In the third century, the escalating persecution of Christians by the Romans led to the need to formalize confession, reconciliation, and penance, especially for those who had denied the Faith by committing apostasy and idolatry to save their lives.[143] We will continue this discussion in the next chapter, but the point for the moment is that when the sacrament of reconciliation was standardized, the absolution of sin came before the assignment of any penance, which proves that the penance was not thought of as "making up for" sin, in the sense of earning forgiveness.[144] Penance was an expectation placed on the person who was already forgiven, as both a demonstration of sincerity and a deterrent to future sin.

Free Will and God's Grace

Around the turn of the fifth century, a monk named Pelagius read some of Augustine's writings and took issue with what the bishop of Hippo was saying. Augustine had struggled with temptation and sin in his own life, and that led him to question whether the human will really was free after all. Eventually, Augustine became pessimistic about the ability of any person to resist temptation and obey the commandments. He came to believe that the human will is not really free—at least not free enough to do anything good—and he reasoned that any good work that a person might do is only an act of God working in and through him.[145] He said we might be free to *want* to do what is right, but we are not actually free to *do* it. Only God's grace can free us to do the right thing.[146]

When it came to salvation, then, Augustine concluded that there was no way we can participate in our salvation or even cooperate with grace, and so our salvation depends on a decision of God, completely apart from anything we might do, and even before we might come to faith. So he taught a doctrine of *election*, which said that God decided before we were ever born which of us were destined to salvation, and which of us were not. This is effectively a *double predestination*, meaning that some are predestined to salvation, and the rest are predestined to damnation, and there's nothing humans can do to change their destiny. This also means that all those who are among the elect must finally persevere and be welcomed into the kingdom of heaven, since it is God who causes the perseverance to fulfill his election. Thus Augustine is the originator of the idea of perseverance as "once saved, always saved."

When Pelagius read what Augustine was teaching, he rejected it on the same basis that all of the earlier Fathers had affirmed free will: that if humans do not have free will, then they cannot be held accountable for sin, and evil is really to be blamed on God. In other words, Pelagius reasoned that if Augustine was right, what was the point of being a monk? Indeed, what was the point of trying to be a good Christian at all? So Pelagius started writing in opposition to Augustine. However, Pelagius did not simply take issue with Augustine's teachings, he went to the opposite extreme: he denied the very existence of original sin, and even went so far as to imply that infants did not need to be baptized. Note that both extreme views, Augustine's and Pelagius's, were virtually unheard of in the Church before their time.

Pelagius became the champion of free will, but to the extent of teaching that the human will was free to turn to God initially even without the help of divine grace. Or perhaps it is more accurate to say that for him, grace was reduced to the information one might need to make an informed decision of faith. "Grace," for Pelagius, is the gift of the Ten Commandments, the Gospels, and the example of Jesus Christ, which is all anyone should need to come to faith by free will. Thus he believed that anyone's salvation was entirely based on how he used his free will. Pelagius was eventually condemned as a heretic, but his way of thinking, which we call "Pelagianism," was carried on by another teacher named Julian of Eclanum.

Thus Augustine and Pelagius became the two extremes of a polarized, and polarizing, controversy in the early Church. For Pelagius, grace is passive (reduced to information) and the human will is active. For Augustine, grace is the active power of God and the human will is passive.[147] In fact, Augustine believed that the human will was so broken that it could not move in any positive direction without the force of grace. This is the origin of the concept of the *total depravity* of the will. In response to Pelagius and Julian, Augustine went even farther to his side and effectively painted himself into a corner, saying that God's grace was irresistible, implying that if one was chosen to be among the elect (saved by predestination), even evil actions could not change that.[148] But this created a logical problem. If some people are predestined to damnation, then either Christ's death on the cross was insufficient to help them, or Christ did not die for them in the first place. Since he could not allow that the death of Christ was in any way ineffective, Augustine instead implied that Christ did not die for all of humanity, but only died for the elect, a concept now known as *limited atonement*.

The Conclusions of the Church

Between these two extremes of Augustine (everything rests on God's grace) and Pelagius and Julian (it's all about the human will), there were two attempts at finding a middle way. The theologian John Cassian, along with some others, proposed what we now refer to as "semi-Pelagianism" (though they would have been horrified at the label, since they rejected Pelagius's teachings as heresy). Cassian agreed with Augustine that grace is a power of God, and a gift of the Holy Spirit, but he said that the human will was truly free to accept or reject grace. Grace is not irresistible (unless God wants it to be, on a case-by-case basis).[149] However, Cassian and the other "semi-Pelagians" seem to have been a bit too optimistic about the human will, implying that it was even free to turn to God apart from grace, or before receiving grace.[150] In other words, in the human-divine relationship, a person can take the initiative by free will, and then grace would be cooperating with, or following, the human will. This position would ultimately be unacceptable because it gave too much power to the human will, and did not sufficiently take into consideration original sin. Nevertheless, Cassian was not considered a heretic.

The true "middle way," and the position that won the day, was the one we now refer to as "semi-Augustinian." Championed by Caesarius, bishop of Arles, the semi-Augustinian position was almost the same as the semi-Pelagian position, except that Caesarius taught that the human will was not free to turn toward God without the gift of prior grace. God's grace must take the initiative, but then the human will was truly free to cooperate with grace or reject it. In this way, atonement is not limited, and Christ died for all, but what determined whether a person was finally saved was the response of the individual's will to God's grace. Thus grace is not irresistible—a person is truly free, even to reject Christ. This position was affirmed as the Church's teaching at the Council of Orange in the year 529, ninety-nine years after Augustine's death.

Of course Augustine was never declared a heretic, and he remains one of the most important of the Church Fathers. However, the Church rejected Augustine's teachings on total depravity, election (as double predestination), limited atonement, irresistible grace, and perseverance, because these negate the reality of human free will, and call into question moral responsibility. However, it accepted Augustine's understanding of original sin as seriously inhibiting the will, and causing all of us to have a real tendency toward sin.

Interestingly, over a millennium later some of the Protestant Reformers picked up the rejected doctrines. Although it is a bit

of an oversimplification of John Calvin's teachings, many people
are familiar with the famous acronym "T.U.L.I.P.," as a memory
device for the main teachings of Calvinism. The letters stand
for *Total depravity* (that Augustinian pessimism about human nature and the lack of true free will), *Unconditional election* (double
predestination based on God's decision without and before any
input from the individual), *Limited atonement* (that Christ died
only for the elect), *Irresistible grace* (the elect are not free to reject
God), and *Perseverance* (the elect must persevere, "once saved,
always saved").

However, the Catholic Church had concluded that the human person is not totally depraved, but does in fact have free
will, and therefore is held accountable for his actions. Furthermore, election is not unconditional; it is conditioned upon a
response of faith as an act of the will. What Jesus called repentance (turning to God), what Paul called faith (or belief),
and what John called accepting (or receiving) Christ, all point
to the reality that although God's grace takes the initiative to
reach out to humanity, each person must respond. Grace is
the invitation; the will chooses how to RSVP.[151] Therefore,
atonement is not limited to the predestined. The invitation is
extended to all by God's grace—yet that grace is not irresistible, and individuals can use their free will to reject Christ.
For those who are not finally saved, this is the result of their
own choice, not because of a preemptive decision of God.[152]
Perseverance, then, is not guaranteed for the elect and out of
reach for the pre-damned; rather it depends on each person's
will cooperating with God's grace, as we accept God's invitation to justification, and then participate in our sanctification,
and "work out [our] salvation" (Phil. 2:12).

Indulgences

One of the things that Martin Luther objected to in his critique
of the Church was the sale of *indulgences*. An indulgence is an
act of the Church by which the merit of Christ and the saints

is applied to the sinner, to release him from some of the consequences of sin in purgatory. Sometimes indulgences were associated with certain acts of devotion, such as going on a pilgrimage
to a holy site for prayer and contemplation. Probably beginning
with the Crusades, indulgences were offered as a reward for service to the Church. So a knight embarking on a Crusade to the
Holy Land would be considered as though he were going on a
holy pilgrimage, and if he died on the Crusade, he would be
considered a Christian martyr.

As time went on, many people came to believe that one could
obtain an indulgence for someone else. This is consistent with
the longstanding acceptance of vicarious faith (one person's
faith standing in for another, for example, that an infant can be
baptized on the basis of its parents' faith).[153] The Church began
granting indulgences that were supposed to apply to the souls of
the departed who were thought to be languishing in purgatory.
So in addition to praying for the transition of one's departed
loved ones, a person could also obtain an indulgence that, it was
believed, would lessen their time in purgatory, or even immediately erase any remaining impurity and release that person from
purgatory into heaven.

In addition, long before the Middle Ages, the concept of
almsgiving as a penance had evolved to include offerings to the
Church. If one could give to the poor indirectly by giving to
the Church (which was supporting the poor), then people reasoned that any gift to the Church was a form of almsgiving, and
therefore a valid penance. When this was combined with the
concept of indulgences, eventually some Church leaders realized
they could raise a lot of money for the Church by offering indulgences in exchange for an offering. Monks were sent out into the
countryside, armed with stacks of indulgence certificates, ready
to hand out absolution for an appropriate donation. According
to the story, one famous indulgence seller even had a little jingle
he would sing as he walked along the roads from town to town.
Translated into English, it goes something like this: *As soon as the
coin in the coffer rings, a soul from purgatory springs.*

Therefore, it is very understandable that Martin Luther would object to the practice of indulgence sales. In fact, the Church would soon see it his way, and the sale of indulgences stopped with Pope Pius V and the Council of Trent, in 1567. Pope Paul VI further reformed the practice of indulgences in 1967, and they now require both confession and Eucharistic communion. So, while the Catholic Church still has indulgences, we no longer sell them.

Just as St. Paul's language of faith over against the law was a response to the Judaizers, Luther's emphasis on "faith alone" (*sola fide*) was a response to the sale of indulgences as an abuse of the practice of penance. And just as Augustine reacted to Pelagius by going to an extreme, Luther reacted by also going to the Augustinian extreme, emphasizing a pessimistic view of human nature and putting all of the burden for doing good on God's grace. But *sola fide* was never meant to imply that good works were impossible, or unnecessary. In fact, "faith alone" is really just shorthand for the Pauline phrase, "by grace . . . through faith" (Eph. 2:8). God's grace takes the initiative, and faith is a response to grace—but that response is only possible because of the grace. In this, Lutherans and Catholics agree, as we will see.

Can a Catholic Have Assurance of Salvation?

It should be said at this point that Catholics do believe one can have a sense of peace about one's salvation. Protestants sometimes criticize the Catholic Church for leaving its people with a feeling of despair over their salvation, and the question is often asked: How do you know if you've done enough good works to keep from losing your salvation?

The answer is in one sense that we don't, and that's why we have to work at it (and that's why we believe in purgatory). To speak of "assurance" of salvation might be going farther than Catholic Tradition would allow, but this does not mean that we can't have confidence in our savior. When we identify with Christ as our Lord, and remain in him through the sacraments and through acts of devotion and charity, we can be confident that we will not "accidentally" lose our salvation because of one slip-up or a few minor ("venial") sins. God wants us to be vigilant, but he does not want us to live a life of worry.

So we believe the promises of Scripture, where Paul tells us that we can have peace (Rom. 8:31–39, Phil. 1:6, 4:6–7), and where John tells us that we can have confidence, and do not need to fear judgment (John 14:1–2, 27–28, 1 John 4:17–18, 5:11–15). The key to having peace of mind about salvation is in ongoing identification with Christ through Church attendance (Heb. 10:25), participation in the sacraments—especially the Eucharist—and by doing good works. These things show us that salvation is not only individual, but it is also communal, and we "stay saved" by staying with the community, the Body of Christ. This is why early Christian writers such as Cyprian of Carthage and Tertullian said that there is no salvation outside the Church—because it would be virtually impossible to remain connected to Christ without the sacraments.

All of this means that the Christian life requires vigilance. It requires a continual participation in the liturgy and other ministries of the Church, and ongoing cooperation with God's grace in the world through good works. Also, when we fall into sin, the separation that sin causes between ourselves and God must be repaired through reconciliation. So perseverance is the result of remaining in Christ (John, chapter 15) and working out our salvation (Phil. 2:12). This work of reconciliation is both private and communal because it requires both repentance (a turning, or change of heart) and confession and penance. In this way, the works of penance contribute to perseverance, and ultimately, to salvation, because (acts of) "love covers a multitude of sins" (1 Pet. 4:8).

So we cooperate with God's grace when we do good works. But it must be pointed out that although the Fathers taught that the works are done by free will, they also taught that they could not be done without grace. God's grace motivates and empowers us to do good, so that we cannot put our faith in the capacity of the human will. Even in salvation, the initial response of faith is itself a work of God, since no one could turn to God without the prior gift of grace. Still, the Church had to reject the Augustinian doctrines of election and perseverance because these logically require irresistible grace (negating free will) and lead to limited atonement (negating the universality of the cross).[154] The Fathers knew that the Church had to maintain that Christ died for all—and it also had to maintain that if someone is not finally saved, they cannot blame God for that.

Does the Catholic Church Over-Emphasize Works?

So does the Catholic Church lean too much toward the Martha side? Not officially, and not intentionally. Of course, as we have seen, there have been abuses of the tradition of penance, and there have been times when Catholics went too far, as there are to this day (and as there are in any faith tradition). But when it is at its best, the Catholic Church strives for a balance of faith and works. And even with faith itself, the Church teaches a balance between two extremes: faith is not completely up to God with no room for free will, nor is it completely an act of the human will apart from grace (which would reduce the faith decision to a kind of work). The Catholic "middle way" is to say that faith is a free-will response to grace, which would be impossible without prior grace. Grace comes first, then faith, then works, and everything that comes after grace is only possible because of the grace.

So faith and works are not mutually exclusive, as if emphasizing one diminished the other. They are complementary, and one completes the other. Specifically, works are part of the life of faith, and make faith complete. In a way, Paul emphasized what was necessary to begin the journey of salvation, and James and John emphasized what is necessary for ongoing faith. But all would agree that faith without works would be just as bad as works without faith. So the problem is not an argument between Paul and James (though there does seem to have been a problem between Martin Luther and James). The point is that the Catholic Church does not teach salvation by works any more than most Protestant denominations teach that good works are unnecessary.[155] As Paul wrote, and as the Fathers knew, we are not saved by good works, but we are created for good works (Eph. 5:8–10).

~

The Church has never taught a salvation by works, in the sense that works earn justification. Salvation is made possible by the cross of Christ and offered to all by God's grace, but it becomes a reality for an individual when there is a response of faith and baptism. However, salvation is incomplete without ongoing participation in the sacraments of the Church, and evidence of the "fruit of the Spirit" and good works of devotion (love of God) and charity (love of neighbor). In other words, the Christian life is not a matter of faith *or* works, but faith *and* works. The life of faith includes moral accountability and a responsibility to love our neighbor, and so it could be said that faith includes works, just as we said Tradition includes Scripture.

All human beings, by virtue of being created in the image of God, have free will. Therefore, we are accountable to God for our choices, and to some extent Scripture teaches that we will be judged on the basis of our works—whether good works or sins. Christian baptism washes away the guilt of original sin, but the tendency toward sin remains, and baptism does not wash away future sins. Therefore post-baptismal sin is a real problem, especially the "mortal," or deadly sins, which are the gravest sins—the ones that break the Ten Commandments. Thus, perseverance in the Faith is not guaranteed, and one can lose one's salvation after baptism through habitual (lifestyle) or mortal sin. In other words, just like we have free will to accept Christ, we always have the freedom to reject him by turning away. In a way, this would be a kind of rejection of the offer of forgiveness that we had once accepted, and if one rejects the offer of forgiveness, one should not expect to receive forgiveness.[156]

Sometimes certain passages in Paul's letters are used to support a *sola fide* approach that diminishes works. But when Paul wrote those passages, he was arguing against the Judaizers. He was not contrasting faith over against works—he was contrasting *justification* by faith over against justification by *the law*. He certainly did advocate participation in good works, even as a way to participate in our own salvation and sanctification. This is how God expects us to use our free will in general, but especially when it comes to repairing the estrangement caused by our own sin. When our sin separates us from God and the Church, we participate in our reconciliation through penance, which is the outward sign of the sincerity of our inward repentance.

The bottom line is that *sola fide*, or "faith alone," does not sufficiently take into account the reality that salvation is not a one-time event in a person's life; it is not only a decision point or profession of faith that a person can look back on and remember when he "got saved." On the contrary, salvation is an ongoing process that includes spiritual growth in holiness (sanctification) and perseverance in and through the Church. We will explore this in greater depth in a later chapter when we look at the meaning of the concept of conversion, but for now the key point is that the Church has never taught that salvation is a done deal. As long as a person lives, he is not so much "saved" as "being saved." A conversion experience, decision point, profession of faith, or baptism may in fact be the beginning of salvation, but it is only the beginning. Salvation is a lifelong process that is not complete until we each find ourselves in the presence of God in the heavenly kingdom. In the meantime, we work out our salvation . . . with fear and trembling, yes, but also with confidence and peace.[157]

Featured Father

Clement of Alexandria: Apologist and Catechist

We call this Church Father Clement *of Alexandria* to distinguish him from Clement of Rome, but this eastern Clement was not a bishop. Born around the middle of the second century (probably A.D. 150 to 160), probably in Athens, he was a Christian philosopher who came to be the head of a famous school of catechesis in Alexandria, Egypt.

Like many of the earlier apologists of the second century, Clement was a philosopher before he was a Christian. He set out to study all of the different philosophical schools, determined to find the best one and devote his life to it. He included Christianity in his survey of philosophies, and eventually concluded that Christianity was in fact the best of all the philosophical options. He followed a Christian teacher named Pantaenus to Alexandria, where he eventually (in about A.D. 190) succeeded Pantaenus as head of the catechetical school. One of Clement's students was the famous Origen, the genius/heretic whom scholars either love or hate. When Roman persecution came to Alexandria around the turn of the third century, Clement fled the city, leaving Origen in charge of the school. Clement traveled throughout the Holy Land, and probably died in Asia Minor (what is now Turkey) by about the year 215.

Clement was a brilliant teacher and a prolific writer. His document called *Exhortation to the Greeks* (or *to the Heathen*) is an excellent summary of early Christian theology up to his time, though his contemporary Irenaeus would take it further. His documents known as *The Instructor* and *The Miscellanies* are very long, often difficult, and reflect his rigorist ethics. He basically said that if you like it, it must be a sin. Everything from gourmet food to imported wine were on his list of sinful luxuries. He also took a very strict approach to sexuality. While many of the gnostic heretics of the time were sexual libertines—advocating extreme sexual freedom, but forbidding procreation—Clement took the opposite position, strongly suggesting that sex is only for the purpose of having children.

Perhaps Clement's most interesting writing is the sermon, *Who Is the Rich Man That Shall Be Saved?* Here he answers the question posed by Jesus' disciples in Matthew 19:23–26/Mark 10:23–27. When Jesus said, "It is easier for a camel to pass through the eye of a needle than for one who is rich to enter the kingdom of God," the disciples responded by asking, "Who then can be saved?" Clement's answer was that a rich person can be saved if he shares and gives to the poor. Here Clement reflects the consensus of the early Church Fathers that almsgiving is a form of penance and contributes to one's salvation.

3

Seven Sacraments

Walk into a Protestant church, especially an old Baptist or Methodist church with traditional architecture, and what do you see? There in the middle of the chancel, at the focal point of worship, is the pulpit—the place where the word of God is preached. Now walk into a Catholic church, and what do you see? The focal point of worship is the altar table—the place where the Eucharist is celebrated.

This architectural difference between the two traditions says a lot. Catholicism is historically focused on the sacraments, whereas the Protestant Reformation signaled a shift away from the sacramental toward preaching. In other words, for Protestants, the primary proclamation of the gospel is done in the sermon; for Catholics, it happens on the altar table, where, the apostle Paul says, we "proclaim the death of the Lord until he comes" (1 Cor. 11:26). From the very beginning of the Church, the Eucharist has been the focus of Christian worship, and in fact the sacraments in general have been the center of the Christian life.

WHAT IS A SACRAMENT?

The word sacrament, from the Latin *sacramentum*, originally meant a sacred oath, like the one a soldier would take when he joined a Roman legion.[158] The oath was understood as a binding vow to a new way of life, and in the legions it came to be associated with the mark, or brand, that identified a soldier. Often the oath was taken in the context of religious (pagan) ritual, which was part of the reason why some early Church Fathers said that a Christian should not join the military.[159] Furthermore, some of these Fathers said that the vow itself put a Christian in a conflicted position, and by swearing an oath to Caesar, the soldier

was submitting to another authority, when he should submit
only to Christ.

In the Church, this idea of a sacred oath was applied to a confession of faith associated with baptism. Thus baptism itself was
described as a *seal* that "marked" one for God—in a way, desig-
nating the Christian as a member of God's legions—but more
important, it spiritually "branded" a person as belonging to
God.[160] This is already evident in the book of Revelation, which
contrasts those who are sealed for God (i.e., baptized) with those
who are marked with the mark of the beast.[161] Within the context of Christian liturgy, the sacred oath came to be combined
with the idea of divine mystery, since something was taking place
that included divine intervention in human life. For example, the
third-century theologian Novatian described the divine visitation to Jacob in Genesis as a *sacramentum* because it was a sacred
mystery in which God intervened in human history, and because
it foreshadowed the visitation of the divine to humanity in the
Incarnation of Jesus Christ.[162] So the word *sacramentum* took on
the broader meaning of a *sacred mystery* which implied miraculous
divine intervention.

Therefore, a sacrament is something extraordinary, in the literal sense of the word: extra-ordinary. It is beyond the ordinary
experience of everyday human life because it is a miraculous
event of divine intervention. This means that it assumes a presence of God that goes above and beyond God's omnipresence
(he is here because he is everywhere). In a sacrament, God is actively present in a more powerful way, though what that means
exactly is part of the mystery. But the point is that a sacrament
is not just something that people do—it is something that God
does, and therefore it is something that changes the people who
take part in it. Novatian also called creation itself "sacramental,"
because God's creative activity is a sacred mystery.[163]

So a sacrament is a miraculous event in which God effects a
creative change in the person who receives it. It is also sometimes called a "means of grace." In other words, it is through the
sacraments that people are given the gift of God's grace. What

is grace, exactly? Grace is God's love, compassion, and forgiveness, but it is also something like a divine energy that empowers a person to live the Christian life. Grace regenerates us (making us "born again"), and enables the gifts of the Holy Spirit. It strengthens us to resist temptation, and it is the fuel of good works. Grace causes spiritual growth and sanctification, and results in our adoption as sons and daughters of God. And while the sacraments are not the only way that God's grace comes to us, they are the primary and most powerful way.

So to answer the question, *What is a sacrament?*: a sacrament is a sacred mystery in which Christians engage in a holy ritual that glorifies God through worship, but in which God is also active, sanctifying the recipients of the sacrament, and through them, the whole Body of Christ.[164] This divine intervention results in a powerful infusion of grace, permanently changing the recipient. Some of the Church Fathers described the Church as being like a hospital, and the sacraments are the Church's medicine.[165] Therefore, the sacraments are not simply rites of commemoration—they heal, they strengthen, and they empower Christians to do what we could not do without the power of Christ in us.[166]

Because of the serious and miraculous nature of the sacraments, the Catholic Church has historically reserved for bishops the authority to preside over them. This has been the case going back as far as we have records of early Christian practice. Of course, as time went on and the Church grew, one bishop in a city could not preside over all of the sacraments needed for an increasing number of Christians. So eventually the bishops were able to delegate authority to their priests. And this is how it remains today. Priests may preside over the sacraments, but only as long as they are given permission by the bishop in their area. But as the successors of the apostles, the bishops had the authority to make sure that the sacraments and the rituals surrounding them maintained their integrity and retained the necessary degree of continuity from one place to another. The bishops made sure that Christians in different places stayed on the same page, so to speak, with regard to the practice and understanding of the

sacraments. This is not to say that every detail was done exactly
the same from one city to the next. But as the guardians of the
Church's teaching, the bishops were responsible for making sure
that the sacraments stayed true to their origins, and that the
Church stayed unified. So as we have already seen, the hierarchy served the need to maintain unity in the one worldwide
Church, and guaranteed continuity with the Tradition.[167]

There are of course other sacred rituals in the Church, such
as funeral rites, the taking of religious vows, special blessings,
dedications, consecrations for particular ministries, pilgrimages
and processions, and even exorcisms.[168] There are also more personal practices of devotion that are considered holy acts, such
as the veneration of shrines and relics, the stations of the cross,
praying the rosary, and almsgiving. We will talk about these
practices in detail later, but for now the point is that any of these
practices could be considered a means of grace, but they are not
sacraments because they do not necessarily require the participation of a bishop or priest and they "do not confer the grace of
the Holy Spirit in the way that the sacraments do."[169] These are
usually called *sacramentals*, since they are considered sacred rites,
but they do not permanently change a person.

But this raises the question: why do most Protestants have only
two sacraments, whereas Catholics have seven? First of all, it is
probably fair to say that all Christians have some rituals that they
hold above the others as more profound. There are some Christians who do not name any particular rites as "sacraments," per se,
in part because they argue that all of creation is sacred—and they
have a point. They simply call their most important rituals *ordinances*, preferring a different word for the same idea. In any case,
virtually all Christians have a certain number of rites they revere
above the others. Then they also have the rest of their special rituals or acts of worship which they believe are important, but not as
important as the primary ones—what Catholics and many Protestants call *sacramentals*. However, some of what Catholics call sacraments are considered sacramentals in the Protestant denominations, such as confirmation, matrimony, ordination, and anointing.

Why Do Catholics Have Seven Sacraments?

Most Protestant denominations acknowledge two sacraments: baptism and holy communion. They usually claim that these are the two sacraments initiated by Jesus himself, by his own participation in them. Jesus was baptized, and Jesus instituted the Lord's Supper at the Last Supper. However, Catholics maintain that Jesus participated in more than just these two. Of course, Jesus had no sins to confess, but he did grant absolution of sins, and gave his apostles the authority to do the same.[170] Jesus blessed the wedding at Cana by his presence, and by performing his first miracle there, changing the water into wine. Therefore he did participate in, and validate, the institution of marriage, even though he himself was not married.[171] He was anointed with perfumed oil in preparation for his death,[172] and by choosing and commissioning the apostles, he instituted what would become ordination.

Nevertheless, it is true that in the earliest centuries of the Church, Christians did not have all seven sacraments as we know them today. At least, they were not all formalized rituals yet. On the other hand, it is not the case that only the two sacraments claimed by Protestants existed in the early Church. There were two sacraments at the beginning, but the two were really four, because each sacrament was, at the beginning, two sacraments in one.

It could be argued that the first sacrament was baptism, since baptism begins with John the Baptist, and the ministry of Jesus began with his own baptism. *Christian* baptism was instituted by Jesus in the command known as the "Great Commission," when Jesus said, "Go, therefore, and make disciples of all nations, baptizing them in the name of the Father, and of the Son, and of the Holy Spirit" (Matt. 28:19). Furthermore, the apostles soon realized that baptism is regenerative, because it results in the indwelling of the Holy Spirit. However, it is clear from the book of Acts that although this Spirit-baptism is associated with water baptism, it is not exactly the same thing.[173] In the early Church, the coming of the Holy Spirit was connected more directly to the *confirmation* of the baptism, which was an imposition (laying on) of hands by the presider. For example, around the turn of the third century, the theologian Tertullian wrote:

> Not that in the waters we obtain the Holy Spirit; but in the water . . . we are cleansed, and prepared for the Holy Spirit . . . After this, when we have issued from the font, we are thoroughly anointed with a blessed unction . . . In the next place the hand is laid on us, invoking and inviting the Holy Spirit through benediction . . . Then over our cleansed and blessed bodies willingly descends from the Father that most Holy Spirit.[174]

So in the early Church, baptism was really two distinct rites—the baptism and the confirmation.[175] Baptism was never done without the confirmation, so—two sacraments in one. Around the third century, the two rites came to be separated, for reasons we will explore later.

Even before giving his disciples the Great Commission, Jesus had instituted the Lord's Supper, on that Thursday night before his Passion. In doing that, he initiated the sacrament of the Eucharist. But in the earliest description of the Eucharist, in Paul's first letter to the Corinthians (11:17–34), we can see that there was a concern in the early Church about receiving the sacrament "unworthily," that is, being unprepared to receive the sacrament because of the burden of sin. So Paul advises that Christians examine their consciences before coming to the table. This is based on Jesus' own words when he said, "Therefore if you are presenting your offering at the altar, and there remember that your brother has something against you, leave your offering there before the altar and go; first be reconciled to your brother, and then come and present your offering" (Matt. 5:23–24).

A few decades later, the earliest manual of Church practice, known as the *Didache*, stated, "On the Lord's own day gather together and break bread and give thanks, *having first confessed your sins so that your sacrifice may be pure.*"[176] Therefore, in the early Church, it was assumed that one did not come to receive the

Eucharist without first confessing sins, so—two sacraments in one. Having said that, at the beginning the confession was probably often a Penitential Act such as the *Confiteor* or *Kyrie Eleison*. Private confession to a priest or bishop came later, as we will see.

Thus we can see that in the earliest days of the Church, there were already four of the seven sacraments in place, though they came in bundles of two. By about the third century, they came to be "unbundled," and expanded into four distinct sacraments. The other three sacraments, although they existed from the beginning, became formalized over time, under the influence of Tradition and apostolic succession. As we will see, marriage and ordination became standardized Christian rituals in the fourth and fifth centuries, and soon after, the anointing with oil.[177]

And so the Catholic Church holds seven sacraments, in three categories. The sacraments of *initiation* are baptism, confirmation, and the Eucharist. The sacraments of *healing* are reconciliation (confession/penance) and anointing (unction). And the sacraments of *vocation* are holy matrimony (marriage) and holy orders (ordination).

What Did the Church Fathers Say About Baptism?

We have already explored what baptism does and doesn't do. It does result in regeneration (being born again) and thus it does save, but it does not guarantee salvation (perseverance).[178] But what is baptism, exactly?

The Church Fathers saw the salvation of baptism foreshadowed in the stories of the family of Noah, and the Israelites under Moses, who were saved by going through water (in the case of the Israelites, it was in the passing through the Red Sea).[179] Thus by going through the waters of baptism, Christians were participating in the salvation of God and God's people. As we have noted, Jesus commanded his apostles to baptize all who would believe in him, and when people asked the apostles what they should do to be saved, the answer was baptism.[180] So we are baptized, and we baptize, because Jesus commanded us to, and because it fulfills God's plan for salvation and demonstrates God's nature as a saving God.

Furthermore, baptism takes a specific form, because by being baptized we are identifying ourselves as people of God (we are "sealed" or marked for God), and we are specifically identifying ourselves as followers of Jesus Christ. So it is important that we are baptized by the right formula, because it is important that we are baptized into communion with the *right* God. (A baptism in the name of Zeus is not Christian baptism.) This might seem obvious; however, there are some people who call themselves Christians who baptize using a formula other than the one Jesus commanded us to use. A valid Christian baptism will use the words of Jesus in Matthew 28:19, when he said to baptize, *In the name of the Father, and of the Son, and of the Holy Spirit.* Any other formula is unacceptable and does not make a valid baptism, because any other formula is ambiguous as to exactly which God one is attempting to be baptized into.[181]

In addition to the pronouncement of the Trinitarian formula, baptism of course included immersion in water. However, here there was room for diversity of practice. According to the *Didache*, the water should be "living" (running) water, and it should be cold, but if running water was not available, standing water was acceptable, and if cold water was not available, warm water was also acceptable. And if there was not enough water for immersion, then pouring water on the head (affusion) was also acceptable.[182] In fact, even sprinkling a few drops would do the job.[183]

Early baptism included an anointing with oil, and sometimes two or even three anointings. The anointings after the immersion or affusion were probably associated more with confirmation, and later, as the two sacraments came to be separated, confirmation became an anointing with imposition of hands to confer the Holy Spirit.[184] In some places, baptisms were preceded by exorcisms, to "clean the house of the soul," and make room for the Holy Spirit who will come to indwell the person being baptized.[185] The *Didache* also advised that an adult who is to be baptized should fast for one or two days before the baptism, and the presider should also fast, as well as any of the congregation who are able.[186]

So an early Christian baptism for adults might have gone something like this: After a time of fasting, the bishop would perform an exorcism, and then when the time came for the baptism, the recipient would strip down and there would be an anointing with oil.[187] Then the immersion in water, three times, with the words, "I baptize you in the name of the Father (dunk/pour) and of the Son (dunk/pour) and of the Holy Spirit (dunk/pour)." After coming up out of the water, the newborn Christian received a white robe, symbolizing purity, and possibly another anointing. The bishop confirmed the baptism with the laying-on of hands.[192] Finally, the baptism was immediately followed by the first reception of Holy Communion, a practice that continues in the Eastern churches to this day. Sometimes the first Eucharist was taken with milk and honey, to symbolize the innocence of the newly baptized believer, as well as the promise of eternal life in paradise.[189] In actual practice, there was a fair amount of difference in the rituals of baptism from one place to another in the early Church, but the one thing that never changed was the formula of baptism, the invocation of God as Trinity.

Theologically, baptism is the initiation into the Church, the Body of Christ. As such, the early Church Fathers understood and taught baptism as a cleansing, an anointing, an adoption (as son or daughter of God), an identification with Christ, and as a seal.[190]

As a cleansing, Christian baptism is the continuation of the Hebrew cleansing bath. In the Old Testament, if someone was ritually unclean, that person would have to take a purification bath in order to resume his or her place in the community and in the worship of God. Christian baptism is like this, in the sense that it is the "washing of regeneration" that cleanses us from sin and gives us a fresh start.[191] Baptismal anointings were also seen as a cleansing, since in the ancient world oil was used the way we use soap. So the oil of anointing has always been understood to have both cleansing and healing properties.[192] And although

Jesus did not need cleansing from sin, the Fathers taught that
he submitted himself to baptism in order to consecrate water
as the element of baptismal cleansing for the rest of us. And so,
as an initiation, baptism is the rite of passage that welcomes us
into the Church, and into the family of God. In this way, it
is also analogous to Hebrew circumcision.[193] In fact, in a way,
Christian baptism combines the concepts of Hebrew purification baths and circumcision, to make an initiation that also gives
us a clean slate.

It is important to point out that baptism does not initiate a
person into one branch of Christianity only. Baptism initiates the
person into the universal Church, and so our baptism is one thing
that all Christians share in common, and that unites us in the universal Body of Christ and the communion of saints.[194] According
to the *Catechism of the Catholic Church*, "Baptism constitutes the
foundation of communion among all Christians . . . [non-Catho-
lics] are incorporated into Christ; they therefore have a right to be
called Christians, and with good reason are accepted as brothers
by the children of the Catholic Church. Baptism therefore constitutes *the sacramental bond of unity* existing among all who through
it are reborn."[195]

As an anointing, Christian baptism is like the anointing of
Old Testament priests and kings, and in this sense Jesus did need
to be baptized, because his baptism was his commissioning by
God for the ministry he was about to begin. At Jesus' baptism,
the Father affirmed that he is the Christ, the *Messiah*, which
means, "anointed one." For us, through our baptism we become
an anointed people, and even a holy priesthood.[196] In fact, the
Fathers taught that by our baptism we become "christs" in the
sense that we, too, are anointed to be followers of Christ. So
the very name "Christian" has a double meaning: it means we
are Christ's, and it means we *are* christs. In the sacrament, the
anointing with oil also symbolized the anointing in the Holy
Spirit, which results in the indwelling of the Holy Spirit.[197]

As an adoption, our baptism makes us a "new creation," and
welcomes us into the family of God as his children.[198] Jesus did

not need this adoption, since he was, from eternity, the divine Son of God; but when we accept him as our brother we are adopted as sons and daughters of God through baptism. Thus baptism is an identification with Christ: we accept him as our savior and Lord, and we submit ourselves to him as belonging to him. We do this by symbolically following him through death and resurrection, by going down into the water (symbolizing death) and rising up from the water (symbolizing resurrection).[199]

Finally, as a seal, baptism is the mark by which God calls us his own.[200] In a second-century Easter homily, bishop Melito of Sardis described the seal of baptism as being like the lambs' blood on the doors of the Hebrews at the first Passover. In the Church, this seal is associated with the sign of the cross; as Christians cross themselves, they recall and affirm their baptismal seal.[201] The seal, and the sign of the cross, protect the believer from evil, and strengthen the Christian against temptation.[202] Some Fathers also said that the sign of the cross on the forehead was analogous to the Old Testament practice of binding scrolls of Scripture to the forehead in containers called *tefillin or phylacteries*.[203] In this sense, both baptism and the sign of the cross together constitute the opposite of (and the guard against) the mark of the beast described in Revelation 13:16–17.

The early Church took baptism very seriously, and "not rashly to be administered."[204] Remember that baptism cleanses one from original sin, and from any sins committed before the baptism, but it does not cover post-baptismal sin. Therefore, the Church had to be relatively certain that a person was ready to live up to the expectations of Church membership before he could be baptized. Once a person requested baptism, the period of instruction that was required to prepare for the sacrament could take up to three years.[205] But this instruction, or *catechesis*, was not so much a training in theology—that could wait until after the baptism. Rather, this period, called the catechumenate, was meant to teach potential Church members how to live as Christians, which often meant a radical change from their former pagan lifestyles. The Church could ask for character references, and so we have the origin of "godparents":

sponsors who would not only shepherd the catechumen through the pre-baptism process, but also vouch for that person's character and readiness for baptism. Church leaders might even interview candidates' relatives, friends, and neighbors to determine whether their faith was sincere and whether they were living a moral life and ready to make the commitment of becoming a Christian.[206]

WHAT ABOUT INFANT BAPTISM?

The reason that the validity of a baptism is not dependent on the way the water is applied, or even on the state of the presider's faithfulness, is that baptism is a work of God, and not primarily a work of humans. The Church demonstrates its faith in this work of God by baptizing infants. And although there are some denominations that do not baptize infants, the Church has historically listened to the words of Jesus when he said, "Let the children come to me, and do not prevent them" (Matt. 19:13–14). In fact, in the early Church, the debate was not over whether to baptize infants, but over whether one should wait until the eighth day after birth.[207]

The Fathers assumed that infant baptism was a fact of the Church. This is because it is based on the concept of vicarious faith—a concept that they accepted. Vicarious faith is the idea that the faith of one person can stand in for, or benefit, another person. For example, Jesus was willing to raise from death the daughter of Jairus, on the basis of *his* faith.[208] In the book of Acts, the apostles acknowledge that a whole household could be saved on the basis of one man's faith.[209] And then, we are told, the whole family was baptized.[210] There is no reason to assume that this family did not include children. Clearly we can see that the power of faith and the reach of God's grace are not limited, and that they can extend beyond the individual.[211]

Baptism, therefore, is not something private, but is a communal act that initiates us into the Body of Christ. As an initiation, it should not wait until adulthood, but should be performed as a new child is welcomed into the Church family. Even denominations that do not baptize infants recognize the need for Christian initiation, since they often create rituals of dedication to welcome infants into their community. They reject infant baptism because it's not explicitly mentioned in the New Testament, but the truth is that this is because there was no second generation Church yet. Most people who responded to the gospel were adults; but we can see that when parents were converted to the Church, their children were also baptized.

So the practice of infant baptism was not something that came along later, but something that existed from the beginning.[212] As the Church grew, and Christians married and had children, they did baptize their children, and infant baptism became widespread.[213] The Third Council of Carthage affirmed infant baptism as the existing practice of the Church in A.D. 253.[214] And when Christianity was legalized, and more people were joining the Church, infant baptism became more prevalent than adult baptism, as many more babies in the Roman Empire were being born into Christian families. And then when infant baptism became the norm, it was determined (in the Western Church) that the confirmation of baptism should be postponed until the Christian could claim the Faith for himself, and that catechesis would have to come later, when the child was old enough to begin to understand the Faith.[215]

Remember, too, that baptism is normally considered necessary for salvation, and in a world with a high infant and child mortality rate, it could be considered unwise to postpone it.[216] A child needs God's grace, too, and the grace of baptism works within a person before he is able to respond to it— and in fact it is a grace that *enables* a person to respond to God in faith. Some theologians call this *prevenient* grace, whereas others choose not to distinguish different kinds of grace, but the point is that God's grace is a kind of invitation that precedes any response a person might have. This grace enables a person to have faith, and empowers the individual to grow spiritually and morally.[217] This means that baptism is not necessarily a sign of something that has already taken place (such as a conversion experience) or something already in a person (such as a faith commitment), but is primarily a sign of God's gift. It is a sacrament of reception of grace, by which God claims a person, and energizes that person to live the Christian life.

And so the Church baptizes infants because we believe that God is already at work in the life of that child. And as the bishop and saint, Cyprian of Carthage, wrote in the third century, baptism should not be denied to anyone, because God's mercy and offer of reconciliation are available to all. In his own words:

> If even to the greatest sinners, and to those who had sinned much against God, when they subsequently believed, remission of sins is granted—and nobody is hindered from baptism and from grace—how much rather ought we to shrink from hindering an infant, who, being lately born, has not sinned, except in that, being born after the flesh according to Adam, he has contracted the contagion of the ancient death at its earliest birth, who approaches the more easily on this very account to the reception of the forgiveness of sins—that to him are remitted, not his own sins, but the sins of another. And therefore, dearest brother, this was our opinion in council, that by us no one ought to be hindered from baptism and from the grace of God, who is merciful and kind and loving to all. Which, since it is to be observed and maintained in respect of all, we think is to be even more observed in respect of infants and newly-born infants, who on this very account deserve more from our help and from the divine mercy, that immediately, on the very beginning of their birth, lamenting and weeping, they do nothing else but entreat.[218]

The rejection of infant baptism creates a serious problem for those denominations that reserve baptism for people over a certain age. If one who was baptized as an infant wanted to join such a community, they would require a *rebaptism* (though they would not call it rebaptism, since they don't count the first baptism). After a controversy over rebaptism in the third century, the Church determined that it is a heresy to rebaptize.[219] That is because the rebaptism is a rejection of the Church's teaching on baptism as a means of grace, and a rejection of God's work in the baptism. Such rebaptism turns the sacrament of baptism into a human work, and implies that God was not active in the baptism of an infant or child. Even more serious is the fact that since baptism should be one of the things that still unites all Christians, those denominations that acknowledge only adult baptism are making the divisions worse by rejecting a sacrament of the vast majority of the world's Christians.

What Did the Church Fathers Say About Confirmation?

As we have noted, confirmation was originally part of baptism, associated with anointing and the imposition of hands for the conferral of the Holy Spirit.[220] All of this attests to a commissioning, a kind of "ordination" into our role as a "holy priesthood" (1 Pet. 2:5, 9). Baptism gives us the grace to grow into that role, and confirmation gives us the grace to live in it, as we claim the gifts of the Spirit.[221] In fact, confirmation was seen by many Fathers as the baptism in the Holy Spirit.[222]

The separation of confirmation from baptism in the West was made necessary not only by the emergence of infant baptism as the norm for Christian families, but also by the rapid growth in the number of baptisms as the Church grew in the second through the fourth centuries. In Rome, by the fifth century, baptisms were taking place every day.[223] This great need for so many baptisms led to an increasing tradition of bishops granting priests the authority to baptize, but reserving for themselves the authority to confirm.[224]

Thus the sacraments of baptism and confirmation came to be two separate rites. As early as the end of the second century, Tertullian described the "seal" of Christian initiation in terms of three distinct sacraments: baptism, confirmation, and Eucharist:

One Lord God does she [the church of Rome] acknowledge, the creator of the universe, and Christ Jesus (born) of the

Virgin Mary, the Son of God the creator; and the Resurrection
of the flesh; the law and the prophets she unites in one
volume with the writings of evangelists and apostles, from
which she drinks in her faith. This she seals with the water
(of baptism), arrays with the Holy Ghost [confirmation], feeds
with the Eucharist, cheers with martyrdom, and against such
a discipline thus (maintained) she admits no gainsayer.[225]

The Church Fathers interpreted Jesus' words about "being
born of water and Spirit" as a reference to the two sacraments of
baptism (water birth) and confirmation (Spirit birth).[226] Cyprian
of Carthage said one is only "fully sanctified" with both sacraments, and used the phrases "baptized and sanctified" and "justify and sanctify" to refer to the two distinct sacraments.[227] Today
confirmation is considered one of the three sacraments of initiation, along with baptism and the Eucharist. Confirmation con-
firms the baptism, and the Eucharist completes it, though confirmation does not necessarily take place before a person's first Holy
Communion.[228] (However, as we noted above, in the Orthodox
and Eastern Catholic traditions, baptism, confirmation, and first
Eucharist all take place at once, even for infants.) Like baptism,
confirmation cannot be repeated.[229] However, if one's faith needs
to be "reconfirmed," that is what the sacrament of reconciliation
is for.

What Did the Church Fathers Say About the Eucharist?

We will look in detail at the Church's understanding of the Eucharist in the next chapter. At this point it will be sufficient to
say a few things about the Eucharist as a sacrament, and as it
relates to the other sacraments.

Just as Christian baptism is parallel to circumcision, the sacrament of the Eucharist is parallel to the Hebrew Passover. Like
the Passover meal, the Eucharist remembers God's past saving
acts, and brings them into the present-day community to encourage the faithful, as "past history is made present mystery."

It also parallels the Hebrew sacrifices of atonement. In this one sacrament, Christ is the Lamb who fulfills completely and permanently what the lambs of the Passover and the sacrifices could only do in an incomplete, temporary way.

The Church Fathers believed that the sacrament of the Eucharist was foreshadowed in the Old Testament by Melchizedek's gift of bread and wine, in the manna from heaven, and in the water that flowed from the rock.[230] They also saw it foreshadowed in Jesus' own ministry, in his changing water into wine and feeding the multitudes.[231] As we will see in the next chapter, Jesus himself connected the bread from heaven with the bread that he would offer.[232] For the Fathers, the sacrament of the Eucharist is the fulfillment of all of these things, and the continuation of Jesus' ministry in the Church.

Like all the sacraments, only to a more perfect degree, the Eucharist carries healing and saving power, as it leads us toward eternal life. Ignatius of Antioch called it "the medicine of immortality."[233] Clement of Alexandria wrote, "He who eats of this meal, the best of all, shall possess the Kingdom of God," and, "To drink the blood of Jesus is to become partaker of the Lord's immortality . . . they who by faith partake of it are sanctified both in body and soul."[234]

What Did the Church Fathers Say About Confession, Penance, and Reconciliation?

Confession, penance, and reconciliation are all together one sacrament, which can be called by any one of these terms. Most often nowadays it is referred to as reconciliation, since that is its goal.[235] Our sin separates us from God, and the sacrament is a means of reconciliation with him. As we have noted, this sacrament was originally part of the sacrament of the Eucharist, in that the Fathers believed it would not be appropriate to approach the communion table without first confessing one's sins.[236] Thus confession of venial (minor) sins was always a part of the Eucharistic prayers. The most serious sins (such as apostasy and idolatry, which resulted in excommunication) were confessed both privately and then publicly at the end of a time of penance, and as part of a rite that may have included an anointing with oil and imposition of hands.[237] This shows that the Church Fathers always assumed that reconciliation with God required reconciliation with the Church. For example, Ignatius of Antioch wrote, "For all those who belong to God and Jesus Christ are with the bishop, and all those who repent and enter into the unity of the Church will belong to God, so that they may be living in accordance with Jesus Christ . . . The Lord, however, forgives all who repent, if in repenting they return to the unity of God and the council of the bishop."[238]

WHY DOES A PERSON NEED TO CONFESS TO A PRIEST?

Confession is acknowledging what God already knows: the particular sins that an individual has committed. So some will ask, "Isn't it enough to confess directly to God? Why does a person need to confess to a priest?" The letter of James tells readers to "confess your sins to one another," because there is healing in confession.[239] Confessing our sins out loud forces us to consciously acknowledge and take responsibility for them. It's harder to fool ourselves into thinking sin is not that bad when we have to say it out loud. So confession is an act of humility that holds us accountable for our actions and encourages us to resist temptation in the future. It's almost a form of therapy, or perhaps something closer to spiritual direction, to bare one's soul to another and confess one's moral failures. It's important to keep in mind that God wants us to be reconciled to him, and so confession is a victory over pride and sin that results in the healing of our relationship with God.[240]

The Fathers believed that confession cannot be completely private because sin is not private. Sin is an offense against God, but it is also an act of injustice toward our fellow children of God. Therefore sin is a failure to keep both of Jesus' commandments: to love God and to love our neighbor. Since sin is not only something that affects the individual, reconciliation is not only for the individual—it is something done by and in the community.[241] In fact, in the early Church, confession and reconciliation of serious sins took place in front of the whole congregation.[242] The reconciliation included a laying-on of hands by the bishop with the assembly praying over the penitent person.[243]

Of course, confession is simply the verbal expression of repentance, so all of this assumes that the repentance must be sincere.[244] The biblical words for *repentance* mean "changing one's mind," or a turning, as in "turning your life around," or "turning over a new leaf." Specifically, repentance means turning back to God. It implies not only regret for past sin, but sincere desire to resist temptation in the future.[245] As St. Ambrose, bishop of Milan, described it in the fourth century, the sacramental element of confession is tears of repentance.[246] So repentance leads to confession. But how does the Church know that one's repentance is real and one's confession is sincere? This is where penance comes in. Penance is considered an outward and visible sign of the inward repentance. Since one cannot prove the sincerity of one's heart, the Church provides an opportunity to demonstrate that sincerity.

But just as excommunication is not for abandonment, but for discipline, the point of penance is not punishment, but spiritual growth.[247] So, even more important than proving sincerity is the fact that penance gives a person a chance to participate in the remedy for sin.[248] Penance is a cooperation in the ongoing process of conversion, as we "work out [our] salvation with fear and trembling."[249] Sometimes the consequences of our sin require making amends directly, repairing the damage done by our actions or words.[250] Other times, penance can take the form of indirect satisfaction, such as "works of mercy, service of neighbor, voluntary self-denial, sacrifices, and above all the patient acceptance of the cross we must bear."[251] In the early Church, penance usually meant prayer, fasting, and almsgiving. To those who had denied Christ to save their lives during times of persecution, Cyprian of Carthage wrote:

Think you that he will easily have mercy upon you whom you have declared not to be your God? You must pray more eagerly and entreat; you must spend the day in grief; wear out nights in watchings and weepings; occupy all your time in wailful lamentations; lying stretched on the ground, you must cling close to the ashes, be surrounded with sackcloth and filth; after losing the raiment of Christ, you must be willing now to have no clothing; after the devil's meat, you must prefer fasting; be earnest in righteous works, whereby sins may be purged; frequently apply yourself to almsgiving, whereby souls are freed from death.[252]

Still, one might ask, "If James says confess your sins to one another, why do we need to confess to a priest?" The answer to this question goes back to Jesus himself. In the Gospels, we read that Jesus gave to Peter and the other apostles the authority to forgive sins.[253] And so, although only God has the power to forgive sin, we see that he has granted his power to the Church, which forgives sins in the name of Christ, and on his authority.[254] The forgiveness of sins is called *absolution*, and just like the authority to baptize, confirm, and preside over the Eucharist, this authority was passed on from the apostles to the bishops (and the priests to whom they delegate it) by apostolic succession.[255] As bishop Pacian of Barcelona wrote in the fourth century, this authority "has descended in the stream from the apostolic privilege."[256]

In the third century, a wave of persecution raised the problem of what do about those Christians who denied the Faith to save their lives. By their apostasy, they had effectively excommunicated themselves. But when the persecution subsided and they wanted to return to the Church, they found that they could not be reconciled without facing the consequences of their sin. Remember that although venial sins could be forgiven by the prayers of confession before receiving the Eucharist, mortal sins such as apostasy and idolatry could not.[257] These required sacramental confession and penance. Some of these lapsed Christians did try to confess their sins to fellow lay people who had not denied the Faith, but the Church quickly clarified that only those who were within the apostolic succession (that is, clergy) had the authority to absolve sin. This probably solidified the separation of the Eucharist and confession as two distinct sacraments. In a letter to Bishop Cyprian written in the year A.D. 250, Novatian referred to penance and reconciliation as a sacrament.[258]

The goal of confession and penance is reconciliation, and reconciliation gives the Christian peace of mind. So the early Fathers often referred to this sacrament simply as the Peace of the Church.[259] Sometimes Protestants ask Catholics how they can know if they have done enough good works to make up for sin. But that question misses the point. Peace of mind is not found in the merit of good works, but in forgiveness for sins. And so the Church gives peace to believers by absolving their sins. Jesus was constantly saying, "Peace be with you," and now he continues to offer peace, through the Church. Catholics do not have to wonder if they are forgiven, because they can trust in the authority of the Church—based on Jesus' own command—to forgive their sins.

The apostle John wrote that if we confess our sins, God is faithful to forgive us.[260] Peter knew firsthand what it meant to deny Jesus and then be reconciled to him.[261] For the Fathers, Peter's reconciliation to Jesus after his Resurrection would become the model for Christian reconciliation. As one anonymous early Christian author wrote, "Even Peter, whom he had previously foretold as about to deny him, when he had denied him, he did not deny, but sustained; and he himself soothed him when subsequently bitterly bewailing his denial.[262]

As we noted, they saw the Church as a hospital, and sin as a sickness. The bishop (or priest under his authority) is like a doctor, administering the medicine of the sacrament. That medicine, confession and penance, results in the cure, reconciliation.[263] And because reconciliation is a sacrament of healing, it is repeatable—the Church offers it whenever the faithful need it.[264]

WHAT DID THE CHURCH FATHERS SAY
ABOUT HOLY MATRIMONY?

The institution of marriage is, of course, older than all the other sacraments, and older than Christianity itself. In fact, one could say that marriage is older than all culture, and is the very foundation of culture.[265] Jesus affirmed marriage when he quoted Genesis: "For this reason a man shall leave his father and mother and be joined to his wife, and the two shall become one flesh" (Matt. 19:5, quoting Gen. 2:24).[266] He also showed his support for marriage when he changed water into wine at a wedding in Cana.[267] The apostle Paul also affirmed marriage, and even compared the marriage relationship to the relationship between Christ and the Church.[268] All of this led the medieval scholastic Hugh of St. Victor to claim that matrimony was the oldest sacrament of all, because it originated in the Garden of Eden.[269] Nevertheless, the *ritual* of Christian marriage is not as old as the sacraments we have discussed so far.

It is important to make a distinction between natural marriage, which can be contracted through a civil ceremony, and the supernatural union that is holy matrimony. We may use the word "marriage" for them both, but holy matrimony is a *sacrament*, a sacred mystery, an act of God that permanently changes its recipients. As Jesus said, "Therefore, what *God* has joined together, no human being must separate" (Matt. 19:6). He didn't say, "what *people* have joined together," or even, "what *religious leaders* have joined together." He said, "what *God* has joined together." The Church believes and teaches that Jesus himself made matrimony a sacrament when he performed his first miracle at a wedding reception.[270]

In the time of the early Church, marriage in the Roman Empire was only a concern of the wealthy, since the legal marriage contract existed primarily for the purpose of ensuring inheritance. To make sure the right people inherited the money of the wealthy, the Romans needed to distinguish between legitimate and illegitimate children. This was done with marriage—and often a dowry was treated like a deposit held in escrow against the event of divorce. Marriage didn't prevent men from having other children with other women; it just meant that those children could not inherit their father's wealth.[271] This means that people who had no inheritance to worry about (the vast majority of people back then) often didn't bother with a legal marriage.[272] They simply made a commitment to live together and raise a family. And this went for many people in the early Church, too. No contract was needed when two people entered into the union by free will and with mutual consent—and what sealed the union was the consummation, making them "one flesh."[273]

Therefore, in the early Church before the legalization of Christianity, many Christians probably only had what amounts to a common-law marriage. In fact, some Christian couples could not have gotten a legal marriage if they wanted to, because there were laws against marriage across certain social class boundaries. In the early days, when many wealthy men avoided Church membership, or postponed their baptism, because of Christianity's moral expectations, single Christian women sometimes found themselves outnumbering single Christian men—and this meant that if they wanted a Christian husband they could not necessarily limit their prospects to their own social class.[274] In any case, the leaders of the Church worried that without a formal commitment the existence of such relationships might be seen as an endorsement of immorality. So the Church had to do something to sanction the unions of Christian couples.

Therefore, from at least the late first or early second century, the Church instructed couples to go to their bishop for permission, and probably a blessing, before forming a union or getting a legal marriage. Although there was no Christian wedding ceremony yet, this bishop's blessing was the beginning of the sacrament of holy matrimony. In about A.D. 110, Ignatius of Antioch wrote to Polycarp of Smyrna, "it is proper for men and women who marry to be united with the consent of the bishop."[275] Eventually, as the Church grew in numbers, the authority to give the Church's blessing to a marriage was extended to the priests.

By the third century, the Fathers were writing about matrimony in sacramental terms, though there was still no formal

Christian wedding ceremony.[276] However, we do know that there was a tradition of announcing the marriage in the Church, at which point we have to assume that the union was blessed.[277] But even though Christian couples were getting the Church's blessing, they were still participating in the traditional (pagan) wedding ceremonies. Tertullian, Cyprian, John Chrysostom, and Augustine were all outspoken in their criticism of these weddings, which often included heavy drinking and singing raunchy songs.[278] Chrysostom preached to his people the following advice:

> When you prepare for the wedding, don't run to your neighbors' houses borrowing extra mirrors or spend endless hours worrying about dresses. A wedding is not a pageant or a theatrical performance. Instead, make your house as beautiful as you can and then invite your family and neighbors and friends . . . they will be content with what you set before them. Don't hire bands or orchestras; such an expense is excessive and unbecoming. Before anything else, invite Christ. Don't adorn the bride with golden ornaments, but dress her modestly. Let there be no drunkenness at the banquets and suppers, but an abundance of spiritual joy. Think of the many good things that will result from weddings like this. The way most weddings—if we can even call them weddings, and not spectacles—are celebrated nowadays ends in nothing but evil.[279]

When Christianity was legalized in the early fourth century, Christian bishops were given many of the same powers as civil judges, presumably so that two Christians who had a dispute could go to their bishop for arbitration, rather than the secular courts. This gave bishops the right to witness marriage contracts, opening the door to the legal recognition of Christian marriages, and the possibility of a Christian liturgical wedding ceremony in places where one did not already exist.[280] The ceremony itself was probably built on the foundation of the announcement and blessing in the church, "sealing" the union between a man and a woman the way that baptism and confirmation seal a person's union with God and the Church. It is clear that the rite of Christian matrimony was created as an alternative to the pagan wedding celebrations, but it is also clear that Christians continued many of the pagan traditions, including the Roman (and Jewish[281]) tradition of the wedding reception. The Christian wedding ceremony continued to evolve, but it is important to clarify that the sacrament of matrimony is not the same thing as the wedding ceremony. Although the Christian wedding liturgy probably did not emerge until after Christianity was legalized, the sacramental nature of the union itself was recognized long before that, in the bishop's blessing and the public declaration of the union within the Christian community. In fact, we know that there were liturgical ceremonies for the consecration of celibates—ceremonies that were parallel to weddings—that evolved prior to the formal Christian wedding ceremony.[282] The point is that holy matrimony as a sacrament is not dependent on the wedding ceremony, but is based on the sacred nature of the union itself.[283] In any case, by the fifth century, both John Chrysostom in the East and Augustine in the West assumed that matrimony was a sacrament.[284]

Matrimony is a sacrament because it permanently changes a person. People can get divorced and become legally single again, but they cannot become "unmarried" in the sense of never married.[285] Matrimony is for life—it is any married person's primary vocation.[286] As a sacrament of vocation, matrimony contributes to our salvation, because it is the primary context in which we learn to be in ministry—to serve others.[287] And so matrimony is not something that only affects the two married people; it is a communal sacrament, in which the couple takes their place in the community of the faithful (and contributes to the growth of that community by raising children in the Faith), and are accountable to the community they are helping to build.[288]

Today, all Christian denominations consider matrimony a sacred and serious union—not to be entered into (or exited from) lightly.[289] But by recognizing it as a sacrament, the Catholic

Church also emphasizes that it is a means of God's grace to those
who receive it, and that they are changed by it. It is also meant to
be a great joy for those who participate in it. As John Chrysostom
wrote, "there is nothing which so welds our life together as the
love of man and wife."[290]

What Did the Church Fathers Say About Holy Orders?

As we discussed in the context of apostolic succession, the hierarchy and succession of authority began with Jesus himself, who
chose and sent his disciples. The disciples of Jesus then became
the apostles, and they in turn chose their own disciples to join
them in the Church's mission.[291] These disciples of the apostles
became their successors, and then appointed others to take over
for them, and to preside under their authority. We can already
see this happening in the New Testament, when the apostle Paul
himself was commissioned as an evangelist, and then when Paul
gave Titus the authority to appoint priests in Crete.[292]

So ordination began as a commissioning of leaders who were
chosen by previous leaders and set apart for the work of the
Church. This was based on Old Testament precedents, such as
Moses choosing Joshua to succeed him, and Samuel anointing
David as king. The early commissioning rituals would have
included prayer, the anointing of the person's hands with oil,
and the imposition of hands for the conferral of authority.[293]
Thus the laying-on of hands granted to the person something he
did not have before. It seals a person, somewhat like baptism and
confirmation, commissioning that person to a new way of life
and a new mission.[294] It is not simply the recognition of gifts, but
as a means of grace, it confers authority and empowers the person
for ministry.[295] Notice that when David was anointed by Samuel,
we are told that, "*from that day on*, the Spirit of the Lord rushed
upon David" (1 Sam. 16:13). The leaders of the Church are only
human, after all, so the recognition of spiritual gifts does not
necessarily mean they have everything they need for ministry,
and therefore the grace of the sacrament of holy orders makes

up what is lacking—in addition to recognizing gifts, it actually *grants* gifts. In the early Church, the congregation prayed that the ordination would *make* the person worthy of the office.[296] All of this is part of the reason why holy orders is considered a sacrament: because the person ordained is permanently changed, both in the sense of embarking on a new mission and in the sense of accepting a new authority.[297] Thus, like baptism, the sacrament cannot be repeated or undone.[298]

In the early Church, as we have seen, it was always understood that authority and hierarchy serve unity. In other words, there could be no unity without the hierarchy. It was the clergy who kept in touch with each other and kept the various local churches on the same page with each other. Therefore, ordination places a person not only into the succession but also into the hierarchy of the Church. When the apostles were gone, their disciples and successors took their place, and took on the role of city-wide or regional overseers, and the title *bishop* (in Greek, *episkopos*) came to be reserved for them.

In places where no apostle had appointed a successor, the house church pastors probably formed a council of priests and elected a bishop to represent and lead them. Eventually, election became the normal way of choosing a bishop from among the priests.[299] In any case, by the end of the first century, the office of bishop as we know it had emerged, taking on the authority previously held by the apostles. In the eighties and nineties of the first century, Clement of Rome became one such bishop, and wrote a letter to the Christians in Corinth exercising his authority over them.[300] Just after the turn of the second century, Ignatius of Antioch wrote about the role and authority of the bishop in a series of letters:

Let us, therefore, be careful not to oppose the bishop, in order that we may be obedient to God . . . It is obvious, therefore, that we must regard the bishop as the Lord himself.[301]
Let no one do anything that has to do with the Church without the bishop. Only that Eucharist which is under the

authority of the bishop (or the one whom he himself desig-
nates) is to be considered valid. Wherever the bishop appears,
there let the congregation be; just as wherever Jesus Christ is,
there is the Catholic Church. It is not permissible either to
baptize or to hold a love feast without the bishop.[302]

The term *ordination*, then, simply means to be entered into
the order, or the office, of the clergy. From the beginning, there
were three levels of authority in the hierarchy. While the apostles were alive, those three levels were apostle, priest/bishop (the
terms referred to the same office at first), and deacon.[303] After
the apostles passed away, the three levels were bishop, priest,
and deacon, and this is how it remains to this day.[304] Although
all three were (and are) considered ordained, only bishops and
priests presided over the sacraments. The role of the deacon was
to assist the presider, and in the case of the Eucharist, bring
the consecrated elements out to those who were not able to be
at Mass. Justin Martyr, in his first apology, written as an open
letter to the emperor, he described the Mass in the mid-second
century. There he wrote, "When our prayer is ended, bread and
wine and water are brought, and the presider in like manner offers prayers and thanksgivings, according to his ability, and the
people assent, saying Amen, and there is a distribution to each,
and a participation of that over which thanks have been given,
and to those who are absent a portion is sent by the deacons."[305]
By the third century, and probably well before that in many
places, ordination had become a ritual in the Church.[306] And
with the formal ritual of ordination, church leadership became
a vocation. But at first, in many places, church leadership was a
volunteer position, and not an occupation.[307] This means that,
as the Church grew, it became increasingly difficult for someone
who had to work for a living to be a leader in the Church. But
eventually holy orders became an occupation as well as a vocation, and clergy[308] started receiving stipends for their labors, allowing those who were ordained to devote all of their time to
the work of the Church.

When Christianity was legalized in the fourth century, Christian bishops were given certain rights and privileges in Roman society, thanks to the Church's patron, the Emperor Constantine. At this point, the ordination ritual (especially for bishops) became something like a ceremony of inauguration to political office, complete with vesting in traditional clothing to set the person apart from the laity and designate him as an authority figure. This, too, could be said to be based on Old Testament precedents, but it also took on some of the pomp and circumstance normally reserved for government officials.[309] Nevertheless, the sacramental character of holy orders predates the post-Constantinian high Church rituals, and was never obscured by them.

Holy orders is a sacrament of vocation, and like the other sacrament of vocation (matrimony) it is dedicated to the service—and the salvation—of others.[310] The three orders of bishop, priest, and deacon, all have their own characteristics. Since the bishops fulfill the role of successors to the apostles, they are the shepherds—that is, they have authority over the Church's sacraments, teaching, and discipline.[311] Another way to say that is that apostolic succession guarantees the validity of the Church's sacraments, the trustworthiness of its teaching, and even its very unity, through the office of the bishop. Without it, doctrine would break down into heresy, and unity would break down into schism.[312] Thus the bishops are the guarantors of the Church's unity.[313] Therefore, since the bishops are "ordered" into the apostolic succession, they are the ones who ordain all new deacons and priests.[314] All bishops are chosen from the ranks of the priests, and all bishops remain priests. This means that bishops are not really ordained again, since ordination is a sacrament that cannot be repeated. Thus a bishop is consecrated to that office, but his ordination as a priest always remains in effect.[315]

Priests may also preside over the sacraments, teach the faithful, absolve sins, and reconcile sinners, but they always (and only) do so with permission from their bishop.[316] As we have noted, all authority of a priest is derived from the authority of the bishops. As Irenaeus of Lyons wrote, one can rest assured that the local priests "expound the scriptures without danger," because a priest can only interpret the scriptures in a way that is consistent with, or at least sanctioned by, his bishop.[317] This is how the laity may have a sense of peace that the teaching of their priest is trustworthy. Otherwise, they are at the mercy of one person's opinions.[318]

When bishops and priests preside over the sacraments, and especially the Eucharist, they act in place of Christ, *in persona Christi*, as the Latin says.[319] Like Jesus at the head of the table of the Last Supper, the presider takes the role of Christ as the head of the Church.[320] And through the clergy, Christ continues to guide the Church.[321] Deacons assist the presiders (priests and bishops) in liturgy and the sacraments.[322] However, unlike priests, who in the Western Church may not ordinarily be married, deacons may be married, if they are already married when they are ordained.[323]

There were other orders in the early Church as well, often referred to as lay orders, which may sound like a contradiction, but they were not technically ordained. These included the order of widows and consecrated virgins, and of course religious orders such as monastic communities. But they were not considered clergy, because they had no formal role in liturgy. Therefore, the consecration to lay orders is not considered an ordination, because it would not include the imposition of hands for the conferral of authority.

Do Catholics Believe in the "Priesthood of All Believers"?

One of the hallmarks of the Protestant Reformation is the idea of the priesthood of all believers—that all Christians are called to do God's work in the world, and are in some sense, priests of God.[324] At the time of the Reformation, this concept was used as a reason to reject the Catholic hierarchy, as well as the sacrament of confession. But since the second Vatican Council, dialogue between Catholics and Protestants have led to an agreement that our common baptism is in a way, an "ordination," by which we are all commissioned to be ministers in the world. Baptism and confirmation together commission us to what the Church calls the general ministry—the obligation of all Christians to do works of love and mercy. However, holy orders is a commissioning to the specific, or particular, ministry of the clergy.[325] So with that in mind, the Catholic Church does teach the priesthood of all believers, but like many denominations, it also teaches that some leaders are set aside for full-time ministry, as a vocation, and also as an occupation. And in the Catholic Church, they are the ones invested with the sacrament of holy orders, which is a sacrament of vocation.

WHY CAN'T CATHOLIC BISHOPS AND PRIESTS BE MARRIED?

Of course, once holy orders was considered a vocation, and especially when it became an occupation, that brought up the question of lifestyle. Should the ordained be celibate, or could they also be called to the vocation of matrimony? As many people know, the Eastern churches would determine that married men with families could be ordained priests, though bishops would have to be celibate.[326] The Western Church, however, determined that priests, as well as bishops, should be celibate. The tradition of clergy celibacy in the West goes back at least to the third century. Probably in the second century celibacy was optional, but the celibate Christians were seen as especially holy, and so they were often chosen to be ordained. In other words, it was not so much a question of requiring the ordained to be celibate, but rather one of ordaining those who had already made the commitment to celibacy. From there it became preferable to ordain those committed to celibacy, since they did not have to divide their time and attention to support a family.[327] In any case, by the early fourth century, there was an assumption that priests should be celibate, even though this was not universally enforced. The Council of Elvira, Spain, in about the year 305, mandated that all clergy be celibate, though this council was probably only considered authoritative in Spain.

In the late fourth century, Pope Siricius explained the rationale for clergy celibacy. The faithful were expected to abstain from sex, for twenty-four hours before receiving the Eucharist. And since clergy were expected to be able to preside over the Eucharist every day, that did not leave them time for a consummated marriage.[328] Siricius chaired a council at Rome in the year 386 that mandated celibacy for all clergy, and from that time on it became the norm in the West, though the rule was not always consistently followed. This was ratified and enforced at the Second Lateran Council in 1139, but as it should be clear by now, the idea was not new then. Therefore, myths about clergy celibacy as a medieval invention are untrue.[329]

Why Do Catholics Call Priests "Father"?

In Matthew 23:9, Jesus said that we should call no one *father* except our heavenly Father. In context, this was part of Jesus' warning against encouraging the Pharisees, who put on airs and flaunted their education. Jesus doesn't want his followers to be prideful, or to enable the pride of others. The command is also an example of *hyperbole*: an exaggeration meant to emphasize a point. Jesus was always using figures of speech, and hyperbole was one of his favorites. For example, in Matthew 18:8–9, Jesus advises people to cut off their hands and pluck out their eyes! Clearly, he didn't really want people to do that, but he uses the exaggeration to show how important his point is. If we were to take literally Jesus' words in Matthew 23:9, then not only would we not have a word for our male parent, we would also have to say that the apostle Paul disobeyed Jesus when he called himself a spiritual father to his own converts.[330] For Catholics, priests are Fathers to us in the way that Paul was a father to his disciples: as pastors, guides, and teachers.

What Did the Church Fathers Say About Anointing?

As we noted, the use of oil for anointing goes further back than the time of the apostles, and even pre-dates Jesus' ministry.

In the ancient world, oil was associated with healing, and the Christian practice of anointing is based on the conviction that Jesus himself is the great Healer. When Jesus sent his disciples out to preach, Mark's Gospel tells us that they "anointed with oil many who were sick and cured them" (Mark 6:13). Therefore, as the apostle James advised, the Church follows Jesus' lead and reaches out to the sick with a healing touch.[331]

From the beginning of the Church, anointing with oil was part of the sacraments of baptism, confirmation, and holy orders.[332] In some settings, it may also have been part of the sacrament of reconciliation. In the third and fourth centuries, we can see that the Fathers considered anointing with oil a sacramental rite of the Church. Origen mentions it, as does bishop Serapion of Thmuis, in his fourth century sacramentary.[333] Also, in the fourth century, John Chrysostom quoted the letter of James on anointing when he wrote of the power of the priests to heal through the sacraments:

> The Jewish priests had authority to release the body from leprosy, or, rather, not to release it but only to examine those who were already released, and you know how much the office of priest was contended for at that time. But our priests have received authority to deal, not with bodily leprosy, but spiritual uncleanness—not to pronounce it removed after examination, but actually and absolutely to take it away . . . God has bestowed a power on priests greater than that of our natural parents. The two indeed differ as much as the present and the future life. For our natural parents generate us unto this life only, but the others unto that which is to come. And the former would not be able to avert death from their offspring, or to repel the assaults of disease; but these others have often saved a sick soul, or one which was on the point of perishing, procuring for some a milder chastisement, and preventing others from falling altogether, not only by instruction and admonition, but also by the assistance wrought through prayers. For not only at the time of regeneration, but afterwards also,

they have authority to forgive sins. "Is any sick among you?"
it is said, "let him call for the elders of the Church and let
them pray over him, anointing him with oil in the name of
the Lord. And the prayer of faith shall save the sick, and the
Lord will raise him up: and if he have committed sins they
shall be forgiven him."[334]

By the sixth century, anointing was recognized as a sacrament
all its own, eventually taking on the meaning of "last rites": a
kind of bookend at the end of life, parallel to baptism at the
beginning.[335] It seemed appropriate to anoint people to prepare
them for their passing into eternal life, just as Jesus was anointed
to prepare him for his death.[336] Therefore, the sacrament was
called "extreme unction," meaning the *last anointing*. It was usually accompanied by confession and reconciliation, and if possible, the *viaticum*, or last Eucharist.

The Church teaches that the Eucharist should indeed be a
person's last sacrament in this life, if possible.[337] But the Church
also teaches that it is not necessary to wait until a person is close
to death to receive the sacrament of anointing. Therefore, the
sacrament is now called the Anointing of the Sick, and can be
performed any time a person is suffering from a serious illness,
about to undergo serious surgery, or is in any life-threatening
situation.[338] As a sacrament of healing, the anointing of the sick
can be repeated.

The sacrament of anointing has the effect of "the uniting of
the sick person to the passion of Christ, for his own good and
that of the whole Church."[339] In this way, the person participates
in the suffering of Christ, and Christ participates in the suffering
of the individual. Having said this, the primary healing of the
anointing is spiritual, especially strengthening against discour-
agement. Physical healing is secondary, if God wills it and if it is
conducive to salvation.[340]

～

Some Protestants criticize the Church for putting more "layers"—such as the sacraments—between us and God. Christ,

they say, should be our one and only mediator. It is important to note, however, that the sacraments, the clergy, and even the Church, are not considered mediators between God and humanity in the way that Jesus Christ is our one mediator. But through the sacraments the mediating presence of Christ is made available to (and effective for) believers. They facilitate a closer relationship with God, through Christ's singular mediation, than we could have without them. This is what the early Church Fathers believed and taught, and this is what the Church believes and teaches today.

All the sacraments receive their power from the Passion, death, and Resurrection of Jesus Christ.[341] All the sacraments are miracles in which God's grace is received and the recipient is changed. The outward signs of water, imposition of hands, bread and wine, penance, vows and rings, vestments, and oil, are evidence of an inward faith on the part of the recipient, as well as a work of God within the recipient, and within the Church. In this way, the Church and its members cooperate with the works of God in the world, and grace expands and propagates, as we become a means of grace to others.

In no other sacrament is Christ present in the way and to the degree that he is in the Eucharist, and this is why that sacrament warrants its own chapter. The Eucharist is *the* mystery, the sacrament of sacraments, and "all the other sacraments are ordered to it as their end."[342]

Featured Father

John Chrysostom: Priest and Presider

John was an easterner, from the city of Antioch, in Syria. He was born around the year 348, in the middle of a time of intense theological controversies. But at first, John did not seem destined for the Church. His father was a military officer, and John was not baptized as an infant in case he should follow in his father's footsteps. In the fourth century, even though Christianity was legal, the government was still full of paganism, and so Christian parents who had hopes that their sons would have upwardly mobile careers in the empire sometimes chose not to baptize them, so that they wouldn't be "burdened" with the moral expectations of Christian baptism. No doubt this was John's father's idea, since his mother was very devout. But John would never really know his father; he died when John was very young. Instead, John was raised by his mother, who was enrolled in the Church's order of widows.

At about the age of twenty-two, John was baptized and decided to enter a monastic community. At first, his mother begged him not to leave home, and so for a few years he lived as a monk at home, dedicating himself to prayer, the study of Scripture, and the service of the Church. Eventually, he moved to the outskirts of the city and lived in a cave as a hermit. He took up a lifestyle of extreme asceticism, which included sleep deprivation, a very limited diet, and extreme fasts. He did eventually gather some others into a monastic community. As an ascetic, he believed that marriage was a hindrance to spirituality, and even wrote some things against marriage. Part of the reason for this was that he was trying to convince a friend of his not to leave the community for a woman. That friend did come back; he was Theodore, who went on to become the controversial bishop of Mopsuestia.

The extreme asceticism took a toll on John's health, and before long he was forced to return to civilization—back into the city. There he was ordained a deacon in 381 (the same year as the second ecumenical council, the Council of Constantinople), and he began preaching, gathering large crowds. Incidentally, *Chrysostom* was not his last name. It's a word that means "golden-mouthed," and it refers to the popularity of his homilies. But as Mike Aquilina explains in his book, *Roots of the Faith* (in chapter 9, "The Mysteries of Marriage"), it was during this time that John got involved in the Christian community of the laity, and realized that families were the lifeblood of the Church. He concluded that family life could be spiritual, marriage was a noble vocation, and matrimony was indeed a sacrament. When he wrote, "there is nothing which so welds our life together as the love of man and wife," he was writing as an unmarried, celibate man. So, by "our life," he didn't mean the life of a husband and wife, but the life of the Church. He believed that the family and the sacrament of matrimony were the very foundation of the community.

In the year 386 (the same year as St. Augustine's conversion), John was ordained a priest, and as he presided over the sacraments and taught catechesis and sacramental preparation, he became one of our most important early Church Fathers who wrote on the sacraments. In 398, he was invited to become the bishop of Constantinople, but his time as bishop was filled with scandals, hardships, and betrayal, and eventually ended with John being exiled. He died in exile, on a forced march, in the year 407. He is considered one of the Eastern Doctors of the Church.

4

The Eucharist

When you hear the phrase, "the Body of Christ," what comes to mind? Maybe you think of the human body of Jesus; that he was fully human, and real flesh and blood. Maybe you think of the way the apostle Paul referred to the Church as the Body of Christ, with Christ himself as the head of the Church.[343] Or maybe you think of the bread in the sacrament of the Eucharist. The truth is, all of these are correct, and it's not a coincidence that all three of these concepts are called the Body of Christ.

When you hear the word *church*, what comes to mind? A building? A parish or congregation? Even if we think of the Church in terms of a group of people, we still usually define that group of people as those who gather in a certain place. But originally, the Church was not defined by any particular place. Christians met in homes, scattered across the Roman Empire, and there were no church buildings. So what defined the Church? What determined who was a member of the Church? It was the sacraments. Certainly baptism was a defining factor, since the sacrament of baptism (with confirmation) was a person's initiation into the community of believers. But the initiation was not complete until the baptized believer was initiated to the table of the Eucharist. In other words, the sacrament of the Eucharist was the culmination of initiation. And so, more than anything else, the early Christians defined the Church as those who gathered around the table.[344]

Another way to say this is that the Body of Christ (the Church) is made up of those who receive the Body of Christ (the sacrament). And by receiving the Body of Christ in the Eucharist, a person becomes a part of the Body of Christ, the Church. This is why the phrase *Body of Christ* has these layers of meaning. The Church is the Body of Christ, gathered and united around

the table of the Body of Christ. And when we take the Body of
Christ into ourselves, we become part of the Body of
Christ. You see, the goal of the sacraments of initiation, culminating in
the Eucharist, is not only individual salvation. The goal is also to
make us into the Body of Christ. You become what you receive.
You are what you eat!

Virtually all Christians celebrate the sacrament of the Eucharist, though they may call it by different names. All of the following names are acceptable, and each one emphasizes different
aspects of the sacrament.

The Lord's Supper

We sometimes call the sacrament the *Lord's Supper* because it
reminds us of the last meal that Jesus shared with his disciples
before his Passion.[345] The Last Supper was a Passover meal, complete with unleavened bread and the traditional cups of wine.
But Jesus gave new meaning to the bread and wine when he
said, "this is my body . . . this is my blood."[346] In doing this, he
connected the bread and wine to his human flesh and blood,
specifically saying that his blood was to be spilled for the forgiveness of humanity's sins. We can see that Paul understood the
connection of the cup of the sacrament to the cup of Passover
when he called it the "cup of blessing."[347] He goes on to say that
because Jesus' body was broken for us, we who receive the one
bread of the sacrament can be the one united Body of Christ.

When Jesus said, "do this in memory of me," he intended
to start a tradition of regular observance—in other words, he
meant for this ritual to be repeated.[348] But not just repeated in a
ritualistic way, rather in a way that brings the events of Christ's
passion back to mind, and back to life, for the believer.[349] We can
see that the earliest Christians understood it this way, since we
are told that "they devoted themselves to [among other things]
the breaking of the bread" (Acts 2:42). According to the book
of Acts, from the very beginning of the Church, the Christians
celebrated the Lord's Supper every day.[350] And when Paul

explained the tradition that he had received, he wrote that "as often as you eat this bread and drink the cup, you proclaim the death of the Lord until he comes" (1 Cor. 11:26).[351]

Jesus himself described heaven as something like a wedding banquet.[352] The Lord's Supper, then, is the Supper of the Lamb—the anticipation of the promise of the heavenly banquet of eternal life.[353] It is a meal that offers spiritual food; food for the soul.[354] For the Christian, the sacramental table combines the altar of sacrifice with the sacred meal, as Jesus himself is both high priest and sacrificial Lamb.

Holy Communion

We also call the sacrament *Holy Communion*, because it is the sacrament of union—the unity of the Church. By this sacrament we are united both to Christ and to each other—in fact we are united to Christians of all times and places.[355] When we come together at the sacramental table, there are two aspects to the communion: a vertical union, and a horizontal union. The vertical union is a union with the divine. In the sacrament we make contact with God in Christ. Jesus said, "Remain in me, as I remain in you. Just as a branch cannot bear fruit on its own unless it remains on the vine, so neither can you unless you remain in me. I am the vine, you are the branches. Whoever remains in me and I in him will bear much fruit, because without me you can do nothing" (John 15:4–5). In communion, we are mystically one with Christ as the members of his Body, and collectively as his bride, and this is how we remain in him, and he in us.[356]

The horizontal union is a union of table fellowship. During Jesus' ministry, he was often criticized for sitting down to a meal with sinners; and to gather at the table with sinners is still a characteristic of his Church. Jesus ate with sinners, and now sinners come to eat with Jesus, and we still receive his grace and forgiveness. When we meet at the table of Holy Communion, we experience the communion of the saints, the unity of all Christians who gather at the table, anywhere in the world, united by the Holy Spirit—we are, to use Paul's words, one body who share one bread.[357] In fact, the communion of saints even extends across the boundary line between life and afterlife, to those who have gone before us.[358] At the table of communion, we unite with all Christians: past, present, and future. This is why we traditionally include prayers of intercession for those who are with us, those who are separated from us by distance, and even for those who have already passed on.[359]

Our third and final name for the sacrament is the *Eucharist*, which is a Greek word meaning "thanksgiving."[360] This is the name most often used in the early Church. The sacrament is not meant simply to remember Jesus' Passion, but to express our gratitude for the sacrifice Jesus made for our sake. Thus the sacrament is an act of worship. Not only do we receive something from God in the sacrament (grace, forgiveness), but we also give something back to God: our thanks and adoration.

It is natural to associate thanksgiving with a meal, but the Eucharist was much more than simply the grace before Jesus' Passover. In fact, the Last Supper was actually eaten in between Jesus' consecration of the two elements of bread and wine.[361] So the early Christians continued what Jesus had started by offering the sacrament of the Eucharist in the context of a meal.[362] Ancient documents and archaeological evidence show that the sacramental meal, or *agape* (love feast) as it was called, came to be combined with the ancient Roman tradition of the memorial meal for the dead, and many Christians celebrated the sacrament at the cemeteries and catacombs as a way of honoring both Christ and the martyrs who followed in his footsteps.[363]

How Did the Lord's Supper Become the Mass?

Eventually, it seems that logistical problems arose, probably due to any number of circumstances—from the dangers of persecution to the selfishness of some Christians.[364] We can already see this happening in Corinth within two decades of the Last Supper, as Paul relates in 1 Corinthians 11. There, the wealthy

Christians were gathering early, eating all the good food, and drinking too much, so that by the time the people who had to work for a living arrived, there wasn't much food left.[365] In the late second century, Clement of Alexandria criticized people for making their agape meals no different from the pagan banquets that their non-Christian neighbors were having.[366]

In addition, the growth of the Church in any given city came to the point where one bishop could no longer preside over the sacrament for all its Christians, and the authority to preside had to be delegated to the house church pastors (the priests). Because of this, the sacrament was separated from the meal, and it seems that in many places the *agape* meal continued in the evening while the sacrament remained the center of Sunday morning worship. In the middle of the second century, the Christian philosopher Justin Martyr wrote a document that includes an early "order of worship." Justin wrote to explain what Christians were doing in their liturgies, and to try to convince the Romans that they were not doing anything politically subversive. So Justin described an early Christian worship service in Rome in about the year 150 AD.[367] There is a wealth of information in Justin's description, but for the moment the important thing to note is that Christian liturgy takes place at dawn on Sunday mornings, and it centered around the Eucharist, but with no *agape* meal. The sacrament became the core of morning worship, while the meal became an evening gathering at which the Church fed the poor.[368]

Bishop Cyprian of Carthage, writing in the middle of the third century, tells us that the sacrament was in the morning because that is when Jesus rose from the dead, but the meal was in the evening because that is when Jesus shared the Last Supper with his disciples.[369] This separation of the sacrament from the meal was not something that happened all at once. In fact, it probably happened earlier in some cities than in others. On the other hand, the combination of meal and sacrament probably lasted longest outside of the cities, at the cemeteries, where the early Christians continued the Roman tradition of the *refrigerium*, or the memorial meal.[370] As this tradition became part of Christian experience, the faithful would gather at gravesites (or above burial sites, in the case of the catacombs), and they would literally have a picnic—a fellowship meal at which the stories of martyrs were read aloud, along with Scripture and prayers. They remembered their departed loved ones, or the martyrs of their city, all of whom were buried close by. Often they might have a bishop or priest come out to the cemetery with them, and he would preside over the sacrament of the Eucharist, sometimes even offering the Eucharist on behalf of the departed. These memorial meals were the beginning of the feasts of the saints, since they were celebrated on the anniversaries of their martyrdoms.

The practice of the *agape* meal continued in the Church as the feast days of the Christian calendar, and in places like Rome, it evolved into an outreach to the poor, even open to non-Christians. Eventually, certain churches in Rome were designated as deacon stations, and were set up to feed the hungry. They also may have provided shelter for people to sleep in the vestibules, and so these deacon stations were, in a way, the first soup kitchens and homeless shelters.

The sacrament of the Eucharist, of course, became the central focus of the liturgical service, or the Mass. The re-enactment of the passion of Christ in the Eucharist was considered the primary proclamation of the gospel, and the high point of Christian worship.[371] Christ is considered present under the appearance of the sacramental elements of bread and wine, and in fact water is mixed with the wine (just as water is mixed with flour to make the bread) to symbolize the two natures of Christ—humanity and divinity.[372]

Therefore, Catholics often refer to the whole worship service as "the Mass." Technically, the worship service has two parts: the liturgy of the Word, and the liturgy of the Eucharist. After receiving the written word of God in the Scriptures, and the living Word of God in the Eucharist, believers are then sent out into the world, to live out their mission as Christians. The word "Mass" comes from the Latin *missio*, or "sending forth" (hence the English word "mission")[373] So when we call the worship service, or more specifically the sacrament, by the word "Mass," it should remind us that we don't simply receive the gifts of God for ourselves, but we receive them in order to take them out into the world, where we will do good works in the name of Christ.

TRUE FOOD AND TRUE DRINK

The early Christians believed that the Eucharist is a sacred mystery that is a means of God's grace. They believed that it was foreshadowed in the Old Testament by the miraculous feeding of the Israelites with the manna in the wilderness, and by the water that flowed from the rock. They believed that it was also foreshadowed by Jesus' feeding of the multitudes and changing water into wine at the wedding in Cana. They also believed that Jesus himself instituted the rite, and meant for it to be repeated in the Church that he founded. Finally, they believed that the sacrament itself foreshadows, and mystically anticipates, the heavenly banquet of eternal life in the kingdom. Now, with this as a foundation, let's take a look at what Jesus himself taught about the Eucharist.

Before he ever instituted the sacrament as a rite, Jesus spoke of his flesh as food and his blood as drink.[374] In fact, he said, "my flesh is *true* food, and my blood is *true* drink." Jesus added the word *true* not for dramatic effect, but to indicate that this saying is no mere metaphor. He was not speaking in parables or allegories, but concretely.[375] We can see that his audience did not hear this statement as a metaphor, since some (including some of his own followers) said that it was too hard a saying to accept, and left him because of it.[376] Yet Jesus never tried to call them back and clarify what he had said. There was no need to explain himself, because they had understood him perfectly.[377]

Those who stayed did so because they realized they had nowhere else to go. "You have the words of eternal life," Simon Peter said (John 6:68). This was not just a general statement on Peter's part—he was referring directly to the teaching about the Eucharist. Jesus had just said, "Unless you eat the flesh of the Son of Man and drink his blood, you do not have life within you. Whoever eats my flesh and drinks my blood has eternal life, and I will raise him on the last day" (John 6:53–54). So the words of eternal life in this context are Jesus' own teaching about his body and blood, and the sacrament of the Eucharist. There is no eternal life without participation in the body and blood of Christ in the Eucharist!

In John's Gospel, one of the important themes is that of the acceptance, or receiving, of Jesus Christ.[378] In the first chapter, we learn that though many people rejected Christ, the children of God are those who accept him.[379] In the sixth chapter, this emphasis on receiving Christ is presented in a very powerful way—literally taking the body and blood of Christ into oneself by eating and drinking. Just as the manna had come down from heaven to feed the people of Israel, Jesus has "come down" to humanity—as a person with a full human nature—and his very humanity is the saving bread of the New Covenant.[380]

If Jesus had intended to institute a ritual in which bread and wine would metaphorically represent his body and blood, he easily could have avoided confusion by using a simile (as he often did). He might have said, "My body will be broken like bread, my blood will be poured out like wine." But he didn't do that. He didn't say, "My flesh is *like* food," he said, "My flesh is *truly* food." He didn't say, "My blood is *like* drink," he said, "My blood is *truly* drink." And these are the words of eternal life, because it is only by taking his body and blood into ourselves that we receive him, and remain in him.

DISCERNING THE BODY

The apostle Paul learned the ritual of the Eucharist from the other apostles who were present at the Last Supper. But he claimed to understand the meaning of the Eucharist from his own encounter with the risen Christ.[381] For Paul, the sacrament of the Eucharist is both a remembering and a reenactment of Christ's Passion.[382] It is in the Eucharist that the Church "proclaim[s] the death of the Lord until he comes." The presentation of the Eucharist is a proclamation of the gospel. But Paul goes on to say that some were receiving the sacrament "unworthily," failing to "discern the body," and this was causing negative consequences for their physical health.[383] This demonstrates that Paul believed that the sacrament was much more than a memorial meal, much more than a symbolic gesture. He believed that it has a mystical power that is not to be disrespected.

So what does it mean to "discern the body"? Here again we find that there are multiple levels of meaning in the phrase, "Body of Christ." On one level, when the Christians of Corinth disrespected each other by their selfishness, they failed to discern that they are all members of the Body of Christ, as the Church, and that they are meant to be unified.[384] But on another level, Paul also indicates that their disrespect for the sacrament is a failure to discern the presence of the Body of Christ in the Eucharist. In fact, it is this concern for the respect for the sacrament and for the possibility of taking the elements "unworthily," that led the Church to insist that only the baptized may receive the elements, and that confession must always come before receiving the Eucharist.[385]

What Did the Church Fathers Say About the Eucharist?

There was another group in the early Church that failed to understand the relationship of Jesus' human body with the Eucharist. Known as *Docetics*, or *Docetists,* they were a group of people on the fringes of the Church who believed and taught a heresy called *docetism*, which was an early form of *gnosticism*. Docetics denied the humanity of Jesus, teaching that he only appeared on earth as a phantom, and that he had no real flesh and blood. We can see evidence of docetism in the "false prophets" mentioned in the first letter of John.[386] This belief led them to reason that since Christ had no real flesh and blood, they should reject the use of wine in their Eucharist, or to reject the sacrament altogether.[387]

The Church Fathers responded to docetism by clarifying a couple of things. First of all, they insisted that Christians must not imagine a dichotomy of spirit and matter than denigrates the human body. Docetics believed that Jesus could not have a human body, because they considered the human body evil and unworthy of the spirit. The Fathers affirmed that the human body was created good by a good God, to be redeemed and raised whole and perfected at the resurrection. Secondly, the Fathers clarified and emphasized the reality of Jesus' human body—not only during his life and ministry on earth, and in his bodily resurrection, but also present in the sacrament of the Eucharist.

Ignatius, bishop of Antioch (c. A.D. 110)

Arguing against the Docetics, Ignatius emphasized both the reality of Jesus' human flesh and blood and the reality of his body and blood in the Eucharistic elements. In fact, he made it very clear that the two are connected. The body and blood in the sacrament are as real as the flesh and blood of the body of Jesus, because they are the same. The body and blood of the sacrament are the same body and blood that were born of Mary, hung on the cross, and were raised on the third day. In a letter to the Christians in the town of Smyrna, Ignatius wrote about the Docetics:

> They abstain from Eucharist and prayer because they refuse to acknowledge that the Eucharist is the flesh of our savior Jesus Christ, which suffered for our sins and which the Father by his goodness raised up.[388]

For Ignatius, the Eucharistic elements do not simply represent the body and blood of Christ—they *are* the body and blood of Christ. This is a powerful mystery, because the elements themselves contain power. They are not symbols or metaphors; they are the "medicine of immortality."[389] Ignatius also emphasized that the table of the Eucharist is the thing that unites believers into the one Church.[390]

Justin Martyr, philosopher and apologist (c. A.D. 150)

Justin followed the lead of the apostles and Ignatius. In fact, he emphasized even more strongly the connection between the Incarnation and the Eucharist, by using the Incarnation as an analogy to describe the sacrament. Just as "the Word *became* flesh," so the elements of bread and wine *become* the body and blood of Jesus by a miraculous change.[391] Justin wrote an open letter to the Emperor Antoninus Pius, in which he explained Christian Eucharistic theology:

> For not as common bread nor common drink do we receive these, but just as Jesus Christ our savior was made flesh by the word of God, and had both flesh and blood for our salvation, we have been taught that, in the same way, the food which is blessed by the prayer of his word, is the flesh and blood of that Jesus who was made flesh, and by the change, our flesh and blood are nourished.[392]

So what happens in the Eucharist is a miracle, analogous to the Incarnation. It is, in fact, like another Incarnation—or perhaps the continuation of the Incarnation in the post-ascension Church. The change takes place at the moment that the presider prays the words of Jesus from the institution of the Lord's Supper, when, as Justin says, the elements are "blessed by the prayer of his word."[393]

Irenaeus, bishop of Lyons (c. A.D. 180–190)

Irenaeus, like Ignatius, was working against the heresies of the Docetics and Gnostics. So, like Ignatius and Justin, he makes a strong connection between the flesh and blood of the Incarnation and the body and blood of the sacrament. The change that takes place is a "becoming," in that the bread and wine *become* the body and blood of Christ. Irenaeus wrote:

> For the bread, which is produced from the earth, when it receives the invocation of God, is no longer common bread, but

the Eucharist, consisting of two realities, earthly and heavenly. So also, our bodies, when they receive the Eucharist, are no longer corruptible, having the hope of the resurrection to eternity.[394]

. . . therefore, the mingled cup and the manufactured bread receives the word of God and the Eucharist becomes the Body of Christ.[395]

Notice that, for Irenaeus, after the consecration at the words of institution there are two realities. One is that the tangible aspects of bread and wine remain, which is obvious. The other is the miraculous change that results in the presence of the body and blood of Christ, which have the power to grant immortality.

The consistency of the two biblical testaments was important to Irenaeus (in part because Docetics and Gnostics rejected the Old Testament), and so he often demonstrated that consistency by a method known as typology. A *type* is a sign that foreshadows a deeper reality that later fulfills and completes it, called an *antitype*. For example, Adam is a type of Christ, and Eve is a type of Mary. When it comes to the Eucharist, Irenaeus and the other Church Fathers interpreted the manna in the desert and the water from the rock as types of the sacrament. They also saw the multiplication of the loaves and the miracle at Cana as New Testament types of the Church's sacrament. These biblical types all pointed to the Eucharist, which would later fulfill them. Note that all of these *types* were miracles, and the Church Fathers all understood the Eucharist to be a miracle as well. Furthermore, the elements of bread and wine themselves are types of the body and blood of Christ, which means that at the words of consecration the type *becomes* the antitype. The sign becomes the deeper reality.

Tertullian, Lay Teacher of Carthage (~200)

Like Ignatius and Irenaeus, Tertullian defended the real humanity of Jesus against Docetics. In fact, Tertullian wrote an extended treatise against the most famous Docetic of them all: Marcion (though by the time he wrote it, it was more Marcion's followers who were the concern). Tertullian followed Irenaeus's understanding of typology and expanded on it; however, whereas Irenaeus had written in Greek, Tertullian wrote in Latin, and so he used the word *figure* (*figura*) to translate Irenaeus's concept of the *type*. Thus for Tertullian the bread and wine are *figures* of the deeper realities of Christ's body and blood.[396] One could say that before the consecration, they *prefigure* the reality they are about to become, as the *type* foreshadows the *antitype*. At the words of institution, the figures become the realities they point to, as the bread and wine turn into the body and blood of Christ.

Arguing that the flesh of Christ must be real flesh in order for it to be able to save human flesh, Tertullian wrote, "The flesh feeds on the body and blood of Christ, that the soul likewise may be nourished by God."[397] We can see that Tertullian understood that this was not just a metaphor, since he criticized Marcion for believing just that: "If, however (as Marcion might say), he pretended the bread was his body, because he lacked the truth of bodily substance, it follows that he must have given [mere] bread for us."[398]

In other words, if Christ had no real flesh and blood (but was only a phantom, as Marcion taught), then there could be no real body and blood in the Eucharist; it would be only bread and wine. But, recognizing that the consecrated elements are no longer ordinary bread and wine, Tertullian also notes, "We feel pained if any wine or bread, even if our own, should fall on the ground."[399] Tertullian refers to the Eucharistic bread as "the bread by which he re-presents his own proper body, thus requiring in his very sacrament the humble elements of creation."[400] Notice that in Tertullian's understanding the human body of Jesus is "re-presented" in the sacramental elements. The bread and wine begin as *figures* of the body and blood of Christ, and then they become what they prefigure. Another way to think of this is that in the figure, or appearance, of bread, we receive the body, and in the figure, or appearance, of wine, we receive the blood.

It is also important to understand Tertullian's use of the term *substance*.[401] Although we can see from his use of the term above that the *substance* of the body is what the Docetics believed Christ lacked, the concept of substance does not refer to material substance—rather it refers to the underlying essence of a thing. It is in this sense that the *substance* of Jesus' body and blood is present in the consecrated elements. The figures of bread and wine become the substance of the body and blood of Christ.[402] Even though they still look and taste like bread and wine, the *substance*, or underlying essence of the elements has become the substance of Jesus' body and blood.

Hippolytus, Theologian and Possibly Bishop (~220)

Hippolytus was still writing in Greek, although this was the time period that the Western Church was shifting from Greek to Latin. He may have been the bishop of a town near Rome called Portus. We know that he was within the metropolitan area of Rome, and that he openly criticized the bishops of Rome. He did not disagree with the Church on the Eucharist, however, as we can see from some fragments of his writings on interpreting the Old Testament. He tells us his understanding of the Eucharist while commenting on the passage from Proverbs 9, which says that Wisdom "has spread her table":

> It also refers to his [Christ's] honored and undefiled body and blood, which day by day are administered and offered sacrificially at the spiritual divine table, as a memorial of that first and ever-memorable table of the spiritual divine supper.[403]

Of Proverbs 9:4–5, which says, "To him who lacks understanding I [Wisdom] say, 'Come, eat of my food and drink of the wine I have mixed,'" Hippolytus goes on to comment, "[B]y which is meant that he gave his divine flesh and honored blood to us to eat and to drink it for the remission of sins."[404]

We can see from these passages that Hippolytus believed the Eucharist to be a re-presentation of the sacrifice of Jesus' Passion, in which the flesh and blood of Jesus are given to us to eat and drink—not as a memorial only, but in a way that is effective for the forgiveness of our sins. We can also see that the Eucharist was being offered daily.

Cyprian, Bishop of Carthage (~253)

Bishop Cyprian was writing during a time of intense persecution of the Church. During that time, some who did not believe in the divine nature of Christ (a heresy known as *adoptionism*) were offering a modified version of the Eucharist that did not include wine. Their cup held only water.[405] Their stated reason for doing this is that they did not want to leave their meetings with wine on their breath and be found out as Christians.[406] Their real reason, though, may have been that they thought drinking wine was a sin, or that they did not believe that Christ's blood could save, since they thought he was only a man. Cyprian responded by reprimanding them for being ashamed of the blood of Christ.[407] Then he clarified that the cup must contain wine, since it is only if the cup contains wine that it can contain the blood of Christ.

Cyprian used the word *symbol* in the same way that Tertullian used the word *figure*: to talk about the elements of bread and wine as types of the reality that they were to become. It may be tempting to read the word *symbol* as though it means "only symbolic," in the sense of a metaphor. However, it is clear that Cyprian did not mean it that way, since he was so adamant that any disrespect of the elements was a direct affront against Jesus himself, and he emphasized that the receiving of these elements directly affected one's salvation. In fact, he wrote that for one to receive the sacrament without reconciliation after having committed apostasy in the persecution (and therefore to receive "unworthily") was to commit an act of profound disrespect for the sacrament: "[V]iolence is done to his body and blood, and they sin now against their Lord more with their hand and mouth than when they denied their Lord."[408]

Therefore, we can see that Cyprian used the word *symbol* the
same way Tertullian used *figure* and the same way the word *sign*
is used in the Gospel of John: to speak of something miraculous, a mystery that points to a deeper reality. He concludes that
without real wine, there could be no real blood, which meant
that the atonement of Christ's Passion could not be applied to
the individual.

For Cyprian, the Eucharist is only effective if it contains the
true symbol, because only the true symbols of bread and wine
can become the true realities of the body and blood of Christ.
And without the true body and blood of Christ, the recipient cannot become part of the Body of Christ, the Church.
This is why Cyprian believed the sacrament to be essential for
salvation. This is also why he was perhaps the most vocal of
the Church Fathers who said that there could be no salvation
outside the Church: because there were no sacraments outside
the Church.[409]

Cyril, Bishop of Jerusalem (~350)

Cyril, perhaps before he was consecrated bishop, delivered a series of catechetical lectures. In two of them in particular, delivered to people who were newly baptized, he explained the
Church's understanding of the Eucharist:

> Whereas the bread and wine of the Eucharist before the in-
> vocation of the holy and adorable Trinity were simple bread
> and wine, after the invocation the bread becomes the body of
> Christ, and the wine the blood of Christ.[410]
>
> He once in Cana of Galilee turned the water into wine,
> akin to blood, and is it unbelievable that he should have
> turned wine into blood? . . . Therefore with full assurance let
> us partake as of the body and blood of Christ, for in the fig-
> ure [appearance] of bread is given to you his body, and in the
> figure [appearance] of wine his blood, that you, by partaking
> of the body and blood of Christ, may be made of the same

body and the same blood with him. For thus we come to bear Christ in us, because his body and blood are distributed through our members, thus it is that, according to the blessed Peter, we become "partakers of the divine nature."[411]

Therefore, consider the bread and wine not as bare elements, for they are according to the Lord's declaration the body and blood of Christ . . . don't judge the matter from taste, but from faith be fully assured without misgiving, that the body and blood of Christ have been given to you . . . Having learned these things and been fully assured that the seeming bread is not bread, though sensible to the taste; and that the seeming wine is not wine, though the taste will have it so, but the body and blood of Christ.[412]

As we can see, Cyril gives his new converts (and us) a nice summary of the Church's understanding of the Eucharist so far. The bread and wine become the body and blood of Christ in a miraculous mystery that parallels the miracles of the incarnation and the wedding of Cana. Furthermore, it is by participation in the Eucharist that we are able to have union with God.

Ambrose, Bishop of Milan (~390)

Ambrose followed Tertullian in his use of the word *figure* to describe the elements of bread and wine as signs that point to—and become—a greater reality. The bread is a figure that becomes the body of Christ, the wine is a figure that becomes the blood of Christ. The figures are signs that, at the words of institution, become the reality of the body and blood of Christ. The element "changes from bread to the body of Christ."[413] And as Cyril had done, Ambrose argues that this miracle should not surprise us, nor should we think it unbelievable, because the miracle of the Eucharist is created by the same Christ who was the agent of creation, and who was incarnate and who performed many other miracles. In a treatise on the sacraments, Bishop Ambrose wrote:

We observe, then, that grace has more power than nature . . . But if the word of Elijah had such power as to bring down fire from heaven, shall not the word of Christ have power to change the nature of the elements? You read concerning the making of the whole world, "He spoke and they were made, he commanded and they were created." Shall not the word of Christ, which was able to make out of nothing that which was not, be able to change things which already are into what they were not? . . . [B]y the example of the incarnation, the truth of the mystery is proven . . . it is the true flesh of Christ which was crucified and buried, is then truly the sacrament of his body.[414]

Notice how Ambrose talks about the change in the *nature* of the elements. This is the same concept as Tertullian's *substance*. Here Ambrose, like Cyril, acknowledges that even after the elements of bread and wine become the body and blood of Christ, they still feel and taste like bread and wine. Therefore, he points out that the change does not affect their physicality; what is changed is their nature, their substance, their very essence. "In that sacrament is Christ," Ambrose wrote, "because it is the body of Christ; it is therefore not bodily food, but spiritual.[415]

By calling the food of the Eucharist "spiritual," Ambrose did not mean that it was only symbolic or metaphorical, as we can see from the passage above. What he meant to clarify was that the miraculous change does not take place on the level of what is tangible, but on the deeper level of underlying reality. Even after the consecration, the elements appear to be bread and wine to the physical senses. But to those who see with the eyes of faith, they are the mystical presence of the flesh and blood of Jesus. This presence is not less real than the tangible presence of the look and feel of bread and wine—in fact, the mystical presence of the body and blood of Christ is *more* real.

Augustine, Bishop of Hippo (~the early 400s)

Augustine was the student of St. Ambrose. However, whereas Ambrose followed Tertullian in using the word *figure* to describe

the elements of bread and wine, Augustine usually followed
Cyprian in preferring the term *symbol*. But Augustine had a long
career and wrote many works, so there are times when he used
figure in the way that Tertullian did, and there were other times
when he used *figure* to mean a metaphor.[416] So it can be a bit con-
fusing, especially when reading Augustine from our modern
vantage point, and in English. Having said that, we can see that
Augustine did not disagree with his mentor Ambrose when it
comes to the miraculous change that takes place in the sacrament
of the Eucharist. Augustine preached these words to his people:

> That bread which you can see on the altar, sanctified by the
> word of God, is the body of Christ. That cup, or rather what
> the cup contains, sanctified by the word of God, is the blood
> of Christ. It was by means of these things that the Lord Christ
> wished to present us with his body and blood, which he shed
> for our sake for the forgiveness of sins. If you receive them
> well, you are yourselves what you receive.[417]

Notice how Augustine even anticipates the objections that
might pop up in the minds of his audience:

> For what you see is bread and a cup. This is what your eyes
> report. But your faith requires far subtler insight: the bread
> is Christ's body, the cup is Christ's blood . . . Inside each of
> you, thoughts like these are rising: "Our Lord Jesus Christ,
> we know the source of his flesh: he took it from the Virgin
> Mary. Like any infant, he was nursed and nourished, he grew
> and became a young man, suffered persecution from his own
> people. He was nailed to the wood, he died on the wood, and
> from the wood, his body was taken down and buried. On
> the third day (as he willed) he rose. He ascended bodily into
> heaven from where he will come to judge the living and the
> dead. There he dwells even now, seated at God's right hand.
> So how can bread be his body? And what about the cup? How
> can it (or what it contains) be his blood?" My friends, these

realities are called sacraments because in them one thing is
seen, while another is grasped. What is seen is a mere physical
likeness; what is grasped bears spiritual fruit.[418]

We can see from St. Augustine's sermons that he agreed with
Ambrose on the reality of the change in the Eucharist: that the
very essence of the bread and wine become the body and blood
of Jesus Christ. We can also see that Augustine, like Ambrose,
did not believe that the change affected the tangible aspects of
the bread and wine. The underlying substance of the elements
changed, not their physicality, so that the result is a presence of
the body and blood of Christ on a deeper level of reality than
what is accessible to the senses.[419] What happens in the Eucharist
is a miracle, and a mystery, but not a magic trick.

Did a "Protestant" View of the Eucharist Exist in the Early Church?

There have been attempts to pit Augustine against Ambrose,
as though student and teacher disagreed on the mystery of the
Eucharist. Sometimes Augustine's theology of the Eucharist is
called "symbolic," as though the elements only represented,
metaphorically, the body and blood of Christ. However, this
view is a misunderstanding of the way the term *symbol* was used
by both Cyprian and Augustine, and it ignores the evidence in
Augustine's own writing. The proof is in the fact that at the time,
there was no controversy. No one who lived at the time thought
there was any disagreement between the two bishops, least of
all the bishops themselves. Neither one ever suggested that they
thought the elements were only (metaphorically) symbolic of
the body and blood. They simply had two different ways to
talk about what is going on in the sacrament. For Ambrose, the
figure becomes the reality; for Augustine, the symbol becomes
the reality; but both of them were saying that the elements of
bread and wine are signs that become the reality to which they
point. The change that takes place is a change in the very nature

of the elements, so that their substance, or essence, becomes the substance of the body and blood of Jesus—it is a miracle, just as the "signs" in the Gospel of John are miracles.

Furthermore, both Ambrose and Augustine made a close connection between the body of Christ as sacrament and the Body of Christ as the Church. As a sacrament, it is a sign of our identification with Christ. Just as in baptism we identify with Christ's death and resurrection by going under the water and rising up from it, in the sacrament of the table we identify with Christ's Passion by receiving his body and blood.

The understanding of the Eucharist we have outlined here so far was assumed in the early Church, almost without exception.[420] There are many more early Church Fathers who could be quoted as evidence of this consensus, including Hilary of Poitiers, Gregory of Nyssa, and John Chrysostom. In fact, there was far less dissension over this doctrine than there was over the doctrine of the Trinity! Therefore, it can be said with confidence that a Reformed (Protestant) Eucharistic theology did not exist in the early Church.

As it turned out, it was not until the ninth century (in the West) that Eucharistic theology came to be a topic of much discussion. Three things happened to cause the issue to come up, and when it finally did, the coming controversies would force the Church to clarify its teaching, just like the earlier heresies had forced the Church to clarify orthodox doctrine.[421] First (as the story goes), missions in northern Europe converted tribal people who were used to the idea of a priest being a kind of wizard. They didn't speak Latin, so they misunderstood the words of institution, *hoc est corpus meum* as magic words (this is apparently the origin of the expression "hocus pocus"). So people started thinking that the sacrament was a kind of magic trick, in which the human eye was fooled into seeing something that was no longer there. Secondly, as the Church spread throughout Europe, an effort was made to standardize liturgy across the Western Church. And finally, Charles the Bald, king of the Franks, read a new treatise on the Eucharist by a monk named Radbertus.

Paschasius Radbertus, Abbot of Corbie (~831)

Radbertus wrote a document called *On the Body and Blood of the Lord*, in which he followed the Church Fathers by connecting the miracle of the Incarnation with the miracle of the Eucharist. He wrote that at the words of institution, the substance of the elements becomes the substance of the body and blood of Christ. Furthermore, he said, this must be the same body that was born of Mary and hung on the cross, or else the sacrament could not be effective for the recipient. For Radbertus, the tangible aspects of bread and wine remain as figures of the body and blood, but the reality of the body and blood are hidden under the figures. This means that after the consecration, the bread and wine are no longer present as to their substance, or essence. Instead, the body and blood are substantially present—in a reality that is deeper than the senses can perceive.[422] This is possible because it is also the same flesh as the resurrected Christ, and so the presence of the body and blood of Jesus in every Eucharist is another resurrection-appearance of the Lord.

> Because he willed it, he may remain in the figure of bread and wine. Yet these must be believed to be fully, after the consecration, nothing but Christ's flesh and blood . . . and to put it in more miraculous terms, nothing different, of course, from what was born of Mary, suffered on the cross, and rose again from the tomb.[423]
>
> For this reason, this mystery is far different from all those miracles which have occurred in this life, because they all occurred so that this one may be believed . . . For the other miracles of Christ confirm this one of his passion, and so the elements are not outwardly changed, but inwardly, that faith may be proved in spirit.[424]
>
> [A] thing capable of intelligible perception through the senses is divinely transformed by God's power through the Word of Christ into his flesh and blood.[425]

However, notice that Radbertus is not advocating a literalistic view of the Eucharist in which recipients chew the flesh of

Christ. Rather, it is the bread that is chewed, and the body of Christ that is received.

> But because it is not right to devour Christ with the teeth, he willed in the mystery that this bread and wine be created truly his flesh and blood through consecration by the power of the Holy Spirit . . . so through the same, out of the substance of bread and wine, the same body and blood of Christ may be mystically consecrated.[426]

Radbertus also clarified that the sacrament is not a magic trick, since the faith of the observers is not necessary for the miracle to take place; though the faith of the recipients is necessary for grace to be received.

Ratramnus, Priest and Monk of Corbie (~845)

Radbertus revised his treatise in about 844 and sent a copy to King Charles the Bald. The king read it, and did not understand the close association of the Eucharistic body and blood with the flesh and blood of the historical body of Jesus. So he posed a question: Are the body and blood of the Lord present *in truth*, or *in a mystery?*

From the same monastery, Ratramnus wrote his reply in a document with the same title as Radbertus's: *On the Body and Blood of the Lord*. However, Ratramnus was not really responding to Radbertus, he was (whether he realized it or not) responding to a caricature of Radbertus, an extreme theology of the Eucharist that assumed a change in the physical properties of the elements— and in responding against that view of the sacrament, Ratramnus ended up saying many of the same things as Radbertus.

Ratramnus, however, thought it best to downplay the Eucharist's connection to the historical body of Jesus, so he spent a significant portion of the document outlining the differences between the body that hung on the cross and the body that is presented on the altar. The sacrament, he said, is the substance of the same body that hung on the cross, but it is not the same in its physical aspects, since we do not literally chew the skin and muscles of Jesus.[427] With this, Radbertus would have agreed. However, Ratramnus was also uncomfortable with the idea that the divinity of Christ (his divine nature, or substance) could be contained within the Eucharistic elements.[428] For all of these reasons, Ratramnus favored those parts of Augustine's writings that described the bread and wine as *figures*, which led to some confusion over whether the body and blood were understood to be "figurative," in the sense of metaphorical.

Ratramnus was trying to answer Charles the Bald's question by saying that the body and blood of Christ are present in a *mystery*: that which is hidden, or veiled. Therefore, he said that after the consecration, the bread and wine are "truly" present (by which he meant tangibly present at the surface level), and the body and blood are "figuratively" present (by which he meant spiritually present at the level of deeper reality). The spiritual presence of the body and blood is not less real than the "true" presence of the bread and wine, but the spiritual presence can only be seen by faith. So to answer Charles the Bald, Ratramnus said that the presence of the bread and wine is "true" (tangible to the senses), and the presence of the body and blood is "in a mystery." The change occurs on the "interior" of the elements, not on the exterior, so that the change is not perceived by the senses, but only by faith. He wrote:

> But that bread which through the ministry of the priest comes to be Christ's body exhibits one thing outwardly to human sense and it proclaims another thing inwardly to the minds of the faithful. Outwardly, it has the shape of bread which it had before, the color is exhibited, the flavor is received, but inwardly something far different, much more precious, much more excellent becomes known, because something heavenly, something divine, that is, Christ's body, is revealed, which is not beheld, or received, or consumed by the fleshly senses but in the gaze of the believing soul.[429]

Notice that Ratramnus is not denying that a change takes place in the elements:

> But since they confess that they are Christ's body and blood and that they could not be such without some change for the better being made, and this change did not take place in a corporeal sense, but in a spiritual, it must now be said that this was done figuratively, since under cover of the corporeal bread and of the corporeal wine Christ's spiritual body and spiritual blood do exist.[430]

Ratramnus even uses the concept of substance to describe how the change takes place on the level of the very essence of the elements:

> From all that has thus far been said it has been shown that Christ's body and blood which are received in the mouth of the faithful in the church are figures according to their visible appearance, but according to their invisible substance, that is, the power of the divine Word, truly exist as Christ's body and blood. Therefore, with respect to visible creation, they feed the body; with reference to the power of a stronger substance, they feed and sanctify the souls of the faithful.[431]

In many ways, Ratramnus was saying the same thing as Radbertus, but using different words. Their disagreement was over the meaning of the word "true." For Radbertus, "true" meant ultimate truth—underlying reality. For Ratramnus, "true" meant that which is on the surface, accessible to the senses.[432] But both agreed that the presence of the body and blood of Christ is the presence that is most real. Neither said that the presence of the body and blood is merely metaphorical, or that the bread and wine are only symbolic of the body and blood.

Both Radbertus and Ratramnus claimed to be in agreement with Ambrose and Augustine (and indeed they were). Both would agree that a miracle occurs in the Eucharist, but they would also agree that it is not the physical aspects of the elements that change. But to answer the king's question, Radbertus said, in effect, "both": the body and blood of the Lord are present in truth, and in a mystery. The truth is the mystery.

During the lifetime of Radbertus and Ratramnus, there was still no major controversy.[433] However, Ratramnus's reluctance to make a more direct connection between the historical body of Jesus and the Eucharistic elements would later lead to his posthumous condemnation. In the eleventh century, Berengar, Archdeacon of Angers (known by his birthplace as Berengar of Tours), read a copy of Ratramnus's treatise. At the time, he didn't even know who wrote it, but he came to believe that Ratramnus was more faithful to Augustine than Radbertus, and he wrote letters to his friends and colleagues about it. Those letters were passed on to Pope Leo IX, and in the year 1051, Berengar was condemned as a heretic. A synod was held in Rome in 1059, where Berengar was confronted and Ratramnus's treatise was also condemned as heresy.

At the synod, Berengar was forced to sign a confession, written by a Cardinal Umberto (or Humbert) of Burgundy, which went to the literal extreme and said that in the Eucharist, recipients actually chew the flesh of Christ. Umberto's view of the Eucharist is sometimes called *annihilationism*, because it assumes that the bread and wine are completely annihilated—no trace of them remains, and the resulting consecrated elements are both the underlying essence *and* the tangible aspects of the body and blood of Christ. In fact, this is the very position that Ratramnus was criticizing in his document. Berengar would later recant this confession and write a pamphlet against the synod of 1059. In it he clarified his understanding of the Eucharist by admitting that a conversion of the elements takes place, but speculated that after the words of institution, even the substance of bread and wine remain, resulting in a double substance of the consecrated body and blood with the substance of bread and wine. In other words, while the tangible aspects remain bread and wine, the underlying reality of the consecrated elements is *both* the substance of bread and wine *and* the substance of the body and blood of Christ. This is a line of reasoning that would later be called *consubstantiation*—the substance of the body and blood added to the elements alongside the substance of bread and wine. Therefore, it could be argued that Berengar was the true precursor to Protestant Eucharistic theology; however, it would be an oversimplification and a misinterpretation to say (as some have claimed) that Radbertus followed Ambrose while Ratramnus followed Augustine, and that somehow Augustine or even Ratramnus exhibit a "proto-Protestant" view of the Eucharist.[434]

Lanfranc of Canterbury (~1062/1079)

Lanfranc, abbot of the monastery of St. Etienne and later the archbishop of Canterbury, wrote his own document called *On the Body and Blood of the Lord*, which not only followed the Eucharistic theology of the Church Fathers and Radbertus, but also provided the Church with a clear explanation of how the traditional view of the Eucharist was a middle way between the extreme literalism of Berengar's forced confession (*annihilationism*) and Berengar's actual belief (*consubstantiation*). In his document, Lanfranc responded to Berengar's pamphlet, demonstrating how Berengar had misread Augustine and how Augustine and his mentor Ambrose were in agreement.

However, at times Lanfranc seemed to think that Berengar believed the Eucharistic elements were *only* symbols (that is, metaphors) and nothing more. This is what is sometimes called *memorialism* (the idea that the sacrament is nothing more than a memorial of Christ, and is not a manifestation of his Real Presence). But Berengar did not believe this, and in fact we have no evidence that anyone did at this time. It seems to be a case of Lanfranc accusing Berengar of going to an extreme that would have been virtually unthinkable at the time, in order to characterize him as an arch-heretic.

As Lanfranc clarified, only the external attributes of the bread and wine remain after the consecration, not their substance.

These external attributes would later be called *accidents*, meaning those aspects that are "accidental" (or, not essential) to the
reality of the underlying substance of a thing. The accidents
of the Eucharist are those aspects of the elements of bread and
wine that are accessible to the senses, which remain unchanged
by consecration. The deeper underlying reality (the substance)
of the elements of bread and wine does change, becoming the
substance of the body and blood of Christ. Thus in the consecrated elements, the substance of the body and blood of Jesus are
hidden under the form (or figure) of bread and wine. Just as both
the human and divine natures of Jesus Christ were contained
within the womb of Mary, the same body and blood of Christ
(his humanity and divinity) are contained within the Eucharistic elements.[435]

Although Lanfranc's thought was consistent with Augustine's,
he owed more of the way he describes the Eucharist to Ambrose.
He begins with Ambrose, "for by the benediction nature itself is
changed,"[436] and then goes on to explain:

> And so that you should not place the power of nature over
> that of the divine, as if God could not change nature in any
> way that he pleases, or that seems proper to him, he adds,
> "Why do you seek the order of nature in the body of Christ,
> when the Lord Jesus himself was born from the Virgin be-
> yond the order of nature?"[437]

In other words, why should we hesitate to believe in the miraculous nature of the Eucharist, when we believe in the miraculous nature of the Incarnation—or any other miracles for
that matter? Lanfranc further explains:

> For in the appearance of bread and wine that we see, we honor
> invisible realities, namely, the body and blood of Christ. Nor
> do we consider these two appearances from which the Lord's
> body is consecrated to be what we once thought them to
> be before the consecration, because we faithfully confess that

before the consecration they were bread and wine, that is, those realities which nature formed. Within the consecration, however, they are converted into the flesh and blood of Christ, and these two realities have been consecrated by the benediction.[438]

We believe, therefore, that the earthly substances, which on the table of the Lord are divinely sanctified by the priestly ministry, are ineffably, incomprehensibly, miraculously converted by the workings of heavenly power into the essence of the Lord's body. The species [appearances] and whatever other certain qualities of the earthly substances themselves, however, are preserved . . . it is the same body that was assumed from the Virgin, and also not the same body, which we receive. Indeed, it is the same body as far as it concerns its essence, true nature, and its own excellence. It is not the same body in its appearance . . . This is the Faith held from ancient times, and is the one that the Church which is now diffused throughout the whole world, and called Catholic, now holds.[439]

Lanfranc's theology of the Eucharist was affirmed at a council in Rome in the year 1079. The council declared that the elements undergo a "conversion of substance," and become—in their essence—the same body and blood of Christ that came into the world through his mother Mary. After the council, as archbishop of Canterbury, Lanfranc updated his treatise, giving it the form it has now.

Ratramnus had written against annihilationism—though whether he thought he saw it in Radbertus or somewhere else is not clear. In any case, by the time of Umberto of Burgundy, there were some people who believed in this crude literalistic approach to the Eucharist—indeed, even the synod of 1059 leaned this way under Umberto's influence. Berengar had followed Ratramnus's lead, saying that what is "real" is that which is visible and tangible. But this led him to go too far, rejecting not only annihilationism, but also the traditional, apostolic

view of the Eucharist, ultimately denying that there was any
true presence of Christ in the elements. Lanfranc provided the
Church with a middle way—affirming the reality of the presence of the very body of Christ that was born of Mary and died
on the cross, without going to the extreme of imagining that
people were literally chewing the flesh of Jesus. Berengar argued
against annihilation and for consubstantiation; Lanfranc argued
against memorialism, and for—though he didn't use the word—
transubstantiation.

A Real and Mysterious Presence

As the name implies, the word *transubstantiation* indicates the
change in substance that the Eucharistic elements undergo. The
substance of bread and wine becomes the substance of the body
and blood, but the accidents do not change, since the appearance
and physicality of bread and wine remain. After the consecration, the substance of the body and blood of Christ are hidden
under the accidents of the bread and wine.

Although the word was not widely used until the twelfth
century, and not officially affirmed until the Fourth Lateran
Council in 1215, *transubstantiation* does express that theology of
the Eucharist that goes all the way back to the early Church.
After the Council of Trent in the sixteenth century, it would
be considered heretical to speak of the body and blood using
words such as *figure*, *symbol*, or *sign*, since these could be taken
to mean that the presence was metaphorical, or in some way less
real than the tangible aspects of bread and wine. Instead, the
Church speaks of the Real Presence, which means what Radbertus meant when he described the presence as both true and
a mystery.[440]

Another way to think of it is that the real, or true, presence
of Christ in the Eucharist, is like the presence of Christ after
his Resurrection, when he was not recognized at first. Looking
at the Eucharistic elements with human eyes only, one might
not recognize the presence of Christ. The senses grasp the signs

(bread and wine); the soul receives the true reality (the body and blood).[441] The eyes of the body perceive, and the mouth accepts, the accidents, or the species (appearances) of bread and wine; the eyes of faith perceive, and the heart accepts, the substance, or the essence (underlying reality) of the body and blood of Christ.[442] What the senses perceive has remained the same, but what the soul receives (the substance) has changed. This change is a miracle, effected by the words of Christ, when the priest speaks the words of institution ("this is my body . . . this is my blood") over the elements.[443] Thus the same Word of God who is the agent of creation also creates the miracle of transubstantiation.[444]

Accordingly, Christians have always held a great reverence for the consecrated elements. The *Apostolic Tradition*, a document that goes back to the third century, advises that those who receive should eat nothing prior to taking the elements, so that the elements should not mix with ordinary food in the stomach. It also warns not to let the consecrated bread fall on the ground, or the cup be spilled, since this would be disrespectful of the elements.[445] It is clear that this kind of reverence and protection would not be necessary if the elements only *represented* the body and blood of Christ. In fact, by the year 1000 it was determined that the Eucharistic bread should no longer be placed in the hands of the recipient, due to the risk of dropping it, and the Church determined that the priest should place it on the person's tongue.[446] This created the need for small, self-contained pieces of bread (hosts) that would not drop crumbs.[447]

This also eventually led to the withholding of the cup from the laity, to lessen the risk of spilling the blood of Christ. However, the Church reminded the faithful that in the mystery of the Mass, since the body and blood of Christ are present in substance, not in material physicality, even when the people only receive one of the Eucharistic elements they still receive both the body and blood of the Lord. The whole presence of Christ— body, blood, and divine substance—is in each Eucharistic species. This is important for those who have food allergies and cannot eat bread, or who cannot drink wine. Only one of the species is necessary to receive the whole presence of Christ.[448] This is called the doctrine of *concomitance*.[449]

As we saw earlier, belief in the powerful presence of Christ in the sacrament, and the great reverence for the elements, also meant that the early Church closely associated confession with the Eucharist.[450] Normally, confession of sins came before the sacrament, since the faithful were conscious of the apostle Paul's advice that those who gather at the table should examine themselves so that they do not receive the sacrament "unworthily."[451] Cyprian of Carthage wrote that those guilty of serious sin (specifically apostasy) would be taking the sacrament unworthily if they failed to first confess their sin, complete their penance, and receive reconciliation.[452]

By the Middle Ages, though, the fear of receiving unworthily was so great that many people stopped receiving altogether. This led to the tradition of *ocular communion*, meaning communion with the eyes. In other words, many people began to feel that it was enough to be present at the miracle of the Mass and watch it happen. The devotional practice of Eucharistic Adoration comes from this time, and continues to be cherished by many people who value the opportunity to pray in the Eucharistic presence of Christ.[453] However, the Church recognized the problem with too many people staying away from the most important sacrament, and eventually mandated that Catholics receive the Eucharist at least once a year, preferably at Easter.[454]

Such is the history of the Church's understanding of the Eucharist. The belief that was always held from the beginning, that in the Mass a miraculous change takes place, and the substance of the elements of bread and wine become the substance of the body and blood of Christ, came to be called *transubstantiation* (meaning, the *change* of *substance*). However, the word *substance* does not mean *physical* substance. The tangible aspects of the bread and wine are signs which point to the deeper reality of the body and blood of Christ, even as their very essence becomes the essence of the body and blood.[455] Another way to say this is that the body and blood of Christ are truly present "under" the accidents (or "species") of bread and wine.[456] The substance of bread and wine changes, while the tangible accidents remain. What results is that the full presence of the body and blood of Christ exists in each of the species of bread and wine. This was affirmed as the correct understanding of the Eucharist at the Fourth Lateran Council, held in Rome in the year 1215.

A helpful analogy is to think of the Eucharist as a Christmas present. As it sits under the Christmas tree, the present consists of a gift, wrapped in packaging—a box, paper, and a bow. But you can only see the packaging, you can't see what's in the box. Imagine that the packaging is made of cardboard, paper, and ribbon; and the gift inside is more cardboard, paper, and ribbon. This is like the elements of bread and wine before the consecration. The "packaging" (the part you can see) is bread and wine; and the essence, or substance, of the elements (on the "inside") is also bread and wine. But imagine if, while you slept on Christmas Eve, someone removed the cardboard, paper, and ribbon, from inside the box, and replaced it with a valuable gift. Now the present consists of cardboard, paper, and ribbon packaging, and on the inside, a valuable gift. This is like the Eucharistic elements after the consecration. The "packaging" still looks like bread and wine, but now the essence of the gift is the body and blood of Christ. The packaging didn't change, but the gift did. That's transubstantiation. The part that is accessible to the senses remained the same, but the part that is the very essence (substance) of the elements—the part that is more real than what can be seen with the eyes—becomes what it was not before.[457]

CHRIST'S TRANSFORMING PRESENCE

In the sacrament of the Eucharist, not one but two changes take place. The substance of the elements is changed at the recitation of Jesus' words of institution.[458] But the people who receive the elements are also changed, at the moment they accept the presence of Christ. All sacraments effect a change in the person receiving the sacrament, but since the Eucharist is repeated, it becomes like a booster shot of grace, bringing forgiveness of sins and empowering the recipient to resist temptation and do God's work in the world.

But the sacrament is much more than a means of grace for the individual. It also completes the transformation of a person into a member of the body of Christ (the transformation that was initiated at baptism), creating a union with the rest of the Church as well as with God. The Eucharist defines the Church, and the Eucharist makes us the Church. You are what you eat. But it can only do that if the presence of Christ in the sacrament is something more than simply the general omnipresence of God, or even the presence of the Spirit in the gathering of believers.[459]

In fact, we can acknowledge that there are different levels of divine presence. On the most basic level, divinity is omnipresent, so God is everywhere, and that includes the divine Son of God. However, we know from Scripture that there are times when God is present in a more powerful way in certain places, such as when the glory of God led the people of Israel, or stayed with the tabernacle, or in the temple.[460] When Jesus was about to leave his disciples, he promised that whenever two or more of them gathered in his name, he would be there with them.[461] We have to assume that this promise implied a more powerful presence than simply the divine omnipresence. And an even more powerful presence than this is the result of the consecration of the Eucharistic elements, when the body, blood, soul, and divinity of Jesus Christ are made present to be received by the faithful.[462] In the sacrament, Christ is not only all around us; not only among us; he is within us.

ARE CATHOLICS SACRIFICING CHRIST ALL OVER AGAIN?

But, the question is sometimes asked, *aren't Catholics crucifying Christ all over again? Isn't the sacrifice of Christ "once and for all"?* It is true that we sometimes call the Eucharist the "sacrifice of the Mass," and it is also true that the letter to the Hebrews makes it clear that the sacrifice of Christ does not need to be repeated.[463]

The Passion of Jesus was indeed, once and for all time. However, Catholics do not believe that the Eucharist is a re-sacrificing of Christ. Rather, it is a re-presentation of the same sacrifice that he suffered once and for all. We remember and re-present the passion of Christ, and it is there at the Eucharistic table that the crucifixion which happened so long ago becomes effective for the Church and for individuals through God's grace.[463] As the *Catechism of the Catholic Church* states, "When the Church celebrates the Eucharist, she commemorates Christ's Passover, and it is made present: the sacrifice Christ offered once for all on the cross remains ever present," and "The sacrifice of Christ and the sacrifice of the Eucharist are *one single sacrifice* . . . the same Christ who offered himself once in a bloody manner on the altar of the cross is contained and offered in an unbloody manner . . ."[465]

The idea that the Eucharist is a "bloodless sacrifice" goes back at least to the second century. The phrase was used by the apologist Athenagoras, as well as the historian Eusebius of Caesarea.[466] This was to distinguish Christian worship from pagan rituals, which of course included animal sacrifices, and which were eventually outlawed at the end of the fourth century. The point is that this demonstrates that the early Christians understood that the Eucharist is not sacrificing Christ again, but in fact for the Christians the Eucharist replaced the sacrifices of Hebrew and Greco-Roman religion, making those bloody sacrifices obsolete.[467]

Why Is Catholic Communion Reserved for Catholics Only?[468]

When the apostle Paul wrote his criticism of the way the Corinthian Christians were gathering for their Eucharist, he warned them that they might incur judgment if they were to receive the sacrament "without discerning the body."[469] This phrase has a depth of meaning that lends itself to multiple levels of interpretation. On one level, it must have something to do with understanding the solemn nature of the sacrament, since the Body and

Blood of Christ are present. In other words, by eating too much and getting drunk at their *agape* meal, the wealthier Corinthians were failing to appreciate the reality of the presence of Christ in the sacrament. Remember that the early Christians believed that one must not approach the table without first examining his or her conscience.[470]

On another level, Paul's rebuke also means that the Corinthian Christians were failing to respect their fellow (poorer) members of the Body of Christ, the Church, when they didn't wait for the others, started eating without them, and ate all the best food and drank the wine before they arrived. This was probably symptomatic of another problem in Corinth, which was a division among the faithful—a division along class lines, which may also have had theological implications.[471] The point is that where there is division among the Body of Christ, the Church, that division affects the sacrament of the Eucharist. And today we live in a world in which Christians are divided by different denominations that are the result of historical conflicts, especially the Protestant reformation. And those other denominations often have a different understanding of what the Eucharist is, and what happens on the altar table.

Therefore, the sacrament is ordinarily reserved for those who are "in communion" with the Catholic Church, both by membership and by agreement with the teaching of the Church on the meaning of the sacrament. For the early Church Fathers, only the baptized could receive the Eucharist, because only the baptized were regenerated and initiated.[472] It was assumed that only the initiated could understand the significance of the presence of Christ in the elements and show them the required respect. Not only may no unbeliever receive the sacrament, but the Church Fathers wrote that care must also be taken that the elements are not eaten by animals, and that the bread would not be dropped on the ground and the cup would not be spilled.[473] Even Christians who were preparing to receive the sacrament should eat nothing before it, to avoid the sacred elements from mixing with ordinary food in the person's stomach.[474]

But it isn't only non-Catholics who are not offered the Catholic Eucharist. Even Catholics who are not in good standing with the Church are asked to refrain from the table until their situation is remedied or they are reconciled to the Church. This demonstrates the intimate connection between the sacrament of Eucharist and the sacrament of Reconciliation. Justin Martyr said that to receive the sacrament, a person must be baptized and, "living as Christ enjoined."[475] As a matter of the Church's discipline, the bishop may *excommunicate*, or *exclude* from *communion*, anyone whose relationship to the Church is in tension, due to unconfessed sin or rejection of the Church's teachings.[476]

Therefore, the Church has always taught that the Eucharist is far too valuable to be given away to the uninitiated. It would be like giving an inheritance to someone who was only a casual visitor to the family household. The inheritance belongs to the family. Or it would be like asking why only the members of a club know the secret handshake. The answer is in the question: the handshake is reserved for members because it is one of the hallmarks of membership, so to reveal it to nonmembers would change the meaning of membership. These analogies may sound trivial, but they are intended to make the point that before receiving the Eucharist, a person must make a commitment to the community that offers it. Thus to give the Eucharist without this commitment would be a form of sacramental promiscuity, like asking for the benefits of sex without the commitment of marriage.

Unfortunately, Catholics are separated even from other baptized Christians, by denominational division, and by theological differences. This division is real, and although there are still some things that unite us as Christians (such as our baptism and our creed), sharing the Eucharist would imply a unity that does not yet exist, and would therefore be a false unity. So the reservation of Catholic Eucharist for Catholics is not meant to be unwelcoming, but it is for the sake of the integrity of the sacrament.

We understand that there are those of our brothers and sisters in Christ who see the table differently. Some Christians believe that hospitality requires an open table. They reason that the invitation to the table, even to a non-Christian, could be a doorway into membership—a form of evangelization. We respect this view, but we do not share it. For Catholics, the Eucharist could not be a doorway into membership, because it is the culmination of membership, and the completion of the sacraments of initiation.[477] In a way, these two views of communion could not be more different. One sees the table as a *symbol* of unity, which can invite people into that which it stands for, as an expression of a hope of future unity; the other (the Catholic) sees the table as much more than a symbol—it is a true *manifestation* of unity, which unfortunately would be diminished by extending it to those with whom we are not united. It is commendable to remember the table hospitality of Jesus, but not every meal Jesus had was a Eucharist. Most meals he was happy to share with the sinners and outcasts. But the Last Supper was in the upper room with his disciples. Catholic Eucharist is the continuation of that upper room experience. It prepares disciples of Jesus to go out into the world, but it does not invite the world in.

On the other hand, the Catholic Eucharist is not a completely closed table. It is not limited to the members of a particular congregation, as some Protestant communions are. And there are even certain cases (of "grave necessity") in which non-Catholics can receive the Eucharist in a Catholic church.[478] Therefore, in a way, the Catholic reservation of the Eucharist is a kind of middle way between a completely closed table and a completely open table. More important, the Catholic communion is based on the practice of the early Church Fathers, in succession from the apostles.

In summary, the Catholic understanding of the Eucharist is that it is a miracle, in which the presence of Christ is powerfully manifested—he is more powerfully present than is implied in divine omnipresence, or even in Jesus' promise to be with his followers whenever they gather.[479] It is the way in which we remain in Jesus, as he commanded us to do.[480] And it is a means, or a channel, of God's grace which we receive for the forgiveness of our everyday sins, and for the strength to resist temptation.[481]

So, like the other sacraments, it changes us. It is not simply a sign of something that has already happened, but it energizes us for living the Christian life. However, unlike the sacraments of baptism and confirmation, it is repeated regularly for ongoing grace and empowerment.

Finally, as a miracle of unity, the Eucharist connects us to the communion of saints, including our loved ones who have gone before us, and are now passed on. This is why we can offer the Mass for the dead, to benefit those who are making their transition through the purification of purgatory into the heavenly realm.[482] And when we gather at the table of the Eucharist, we are receiving a foretaste of heaven—a down payment on our inheritance as children of God and brothers and sisters of Jesus Christ. For the Church Fathers, the Eucharist was the very manifestation of the unity of the Church.[483] Thus, along with baptism and the other sacraments, the Eucharist defines the Body of Christ, as those who share the Body of Christ in the elements. As the Catechism says, "the Eucharist makes the Church."[484]

Source and Summit

As the apostle Paul said, "[A]s often as you eat this bread and drink the cup, you proclaim the death of the Lord until he comes" (1 Cor. 11:26). So the sacrament of the Eucharist is a proclamation of the gospel, and as such, it is the center of Catholic worship.[485] We can see this in the way that traditional Catholic architecture places the altar at the center of the worship space, whereas traditional Protestant architecture gives that place of prominence to the pulpit.

In the Eucharist we remember the Passion of Jesus Christ, in the same way that the Hebrews remembered the Exodus at their Passover.[486] *Past history becomes present mystery*, as we remember the cross with gratitude, just as Jesus asked us to. We think back to the saving activity of God in history, and we re-present the Passion in the Mass, and we do it regularly, so that we might never forget what God has done for us in Christ.[487]

Throughout the history of the Church, this re-presentation of the sacrifice that Jesus Christ made on the cross is itself called a sacrifice.[488] In the Mass, the one sacrifice of Christ is made present again, not because the sacrifice itself needs to be repeated, but because it needs to be proclaimed again and again for our benefit. Therefore, the Mass has historically been called a "bloodless sacrifice," since the blood of Christ was spilled once and for all, and does not need to be spilled again.[489] The sacrifice of Christ is reenacted and celebrated—this celebration of the Eucharist is a spiritual sacrifice, and a "sacrifice of praise."[490]

But this reenactment of the sacrifice of Christ's Passion is not for remembering only. Each time it is re-presented, the benefits of the Passion are applied to the believer who receives the elements.[491] Those who participate receive the forgiveness of sins, and the strength to avoid temptation in the future.[492] The result is a union with Christ that he referred to as "remaining" in him.[493] "Remain in me," he said, "as I remain in you. Just as a branch cannot bear fruit on its own unless it remains on the vine, so neither can you unless you remain in me" (John 15:4). Thus the sacrament of the Eucharist becomes the center of the Christian experience, and so it is the "sacrament of sacraments," the "source and summit" of the Christian life.[494]

The Eucharist is a little bit like time travel. In this one sacrament is contained the past, present, and future, all wrapped up in one moment. It's as though at that moment there is a convergence of the time continuum—where past, present, and future all come together in a moment when eternity breaks through into our time. On the altar, the past sacrifice of Christ's Passion is re-presented in a mystical way that makes it present again, because it is effective for those who receive. In the past, he suffered to take away the sins of the world, and as people receive the elements of his body and blood, they find forgiveness of their sins and they express their gratitude. In the present moment, the Church is unified around the table—the Church of the past in the communion of saints, and the Church of the present, wherever in the world believers gather. And finally, the Eucharist foreshadows our future hope of eternal life at the heavenly banquet. We who gather at the Church's table take comfort in the promise of a place at the table of the kingdom.

Given the reality of Christ's presence in the sacrament, and our conviction that the benefits of Christ's Passion come to the recipient in the sacrament, it is only natural that it should be offered daily, and received at least weekly. Sometimes people are concerned that receiving the sacrament every week would cause them to take it for granted, and perhaps it would lose its meaning—and if the sacrament was only a symbol, then that might be a concern. However, if we assume that the presence of Christ is real, then the transformative power of the sacrament is not diminished with frequency, even if some people do fail to understand its significance. We would never say that if I eat every day, food will lose its meaning, or if I breathe every minute, air will lose its meaning. Would a diabetic say that by taking insulin every day, insulin will lose its meaning? Would a kidney patient say that by having dialysis every week, dialysis will lose its meaning? No, because the "meaning" of those procedures is in their power to sustain the person who receives them. And that's what the Eucharist is—the power to sustain us in the Christian life.

It is true that the divine Son of God is omnipresent, and so he is always around us. And it is also true that he said he would be present with us in a special way whenever we gather in his name.[496] However, like the air that is all around us all the time, if we don't take it into ourselves, we will suffocate and die. In the same way, the presence of God is all around us, but if we never take Christ into ourselves in the way that he himself said we must, we will always be disconnected from him. The key is to make the Eucharist a part of a natural rhythm, like breathing. Imagine confession and the Eucharist like the two parts of breathing. Confession is like breathing out, expelling the bad air; receiving the Eucharist is like breathing in, taking in the good air—taking in God's grace with the body and blood of Jesus.

~

Many Protestant denominations have the tradition of the "altar call": an invitation for people to get out of their seats, come to the front of the worship space, and dedicate (or rededicate) their lives to Christ. For Catholics, every Mass includes an altar call, when the faithful are invited to come to the altar/table and rededicate themselves to Christ by receiving his body and blood. The altar and table are one as the sacrifice of Christ is re-presented and the invitation to fellowship with God is extended.[496] Those who come forward are saying "yes" to the invitation, and "accepting Christ as their savior."[497] Just as in any sacrament, by participating we are identifying with Christ—he is our savior, and we are his followers. So, for those Protestants who may ask if a Catholic has "received Christ as personal savior," the answer is: Yes! We do every week (at least). And in receiving Christ, we receive God's grace, and we give thanks, expressing the meaning of the word, "Eucharist."

So for the Catholic, eating is believing. When we take the body and blood of Christ into ourselves, it is a very intimate way of demonstrating our faith. And to believe that the Eucharist does not contain the Real Presence of the body and blood would be to eat and drink "without discerning the body" (1 Cor. 11:29). And so we come full circle back to the scriptures, and the biblical witness to the meaning of the sacrament. If the Eucharistic elements were only metaphorical symbols representing the body and blood of Christ, then the sacrament of the Eucharist could only be a metaphor for the unity of the Church, not an expression of the communion of the saints; and the sacrament could only be a metaphor for the healing and empowerment of God's grace, not an actual channel of that grace. And if the elements were only metaphors for unity, then the sacrament could be shared with those with whom we have no real unity, but only the hope of future unity. However, if the sacrament is an expression of real unity, then unfortunately it cannot be shared where real unity does not yet exist.

Pope St. John Paul II, in his apostolic letter, *Mane Nobiscum, Domine* (*Stay With Us, Lord*), reminds us that what we experience in the Eucharist is a power that motivates and enables us to transform our daily lives. In other words, after we have been to the table and received Christ into ourselves, we take him out into the world with us, to love our neighbor and work for peace. The Mass (*missa*) is a sending out (*missio*), so that everything we do should be motivated by gratitude for the sacrifice Christ made to reconcile us to God.[498]

Featured Father

Ambrose of Milan: Defender of Orthodoxy

St. Ambrose was born in Gaul (what is now France) in the year 340. He was the younger brother of St. Marcellina, who is known for her commitment to ascetic vows and her humility. Their father died when Ambrose was about fourteen, and so his mother moved the family to Rome, where he was educated. He studied law, and then followed in his father's footsteps and entered a political career. Eventually, Ambrose became the governor of northern Italy, with its capital in Milan. There he gained a reputation as a respected leader and an eloquent speaker. He was also known to be a faithful supporter of the Nicene Creed. This was important, because in the Roman Empire at that time there was an Eastern emperor who was promoting the heresy of Arianism, which said that the Son of God was a created being; that Christ was not God who became human, but a man who became a god.

In fact, the bishop of Milan was also an Arian, having gained the office through interventions by the emperor, and the forced exile of his orthodox predecessor. When the Arian bishop died in the year 347, the people of Milan were up in arms over who would be the next bishop. Would he be a faithful Catholic and supporter of Nicene orthodoxy, or would he be another heretic? When the crowd gathered at the cathedral threatened to turn into a riot, Ambrose was there to keep the peace. According to the story, Ambrose rode in on his horse, and quieted the mob, and in a moment of silence, the voice of a child was heard saying, "Ambrose . . . bishop . . ." The crowd began chanting this, and Ambrose was acclaimed as bishop—even though he was not ordained. In fact, he had never even been baptized, since at that time it was fashionable for wealthy families to refrain from baptizing their sons if they thought the boys might grow up to pursue a career in politics or law. They didn't want the moral expectations of a baptized Christian to interfere with their upwardly mobile careers!

So Ambrose was baptized, ordained a priest, and consecrated bishop, and he accepted his new role with both humility and zeal, giving his possessions to the poor, donating his property to the Church, and embracing a life of simplicity for the sake of the office. Ambrose resisted the efforts of the Eastern rulers to impose Arianism in the West, even to the point of organizing a sit-in at a church that the Arians were trying to acquire. He became a beloved preacher, whose sermons had such a reputation that they attracted—and later converted—the man who would become St. Augustine. It was because of Ambrose that Augustine understood the danger of Arianism, and the urgency to refute it theologically. Augustine would eventually write his important document *On the Trinity* based on that understanding. Ambrose also wrote hymns and theological treatises, including some important ones on the sacraments. It was in these documents, *On the Mysteries* and *On Christian Faith*, that we have the Eucharistic theology of Ambrose that is included here.

Ambrose died on Good Friday in 397, the same year that his saintly sister Marcellina died, and today he is considered a Doctor of the Church.

5

The Communion of Saints

When the apostle Paul wrote his letters to the Christian communities in places like Rome and Corinth, he referred to his audience as *saints*.[499] That English word comes from a Latin translation of the Greek term that means, "holy ones." But when Paul uses the word, it doesn't imply a higher level of holiness, as if he were writing to a special group of Christians. He means that all of his readers are "called saints," or are "saints by calling."[500] In other words, all Christians can be called saints because, by our faith in Christ and membership in his Body the Church, we are set apart as belonging to God.[501] As Christians, we are all holy because God declares us holy, and because God makes us holy.

So why does the Catholic Church also designate certain Christians throughout history as "saints," in a way that doesn't apply to all Christians? To answer that, we have to go all the way back to the early Church, to the time when Christianity was illegal and the Roman government persecuted Christians. Remember that the early Church Fathers taught that baptism washes away original sin and any sins committed up until the time of the baptism, but that post-baptismal sin must be dealt with by confession and penance. This means that one can lose one's salvation after baptism. The ancient world had an expression, shared by many of the world's cultures and religions, that went something like this: *Call no man blessed while he lives*.[502] It means that as long as a person is still alive, there is time for him to fall from grace, so we can't know how his life has turned out until he is dead. In fact, since we don't know what people did behind closed doors, we can't even say for certain whether a person is a saint *after* his life is over . . . with one exception.

If a person is martyred, that is, executed for refusing to deny the Faith, that martyrdom is considered a baptism in one's own blood—canceling any and all sin, even previous apostasy. In a way, martyrdom is the ultimate penance—suffering death for the Faith—and it means certain salvation.[503] All Christians can be called saints in one sense, and any Christian could become a saint in another sense, but you'd never really know for sure unless a person died a martyr's death. Therefore, the martyrs of the early Church were considered the "saints for sure."[504]

The "saints for sure" were held up as examples for all Christians to follow, and this made sense during a time of persecution when Church leaders wanted their flock to imitate the bravery and conviction of the martyrs. But their example went beyond standing firm in the face of persecution—the martyrs came to be known for their other virtues as well, and so it was not only their deaths, but also their lives, that were seen as exemplary. The stories of the martyrs were written down, and the records of events surrounding their trials and executions were read as part of the feasts on the anniversaries of their deaths. Although many of these martyr documents came to be embellished with some legendary material, they are based on actual events, and Christians—both during the persecutions and afterward—were encouraged by these stories of the miraculous ways that God had intervened in the life of the Church.[505] The moral of the stories was that, although the martyr had been killed, he had really won a victory over death by standing firm in the Faith and receiving salvation and resurrection.

When the Roman Empire was converted, and persecution was no longer a daily threat, a new kind of martyrdom emerged. This was a voluntary martyrdom in which some Christians "gave up their lives" by giving up their lifestyles, becoming hermits and eventually monks. These Christians desired to withdraw from the world as a way to resist temptation and live in solidarity with the poor. They pursued a life of *asceticism*, which implies an austere lifestyle of celibacy, limited diet, and even sleep deprivation, all so that they could focus on prayer and contemplation. When literal martyrdom declined, these ascetics became the spiritual martyrs, daily dying to the world in such a way that the Church could be relatively certain they really were very holy people. Thus they became the new "saints for sure," and their way of life was held up as an ideal Christian lifestyle that, even if it could not be perfectly imitated by most Christians, should be admired.

So even though Paul uses the word *saints* to mean all Christians, the early Church used the word in two ways. It could still mean all Christians, in the sense of those who are called holy and being made holy. But it also came to refer to those who are holy in an exceptional way—examples for other Christians to follow.[506] The lives of the saints were a witness to the kind of watching and waiting that Jesus referred to in parables, such as the parable of the ten bridesmaids.[507] As the wise bridesmaids were diligent in waiting for the return of the bridegroom, the saints were the ones living lives of detachment from the world, so that they could be all the more ready to meet their Lord.

Of course, over the centuries, other people who were not martyrs or ascetics have been added to the list of exemplary saints. Eventually, the Church came up with a process for determining who was most likely to be one of the "saints for sure." But the point has never been to separate these saints from the rest of the Church; in fact it is just the opposite. The point is to make the faithful aware of the way that all Christians, in all times and places, are connected in what we call the *communion of saints*. It means that all Christians (not just the exemplary ones) are in union with each other through their connection to God, by the indwelling of the Holy Spirit.[508] And that connection goes across the divide between life and afterlife, so that we are also connected to all Christians who have come before us and are now in the spiritual realm.[509]

As the Second Vatican Council document *Lumen Gentium* says, "Being more closely united to Christ, those who dwell in heaven fix the whole Church more firmly in holiness, add to the nobility of the worship that the Church offers to God here on earth, and in many ways help in a broader building up of the Church."[510] The saints in heaven (those who have been perfected in holiness) are connected to all the saints on earth (those who are being made holy) in a way that benefits every member of the Body of Christ.[511] In a way, it could be said that the Church *is* the communion of saints.[512] *Lumen Gentium* goes on to say, "Exactly as Christian communion among our fellow pilgrims brings us closer to Christ, so our communion with the saints joins us to Christ."[513]

Nowhere is the communion of saints more evident than in the sacraments. Because all the sacraments are sacred mysteries, they are shared by—and are manifestations of the union of—all the faithful, including those who have already passed on.[514] And as we have seen, the Eucharist is the sacrament that is the "source and summit" of the Christian life. So it is in the Eucharist that the communion of saints is most powerfully realized.[515] *Lumen Gentium* concludes, "When, then, we celebrate the Eucharistic sacrifice we are most closely united to the worship of the heavenly Church."[516] Like John's visions into the heavenly realm in the book of Revelation, the Eucharist gives us a foretaste of that final union of the Church at the "wedding of the Lamb."[517]

In fact, the book of Revelation says that John saw the souls of the martyrs "underneath the altar" (Rev. 6:9). And as it turned out, in the early years when the feasts of the martyrs were held at the cemeteries, or sometimes even in the catacombs, and when they shared the Eucharist, sometimes the top of a sarcophagus (the coffin lid) served as the altar table. Eventually, churches were built so that the altar was directly over the tomb of a martyr, and sometimes even the tomb itself (or a repurposed sarcophagus lid) became the Eucharistic table. This may seem strange, or even morbid, but it demonstrates the close connection between incarnation and mortality, between the Eucharist and the communion of saints. As Clement of Alexandria wrote in the late second century, "He (the Christian) also prays in the society of angels, as being already of angelic rank, and he is never out of their holy keeping; and though he prays alone, he has the choir of the saints standing with him."[518]

Therefore, the saints in heaven share in our union with God in Christ, not by glorifying themselves, but by pointing to Christ.[519] Still, the Catholic Church has been criticized for an inappropriate devotion to the saints. In part, this is because some people assume that prayer is automatically a form of worship. So what does it mean to pray to the saints?

DO CATHOLICS WORSHIP THE SAINTS?

Is it wrong to go beyond simply following the example of the saints, to the extent of expressing *devotion* to them? Does prayer and devotion to the saints constitute a form of worship? If so, Catholics would indeed be guilty of idolatry, and of breaking at least a couple of the commandments.[520]

Let's begin by asking, what is worship? Going back to our Jewish roots, worship is really two things: service and submission. To worship God is to serve God and to submit to his will. Service includes liturgy: for the Old Testament, that meant sacrifices, but of course in the Church that means the sacraments, as well as songs of praise and adoration and the recitation of creeds or statements of faith. In fact, the English word "worship" comes from an old English word, *worthshippe*, which meant "worthy-ness," as in, worthy to receive adoration. To worship God, then, is to proclaim that he is worthy of our adoration. Service also includes working for God's purposes in the Church and in the world, and doing the will of God in the name of God. Submission means to recognize our place relative to God, and to pledge to do his will.

In contrast, Catholics have never aspired to do the will of the saints, and we do not make them the focus of our liturgy. The commandment to have no other gods is a commandment to serve no other gods, and to submit to no other gods. Catholic adoration is directed only to the Trinity. We don't serve the saints, and we don't submit to the saints.

But Catholics do pray to the saints. Isn't praying to the saints the same thing as worshipping them? Notice that our definition of worship didn't include prayer. Certainly prayer *can be* a medium for worshipping God, but it is not the case that all prayer is worship. When we pray to God, often we are asking him for something—but we can also "pray," or ask, for something from anyone. In fact, we can "pray" (ask) a person to pray to God for us. Christians do this all the time, and it's called *intercession*—to pray to God on behalf of another person. The apostle James advises that we pray for each other, even for healing from sickness, and says that, "The fervent prayer of a righteous person is very powerful" (Jas. 5:16). And just as we might ask our fellow Christians who are still living to pray for us, we can ask our fellow Christians who have already died to pray for us. This is actually an expression of our belief in the communion of the saints—our brothers and sisters in the Faith can pray to God for us, whether they are living or passed on. When Catholics pray to the saints, we are asking for their intercession.

What about the Old Testament prohibition against necromancy? Isn't speaking to the dead a sin? In the book of Deuteronomy, the people of God are told not to "consult ghosts or spirits or seek oracles from the dead" (Deut. 18:10). This certainly is a prohibition against occult practices such as fortune telling, tarot cards, and séances. But prayer to the saints is not an attempt to wield spiritual power or gain information from the dead. It is simply an expression of the communion of the saints, in the unity of the Holy Spirit that extends across the boundaries of life and afterlife. Notice that in the Transfiguration, Jesus himself spoke with Moses and Elijah.[521]

But how can the saints hear our prayers if they're dead? This can cause confusion if we think that in order to hear our prayers a saint would have to be omniscient. Omniscience (knowing everything) is an attribute of divinity, and if we thought it applied to the saints, that would be a problem. But it is not required that the saints be omniscient. The Church Fathers believed (and the Church has always taught) that they can hear our prayers because they are in the presence of God.[522] In fact, we would say with the apostle Paul that they are not dead, but that they are more alive than ever.[523] They have already begun to reign with Christ.[524] Therefore, they are no longer bound by the limitations of earthly life.[525] They are that "great cloud of witnesses" who surround us and cheer us on as we run the race of faith (Heb. 12:1). And because we are all connected in the communion of saints, not to mention their proximity to God being in his presence, it is a gift of the Holy Spirit that they can hear our prayers, and intercede for us.

In Jesus' parable of the rich man and Lazarus, we read a story of a selfish man who died and went to hell.[526] From his place in hell, the man called out to Abraham and asked for some water. Abraham replied that because of the "great chasm" between heaven and hell, he could not grant the man's request. It seems that when Protestants read this parable, they see the chasm. When Catholics read this parable, they see that Abraham could hear the prayers even of a man in hell. Now, of course, this is a parable—a kind of fable told for the moral of the story. It's not necessarily to be received as the historical account of something that actually happened. But would Jesus tell a morality tale that included the possibility of a "saint" hearing prayers if he didn't want his followers to accept that possibility? In fact, we know that Jesus' Bible included the books of the Maccabees, which tell of a vision of the (long-dead) prophet Jeremiah praying for the people.[527]

But, one might still object, if we pray to the saints thinking they can do something to help us doesn't that ascribe some measure of divine power to them? Perhaps it would, if we thought they were helping us directly, by their own power. But we do not expect the saints to help us directly, only to pray to God for us. In other words, we are asking for their intercession, not their intervention. Thus, prayer to the saints doesn't assume that they are omniscient or omnipotent. But it does acknowledge that they are alive in Christ and connected to us through the communion of saints. It is true that some Christians, in their private spirituality, have taken their devotion to the saints too far, praying for the intervention of the saints in a way that leaves God out of the process. This is an abuse of the Tradition, but to abandon the Tradition just because some people have misunderstood or misused it, is to throw the baby out with the bathwater.

Therefore, prayer to the saints is not a form of idolatrous worship. Still, Martin Luther and the other Reformers worried that prayer to the saints effectively created additional mediators between God and the Church. But this was never the intention, and the Church affirms that Christ is our only mediator.[528] The ability of the saints to intercede depends wholly on the sole and perfect mediation of Christ. And, as St. Jerome wrote, "If apostles and martyrs while still in the body can pray for others, when they ought still to be anxious for themselves, how much more must they do so when once they have won their crowns, overcome, and triumphed?"[529] That is, if we can ask our living brothers and sisters in Christ to pray for us, and their prayers are affective as James said, then how much more effective are the prayers of those who are in the presence of God![530] And just as we can pray for the dead (as we saw regarding purgatory), the dead can also pray for us.[531] The truth is, prayer to the saints is not a form of worship, but a form of reverence, the same kind of reverence mandated by the commandment to honor one's parents.[532] In the biblical and spiritual context, a person's "parents" can be defined broadly to include ancestors, and we honor our ancestors in the Faith when we show them reverence, by following their example, and by communicating with them in prayer.[533]

In addition, intercession is the *ministry* of the saints in heaven.[534] Therefore, it has always been assumed that it is appropriate to ask for their prayers. In fact, some of the earliest Christian inscriptions are actually graffiti at the sites of catacombs where the memorial meals were held. In one place, for example,[535] the wall near the "picnic site" is full of petitions such as, "Peter and Paul, pray for me." Remember that this is where the feasts of the saints began, and they continued on as holidays—or holy days—on which to reflect on the lives of the saints and the examples they set for us, and to see how we measure up. They also became occasions to practice the Faith by feeding the poor and inviting them to the Church's *agape* meal (love feast) in memory of the saints.

What Did the Church Fathers Say
About Praying to the Saints?

In an account of the second-century martyrdom of Polycarp, bishop of Smyrna, the author clarifies the difference between the adoration due to the Trinity alone and the reverence given to the saints:

> We will never be able either to abandon the Christ who suffered for the salvation of the whole world of those who are saved, the blameless on behalf of sinners, or to worship anyone else. For we worship this one, who is the Son of God, but the martyrs we love as disciples and imitators of the Lord, as they deserve, on account of their matchless devotion to their own King and Teacher. May we also become their partners and fellow disciples![536]

Thus, although the Church affirmed the intercession of the saints, it was also clear that worship belonged to God alone.

Methodius, bishop of Olympus (end of the third century)

Bishop Methodius preached a sermon on Simeon and Anna, who met Mary and Joseph when they brought the baby Jesus to the temple in Jerusalem.[537] He ended the sermon with a prayer to Simeon and Anna, as well as to Mary. The prayer asks these saints to be advocates before the Lord, and remember those assembled for the sermon in their prayers. (Perhaps he was following the practice of Cyprian of Carthage, who used to preach to his people that if they died in the persecution, they should remember thereafter to pray for those still living.) Methodius then asks the saints to join him in praising Jesus: "We, together with you, sing our praises to Christ."[538] The fourth-century Liturgy of St. Basil includes a similar prayer: "Grant that we may worship and serve you in holiness all the days of our lives, by the intercessions of the holy Mother of God and of all the saints who have pleased you throughout the ages." So, asking for the

intercession of the saints was even built into the worship services
of the early Church.

Athanasius, bishop of Alexandria (c. 327)

Like the other Church Fathers, Athanasius writes of the saints in
a matter-of-fact way, with no sense of the need to defend what
he believed about them. In the closing comments at the end of
one of his theological documents, he wrote:

> He that would comprehend the mind of those who speak of
> God must needs begin by washing and cleansing his soul, by
> his manner of living, and approach the saints themselves by
> imitating their works; so that, associated with them in the
> conduct of a common life, he may understand also what has
> been revealed to them by God, and thenceforth, as closely
> knit to them, may escape the peril of the sinners and their
> fire at the day of judgment, and receive what is laid up for the
> saints in the kingdom of heaven.[539]

Bishop Athanasius is making the point that in order for us to
hope to receive the heavenly reward that awaits the saints, we
have to be in a kind of relationship with the saints in this life:
imitating them, reading what God revealed to them, and acknowledging their influence on our lives. Like the other Church
Fathers, he does not feel the need to defend the practice of prayer
to the saints, because it was not a matter of controversy at the
time—it was an uncontested practice.

Cyril, bishop of Jerusalem (c. 350)

In his *Catechetical Lectures*, given to those preparing for baptism
and to the newly baptized, Bishop Cyril explained what happens
in the Mass. Regarding the prayers of intercession, he wrote:
"We commemorate also those who have fallen asleep before us,
first Patriarchs, Prophets, Apostles, Martyrs, that at their prayers

and intercessions God would receive our petition."[540] He is clearly saying that the prayers of petition of those on earth are enhanced by the intercessory prayers of those in heaven.

Gregory of Nazianzus (c. 374)

When Gregory preached the funeral sermon for his father, he said, "I am well assured that his intercession is of more avail now than was his instruction in former days, since he is closer to God, now that he has shaken off his bodily fetters, and freed his mind from the clay which obscured it."[541] As with the other early Fathers, here it is clear that Gregory understood that it is the ministry of the departed to pray for the living.

Augustine of Hippo (c. 416)

About the martyrs Augustine preached:

> We do not commemorate them at that table in the same way, as we do others who now rest in peace, as that we should also pray for them, but rather that they should do so for us, that we may cleave to their footsteps; because they have actually attained that fullness of love, than which, our Lord has told us, there cannot be a greater.[542]

He's saying that although it is appropriate to pray for the deceased, there is no need to pray for the martyrs, since their salvation is assured—instead, they pray for us.

There are many more Church Fathers who could be cited in support of the intercession of the saints, and all of them speak of it as though it were assumed, not something they had to argue for.

Do Catholics Worship Mary?

It's probably safe to say that all Christians respect Mary as the one whom God chose to be the mother of Jesus. But do Catholics

take that respect too far? Even if the intercession of the saints
can be demonstrated to be something that has been a part of
Christianity from the beginning, do Catholics elevate Mary to a
position that comes too close to God?

Let's begin to answer that question by asking another question: Who is Mary? To say she is the mother of Jesus is saying a
lot more than it may seem on the surface, and in fact it makes her
not only unique among mothers, but unique among humanity.
Mary is the Virgin Mother, which sounds like a contradiction,
but is really one of those paradoxes that only God can accomplish.
The apostles believed and taught that Mary is the virgin whose
motherhood was prophesied in the book of Isaiah.[543] And Matthew's Gospel records that the early Christians believed that Jesus'
conception was both the fulfillment of prophecy and a miracle.[544]

The virginity of Mary and the virginal conception of Jesus are
important for three reasons. First, the miraculous nature of Jesus'
conception and birth demonstrate that it is ultimately God who
creates life, as in the stories of barren women who are granted
the gift of pregnancy by God. This happens several times in the
Old Testament, but it also happens with Jesus' cousin, John the
Baptist. Second, the miraculous conception and birth of Jesus is
important because it makes it clear that the Incarnation is divine
intervention. Something of cosmic significance is happening,
as God intervenes decisively in human history. And third, all
of this is important because it shows that Jesus is unique among
humanity. He is one of us, to be sure, but he is unique because
his Father is God, and so he has the divine nature. Without the
virgin birth, Jesus is reduced to a mere man, no more able to
save us than we are able to save ourselves.

Mary was the first Christian, because she was the first to say
"yes" to Jesus—to receive him into her life, and as her Lord and
savior. As the apostle John wrote, "to those who did accept him,
he gave power to become children of God" (John 1:12). Mary
was the first to accept him.[545] She believed the angel when he said
that nothing is impossible for God, and so she is our first example
of Christian faith, and a prototype of faith in God, rather like

Abraham was.[546] It is important to be clear that Mary had free will to accept or reject the angel's proposal.[547] She was not coerced by God. And because she said "yes" to God, she is the Church's primary example of obedience to God's will, after Jesus himself.[548]

Mary is also the Queen of the Saints, not because she was a martyr, or even an ascetic, but because she is the first Christian, and because she is the "New Eve." The Church Fathers taught that Mary undid, with her obedience, what Eve did with her disobedience. Irenaeus, the second century bishop of Lyons wrote, "The knot of Eve's disobedience was untied by Mary's obedience."[549] This is not to blame the first sin on Eve alone, especially since the apostle Paul connects it to Adam, but just as Jesus is the second Adam, Mary is the second Eve. What went wrong with Eve and Adam is made right in Mary and Jesus.[550]

Mary is also the "New Ark." Just as the Ark of the Covenant was a vessel that held the tablets of the written word of God, the New Ark is the vessel that held the living Word of God, the Word made flesh. Mary is the one through whom the divine Son of God became incarnate and entered the world. After she gave her consent at the Annunciation, the "power of the Most High" overshadowed her, and this was described by the angel using the same kind of language we find in the Old Testament to describe the way that the glorious presence of God hovered over the ark and the tabernacle.[551] So Mary is the Ark of the New Covenant. She is also called the "seat of wisdom," because it was in her womb that wisdom entered the world in the person of Jesus.[552] And it was on her lap that the Divine Wisdom/Word once sat.

Because the eternal divine nature of Christ was joined to his humanity in the womb of Mary, she is also called Mother of God. This title has been used of her at least since the second century, based on the fact that Elizabeth called her, "the mother of my Lord."[553] Use of the title was confirmed as appropriate at the third ecumenical council of Ephesus, in the year 431.[554]

It's important to note that the doctrine of Mary as Mother of God is really, at its heart, a doctrine of Christology. In other words, it's really more about Christ than it is about Mary. The doctrine emphasizes the unity of the person of Christ (called the *hypostatic union*), and affirms the union of the two natures (divine and human) against any heresy that would want to separate the two natures or deny one of them. As is true with all of the Marian doctrines, at their heart they are founded on important doctrines about Jesus Christ.

Finally, since Mary is the mother of Jesus, and his followers are called his brothers and sisters, Mary is also our mother, too. We can already see this concept in the New Testament. In the book of Revelation, Mary is described as the woman crowned with twelve stars, who gives birth to the male Child. Clearly this male Child is Christ, and John goes on to record how the forces of evil (the dragon) attempted to kill the Child—a reference to Herod's attempt to get Jesus by killing all the babies of Bethlehem. But the dragon's plan fails, and as Revelation tells us, he then turned his attention to the woman's other children, "those who keep God's commandments and bear witness to Jesus."[555] This is a reference to the persecution of the Church, and the woman's other children are the Christians. In a way, when Jesus entrusted his mother to John, and said to him, "Behold your mother," John stands for all of us.[556] Therefore, Mary is called the Mother of the Church.[557]

The Second Vatican Council, quoting St. Augustine, declared,

> Because of this gift of sublime grace [Mary] far surpasses all creatures, both in heaven and on earth. But, being of the race of Adam, she is at the same time also united to all those who are to be saved; indeed, *she is clearly the mother of the members of Christ . . . since she has by her charity joined in bringing about the birth of believers in the Church, who are members of its head.* Wherefore she is hailed as pre-eminent and as a wholly unique member of the Church, and as its type and outstanding model in faith and charity.[558]

Thus she is not only the Mother of the Church, but also a model for the Church, as it should be "without spot or wrinkle," and although its members are imperfect, she is the pure one who shows us how it's done, and through her we as the Church become more like the Bride of Christ that we should be.[559] She is our model of faith, obedience, and purity, the ultimate example of what it means to cooperate with the work of God in the world.[560]

So Mary is the first Christian, the Virgin Mother, the Queen of the Saints, the Ark of the New Covenant, the Mother of God, and the Mother of the Church. She is one of a kind, unique among Christians, among mothers, and among humanity. All of this is based on the historical fact of her voluntary participation in the incarnation of Jesus Christ, and on Scripture and early Tradition. But Catholics do not worship Mary, because we do not try to do *her* will, but rather her son's. We do not recite creeds that make her the center of our faith, and we do not conduct sacraments in her name. Still, it may be asked: do Catholics go too far? What about the Catholic Church's doctrines about Mary?

WHAT IS THE IMMACULATE CONCEPTION?

First of all, we should say what the Immaculate Conception is not: a reference to the virginal conception birth of Jesus, in which a human man did not participate. The Immaculate Conception refers to Mary's own conception. It does not mean that her conception was virginal, it means that it resulted in a conception without the transmission of original sin. Mary's conception was the natural result of both of her parents' contributions, but it was a miracle (in the sense that it involved God's extraordinary intervention) because she was conceived without original sin.

The apostle Paul understood that original sin was a reality, something shared by all of humanity.[561] With one exception, that is. In order for Mary to be the Ark of the New Covenant, the pure vessel through which Christ would enter the world, God ordained that she be born without the stain of original sin. Based on God's foreknowledge of her cooperation in his plan of salvation, through Christ's merits he retroactively redeemed and justified her from the moment of her conception.[562] When the angel greeted her in Luke 1:28, he addressed her with a title that means "grace-filled one." Mary embodied the fullness of grace, was infused with grace from her conception, to the point of being entirely sanctified. As the Second Vatican Council declared, "Enriched from the first instant of her conception with the splendor of an entirely unique holiness, the virgin of Nazareth is hailed by the heralding angel, by divine command as "full of grace."[563]

Already in the second century, the document known as the *Protevangelion of James* (sometimes spelled "protoevangelium") recorded the Church's belief about Mary's birth. Although it was probably not really written by one of the apostles named James, it does express the very early faith of the Church on the events surrounding the birth of Mary. The word *protevangelion* means the "pre-gospel," or the "first gospel," and this is something like a prequel to the gospel accounts found in the New Testament. There we read that Mary was born under miraculous circumstances, something like the birth of John the baptizer.[564]

To be in this state of the fullness of grace is to be without personal sin, as well. So the early Church affirmed that not only was Mary conceived without original sin, but she never committed any sinful act in her life, either before or after the birth of Jesus. This was a gift of God, not a work of merit, that resulted in a unique situation: a sinless perfection that had not existed in humanity since before the fall. To quote Mary's own words, "From now on will all ages call me blessed." And so "Mary has by grace been exalted . . . to a place second only to her son."[565]

The Church Fathers repeatedly attested to Mary's Immaculate Conception, and to her sinlessness. We might note a few passages:

He (Jesus) was the ark formed of incorruptible wood. For by this is signified that his tabernacle (Mary) was exempt from defilement and corruption.[566]

You alone and your mother are more beautiful than any others, for there is neither blemish in you nor any stains upon your mother. Who of my children can compare in beauty to these?[567]

Lift me up bodily and in the flesh, which is fallen in Adam. Lift me up not from Sarah but from Mary, a virgin not only undefiled but a virgin whom grace had made inviolate, free of every stain of sin.[568]

The Immaculate Conception does not mean that Mary didn't need a savior. She did need a savior, and she was saved by her son.[569] As Irenaeus of Lyons wrote in the second century, "Mary, having a man betrothed [to her], and being nevertheless a virgin, by yielding obedience, [became] the cause of salvation, both to herself and the whole human race."[570] Christ saved her, but retroactively, before she ever sinned, and thus proactively ensuring her sinlessness. We can think of sin as being like falling into a deep pit. All other humans fall into the pit and need to be rescued from it. Mary, on the other hand, was prevented from falling into the pit, and so was saved by prevention.

Mary's sinlessness does not make her any less human than the rest of us. It is a mistake to think that sin is a necessary part of humanity. In fact, the truth is that by being sinless, Mary was more fully human than the rest of us. When we sin, we fall short of our true humanity.[571] When Mary did not sin, she lived up to the potential of what all humans were created to be. (This also means that when she was presented with God's plan and gave her consent by free will, her will was truly free because it was not encumbered by sin.) So, like her son, Mary is fully human and one of us, but also unique among us. However, unlike her son, she is not divine, she does not have a divine nature, and she is not the product of a virgin birth. So Catholics do exalt Mary to the level of highest of all human beings (second only to her son), but we do not exalt her to the level of divinity.

In the Catholic Church, the feast of the Immaculate Conception is celebrated on December 8. On that day in 1854, in response to Protestant scholars' critiques of the miraculous, Pope Pius IX clarified what the Church had believed from the earliest centuries: that Mary's conception was miraculous and immaculate, resulting in her birth free of original sin, which in turn

resulted in a sinless life.[572] This made her a fitting vessel in which
the divine Word of God could become incarnate, and through
whom he could enter our world. It is important to be clear that
Pius IX did not create the doctrine of the Immaculate Conception. Rather, he was responding to Protestant scholars' criticism
of the doctrine (and of the miraculous in general) by clarifying
and affirming what the Catholic Church had traditionally believed about Mary.[573]

WHAT IS THE PERPETUAL VIRGINITY OF MARY?

The *Protevangelion of James* also reflects the early Church's tradition that Mary was dedicated to lifelong celibacy, and that she
remained so even after the birth of Jesus. In fact, the *Protevangelion* says, and the Church Fathers taught, that she remained
physically a virgin, even after Jesus' birth.[574] Therefore, she is
called Ever-Virgin, since her virginity (and the purity it implies)
characterized her whole life.[575] Augustine once preached in a
homily, "A virgin conceives, yet remains a virgin; a virgin is
heavy with child; a virgin brings forth her child, yet she is always a virgin. Why are you amazed at this?"[576]

If Mary was always a virgin, then who were the brothers and
sisters of Jesus, mentioned in the New Testament?[577] There was
some debate about this in the early Church, but the majority
of the early Church Fathers maintained that these brothers and
sisters were not the biological children of Mary, and that she had
no children other than Jesus.[578]

Some said that these brothers and sisters were Jesus' cousins,
and in fact the biblical words are not so specific as to require that
they be siblings. Cousins, or any relative, could also be described
by the Greek words for "brothers" and "sisters." Even people
who were unrelated could be called brothers if they were part of
the same fellowship, as we know from early Christian practice.[579]

But most of the Church Fathers believed that the brothers and
sisters of the Lord were children of Joseph from a previous marriage.[580] They taught that Joseph was a widower, and that's why

he is often depicted as much older than Mary in paintings of the Holy Family. They also noted how Jesus himself implied that Mary had no other children, when from the cross he entrusted her to John: "When Jesus saw his mother, and the disciple whom he loved standing near, he said to his mother, 'Woman, behold, your son!' Then he said to the disciple, 'Behold, your mother!' And from that hour the disciple took her to his own home" (John 19:26–27).[581] If Mary had another child, it would be that person's responsibility to take care of her. But since Jesus entrusted her to John, he shows that she had no other children. And surely if there were others in the Bible (such as James, for example) who were also sons of Mary, they would have claimed that in their writings, or it would be clearly pointed out in the Gospels.

The witness of the Church Fathers to their belief in the Perpetual Virginity is too vast to survey here.[582] Suffice it to say that one can find references to it in every century of the Church, and in most cases, the Church Fathers are not making arguments for the doctrine, but simply stating it as an assumption. For example, St. Athanasius stated, "Let those, therefore, who deny that the Son is by nature from the Father and proper to his essence deny also that He took true human flesh from the ever-virgin Mary."[583] Notice how the phrase "ever-virgin Mary" functions almost as a title—something that the author can assume everyone already agrees on.

It is interesting to note that not only the Church Fathers held to Mary's perpetual virginity, but, also the Protestant Reformers! It may seem difficult to believe, but Martin Luther, Ulrich Zwingli, John Calvin, and John Wesley all accepted the doctrine.[584] This means that they did not see it as a particularly "Catholic" doctrine, but simply a Christian one, not in any way conflicting with their own convictions.

What Is the Dormition and Assumption of Mary?

The *dormition* of Mary is her "falling asleep," or her death. The earliest Christian writings don't say much about the death of Mary, so eventually some legends started popping up that claimed she never died. These stories said that she was like Enoch or Elijah, taken up into heaven without dying.[585] But Mary did, in fact, die, and so the story of her death, or her *dormition*, was written to correct the false rumors.[586]

However, it was generally agreed that Mary's sinlessness meant that her body could not decay, since bodily corruption is a result of sin.[587] In addition, nowhere in early Christian writings is there mention of a tomb of Mary, which would surely have been visited and venerated if it existed. So if Mary died, where was her body? The Church Fathers taught that after Mary died, her body was assumed into heaven, where her body and soul were reunited. Like Jesus, she lives the resurrection life in the heavenly realm with her whole humanity (including her human body) intact.

However, unlike Jesus, she did not "ascend." Jesus' Ascension was an exercise of his own divine power to raise himself.[588] In other words, the Ascension of Jesus was active. Mary was taken up in a passive sense, since she is not divine and could not ascend herself. Rather, she was "assumed" into heaven, and this is what we call her Assumption.

So Mary's dormition is her death, and her Assumption is the transportation of her body into heaven. Therefore, she was not only the first Christian, she was the first Christian to experience the resurrection after Christ. The rest of us have to wait until the end of the age for the resurrection, and for our bodies to be reunited with our souls, but Mary's (resurrection) body and soul are already united in heaven.[589] Her Assumption anticipates our hope of resurrection—she is the proof of the promise we have been given.[590] The *Catechism* states, "The Assumption of the Blessed Virgin is a singular participation in her son's resurrection and an anticipation of the resurrection of other Christians."[591]

Many early Church documents that describe Mary's dormition and Assumption are embellished with layers of pious legend.[592] But there is a common core synopsis that can be gleaned from them, which points to a consensus of belief in the early

Church. That consensus suggests that Mary did not live for more than a few years after her son's Ascension, dying around A.D. 35 or 36. Shortly after the events described in the first chapters of the book of Acts, she went with the apostle John to Ephesus, where he continued his apostolic ministry, and she became the leader of a group of celibate women (which included Mary Magdalene, who would succeed her as the leader). Just before her death, Mary discerned that she would soon be joining her son in heaven. Some sources record that all of the apostles were miraculously transported to her bedside from wherever they were in the world, to be with her in the hours before her death.

According to the story, when Mary died, her body emitted miraculous light and sweet odors. Then Jesus arrived to take her soul into heaven, leaving her body to be prepared for burial. Her body was wrapped in luminous fabric that miraculously descended from heaven. It was then placed on a stretcher, to be carried along in procession to what was supposed to be her tomb. However, during the procession, an angry mob rushed the pallbearers, and attempted to steal Mary's body, with the intention of desecrating it. But the first person to touch the stretcher suffered the loss of his hands, as they withered and fell off (sticking to the stretcher), as he and the rest of the mob was struck blind. All they could do was call out to the apostles to heal them, which of course the apostles did, and they immediately converted to Christianity. Mary's body was placed in the tomb, but before long (in some versions after three days), Jesus returned from heaven with her soul, to reunite it with her body. Once Mary's soul and body were reunited, Jesus escorted her into the heavenly realm.

Whether one chooses to believe the legendary embellishments that have become attached to the story is a matter of personal faith. However, it is clear that the doctrine of Mary's Assumption was universally held in the early Church, as it continues to be held in the Catholic and Orthodox churches today. And the core truth of this doctrine is this: after Mary died, her whole person, body and soul, was assumed, or taken up, into heaven.

Now she lives there, resurrected and with her whole humanity intact. It was not fitting for the pure vessel, the Ark of the New Covenant, to suffer corruption in her body, and so God received her into heaven before her body could experience any decay. In fact, this is the meaning of the episode with the angry mob. When one of them touched the stretcher that held Mary's body, he was maimed and his hands fell off. This is supposed to remind the reader (or hearer) of the story of a man who tried to support the Ark of the Covenant, but when he touched it, he was struck dead.[593] The point is that Mary is the new ark, and specifically her body, which held Jesus in her womb.

In 1950, Pope Pius XII re-affirmed and defined what the Church had consistently believed throughout its history. He consulted a large number of bishops, and after determining that he was in fact speaking for the faith of the whole Church, he proclaimed the doctrine of the Assumption of Mary as a dogma of the Catholic Faith.[594] The Feast of the Assumption dates back to at least the fifth century, and since the sixth century has been celebrated on August 15th.

We can see how the Marian doctrines of the Immaculate Conception, Perpetual Virginity, and Assumption are all connected, and that they are all founded on Mary's relationship to her son. When we look at the early Church Fathers, we see that there was very little debate over these doctrines—the consensus of Tradition supports them, and there are no Scriptures or authoritative Church writings that deny them. In the end, everything the Church teaches about Mary is really all about Jesus. Everything we say about Mary says something important about Christ, especially emphasizing his divinity, and his uniqueness among humanity. And so to call her Mother of God is a witness to the union of humanity and divinity in the person of Jesus Christ—a union that took place in her womb, where the Word became flesh. Thus "Mariology" (what we believe about Mary) is really a branch of Christology (what we believe about Christ).[595] Mary is inseparable from Christ.[596] So we do not worship Mary, but what we believe about Mary leads us to a deeper and richer worship of her son.

What Is a "Patron Saint," and How Is Mary Our Patron?

We have already noted that Irenaeus, the second-century bishop of Lyons, wrote, "By yielding obedience, (Mary became) the cause of salvation, both to herself and the whole human race."[597] This idea that she is the "cause of salvation" might sound strange to some, as though Mary is being given too much credit. But it does not mean that she is our savior, it means that she is the instrument through whom God chose to accomplish our salvation. She is the "cause," in the sense that she is the means by which the Incarnation was accomplished.[598]

That passage demonstrates just how important the early Church Fathers understood Mary to be. It also shows that, for the Fathers, the Incarnation was the cosmic event that made our salvation possible. Christ's salvific work included his Passion, death, and Resurrection, to be sure—but the Church Fathers often wrote and preached as though the real instrument of our salvation was not so much the cross (the place of Jesus' death), but the womb of Mary (the place where the Word became flesh).

For this reason, we owe Mary our gratitude.[599] She has helped us in such a way that we could never express proper thanks. That's one way to think of the word "patron": someone who is in a position to help you, but it's not an equal relationship because you're not in a position to help them.[600] So you accept that person's help with gratitude, and all you can really offer in return is your thanks and your love. This is why many people, and not just Catholics, feel a sense of devotion toward Mary. She is the mother of our savior, but she is also the compassionate Mother of all Christians, a great patroness who continues to be a cause of our salvation through her intercession.[601] Mary's ministry of intercession began at the wedding in Cana, when she petitioned Jesus on behalf of someone else, prompting him to perform his first miracle.[602] Now, after her Assumption, she lives the resurrection life in the heavenly realm with Jesus—putting her in a unique position to be our intercessor, even above all the other saints.[603]

This is why Mary is considered the Queen of the Saints, or even the Queen of Heaven. In fact, sometimes her Assumption is associated with the concept of a regal coronation. As the "queen mother," so to speak, she is our advocate, speaking on our behalf with her son, and then speaking to the Church the same message she spoke to the wedding stewards: "Do whatever he tells you" (John 2:5).[604]

A very early liturgical prayer, from the mid-third century, describes Mary's role as patron and intercessor quite beautifully.

We fly to thy protection,
O Holy Mother of God;
despise not our petitions
in our necessities,
but deliver us always
from all dangers,
O glorious and blessed Virgin.

Mary is not the only saint the Church recognizes as a patron. Any of the saints, and in fact any Christian who has passed on to heaven, can be our intercessor with God. There is no harm even in asking for prayers from favorite relatives (or ones who were especially devoted to God) who have passed on—even if the Church has not designated them as "saints for sure." We can ask them to pray for us, and we can ask them to pray with us. There are many saints whom tradition has associated with various things one might pray for. Usually, saints are associated with something related to the suffering they endured in life. For example, St. Monica is known as the patron saint of mothers who pray for their wayward husbands and sons, because she prayed (successfully) for the conversions of her husband and her famous son, Augustine. The martyrs of the early Church especially became known as patrons of their occupations: for example Sts. Cosmas and Damian were surgeons, so today they are considered patron saints of doctors and pharmacists.

The point is that no matter who you are, or what you're dealing with, there is someone from the history of the Church—one of your ancestors in the Faith—who knows what you're going through. And this person can be your patron, that is, your special intercessor and advocate with God.

If the idea that saints are our patrons in heaven can be off-putting to Protestants, the prayer that expresses Mary's unique patronage for all Christians, the *Hail Mary*, is often especially so. They think it's unbiblical, and that the rosary—a devotional practice that includes numerous Hail Marys—is an example of the "vain repetition" they think Jesus explicitly condemned.

In truth, the Hail Mary is a very biblical prayer. It goes like this:

Hail Mary, Full of grace, the Lord is with you
Blessed are you among women,
and blessed is the fruit of your womb, Jesus
Holy Mary, Mother of God
Pray for us sinners,
now and at the hour of our death. Amen.

The first line is a direct quotation of the angel's greeting at the Annunciation, in the Gospel of Luke, with the addition of Mary's name.[605] The second line is a direct quotation of Elizabeth's greeting, when Mary came to visit her, with the addition of Jesus' name.[606] The third line addresses Mary with the early Christian title *Mother of God*, acknowledging her role in the Incarnation that makes our salvation possible. And the fourth line is the part where we ask for her intercession. It's a very simple, beautiful prayer.

The rosary is a way of praying that includes the Our Father, one of the historic creeds of the Church, and the Hail Mary. It includes meditations on the central mysteries in the life of Jesus. Many people find that it helps them with their personal devotion to God, by giving them a set and organized way to pray. However, it does include several repetitions of the prayers. Does this repetition contradict the command of Scripture?

In Matthew's Gospel, Jesus is recorded as saying, "In praying, do not babble like the pagans, who think that they will be heard because of their many words. Do not be like them. Your Father knows what you need before you ask him" (Matt. 6:7–8). Some translations of this verse include phrases like, "meaningless repetition."However, this is a mistranslation of the Greek text of the Gospel, which says nothing about repetition.[607] What Jesus is criticizing here are "empty words" (that is, insincerity and praying for show), and "many words" (focusing on eloquence over meaning). Clearly Jesus was warning his followers against getting caught up in trying to impress God (or others) with their eloquence of their pleading.

This becomes even clearer when one reads the passage in context, including the preceding verse, where Jesus begins with, "When you pray, do not be like the hypocrites, who love to stand and pray in the synagogues and on the street corners *so that others may see them*" (Matt. 6:5).[608] So did Jesus really mean that we should not repeat prayers? He couldn't have, since immediately after this passage, he went on to teach his disciples the Our Father, also called the Lord's Prayer. Clearly he expected his disciples to repeat this prayer.

Repeating pre-written prayers is as old as the Psalms, and it was a common practice in the early Church. To pray someone else's prayer is to connect to the history of God's relationship with people, and to connect with the Church universal who share the same prayers. When we pray the historic prayers of Scripture and of the Church, we are praying with the communion of saints, in the unity of the Holy Spirit. And when we recite the historic creeds of the Church, we are proclaiming the one faith that the apostle Paul wrote was manifest in our common baptism.[609]

SAINTS' BODIES AND HALLOWED GROUND

The early Church's practice of venerating relics also illustrates the value Christians have always placed on the patronage of the saints. The Latin word *relicta* means "remnants" or "things left behind." The early Christians reasoned that since a saint was in the presence of God, and since a saint's spirit was still mystically connected to his body (which would someday be raised and reunited with the spirit), then to be near a saint's physical remains was to be near that saint, and consequently, to be nearer to God. In other words, the presence of a saint's remains turned a place into a holy site. The tombs of the martyrs quickly became shrines and places of pilgrimage, as people visited the graves of their ancestors in the Faith in much the same way that the Romans had always visited the graves of their loved ones.

As we saw in the chapter on the Eucharist, the Roman tradition of the *refrigerium* continued and became the feasts of the saints. These feasts were originally held at the martyrs' tombs, sometimes even in the catacombs. When the Eucharist was celebrated in the family tombs within the catacombs, the top of a sarcophagus would serve as the altar table. Later, when basilica churches were built over the catacombs, they were built so that the altar would be directly over a tomb of an important or popular martyr. (The book of Revelation says that the martyrs are "underneath the altar.")[610] Sometimes the tomb was even raised to be closer to the surface (but still directly over its original resting place), and in a few cases, the church itself was built halfway underground so that the altar would be right over the tomb. When churches were built within the city walls, the remains of the martyrs could be brought to the church, and placed within or just below the altar, so that the Eucharist would still be celebrated in close proximity to the relics of a saint.

This connection between the Eucharist and relics tells us a lot about the way the early Christians understood life and death. The presence of a saint's remains made the saint mystically present, and the place of worship became holy ground. And the Eucharist itself, being a miracle of incarnation—a miracle of life—reminds us of the double-edged sword that is our own mortality.

Now, the Church recognizes different kinds of relics. Primary (or first-class) relics, are the actual physical remains (body parts) of a saint. Secondary (or second-class) relics include clothing or other personal effects left behind—things that touched a saint's body while the saint was alive. A third-class relic is something that touched a first- or second-class relic. These reflect

the ancient tradition of the faithful touching something of their
own to a relic while on pilgrimage, in order to have something
holy to take back home with them. For example, if one went on
pilgrimage to the tomb of a martyr, one might touch a handkerchief to the tomb, and then treasure that handkerchief as a
spiritual souvenir.

The earliest mention of relics in existing Christian literature
comes from the second century *Martyrdom of Polycarp*.[611] This
is one of a genre of documents known as the *martyr acts*, and
these documents were often read during the celebrations at the
martyrs' tombs. In this account, after the bishop Polycarp of
Smyrna was executed and his body was burned. The author of
the document tells us, "Later on we took up his bones, which
are more valuable than precious stones and finer than refined
gold, and deposited them in a suitable place. There, when we
gather together as we are able, with joy and gladness, the Lord
will permit us to celebrate the birthday of his martyrdom."[612]

In the earliest Christian history book, we learn of a story of a
miracle in Jerusalem. In the year 211, the lamp oil ran out during the Easter vigil. St. Narcissus, who was at that time bishop
of Jerusalem, prayed that God would change water into oil to
keep the lamps going. Although this simple story seems to be a
combination of the miracles of Hanukkah and Cana, what is significant about it is that we are told that the people saved a little of
the oil, and kept it as proof that a miracle had occurred.[613] This
demonstrates how the faith-lives of the early Christians included
elements of the physical world that could be connections to, or
reminders of, holy people and events—and how the presence of
these elements could render a place holy.

When the Emperor Constantine granted freedom of religion
in the early fourth century, one of the first things his mother
did was to go on a pilgrimage to the Holy Land. Once there,
she asked around and found many of the holy sites where Jesus
walked, and where important events in his life and ministry
took place. She is also said to have found the tomb in which
he was laid (and raised), and there she found the wood of his

cross.[614] This was immediately venerated as a relic known as
the "True Cross," and eventually the wood was broken up into
small pieces so that it could be appreciated by Christians all over
the world.[615]

But what does it mean to "venerate" a relic? Is that the same
thing as worshipping, and if so, wouldn't that be a form of idolatry? This brings us to the larger question of icons.

Are Icons "Graven Images"?

Typically, when we talk about icons, we think of the stylized
paintings so common in Byzantine Christianity,[616] but icons can
also include mosaics, statues, sculptures, and stained glass windows. Even the cross itself is an icon.[617] An icon is a symbol or
image, and in the Christian context, it implies an artistic depiction of something holy—usually a holy person—that is meant
to remind believers of some aspect of the Faith, and encourage
them to be devoted to God in Christ and to emulate the lives
of the saints. But icons are much more than simply a reminder:
they are windows into the spiritual realm. In fact, it could be
said that relics are a kind of icon, though they are a special kind,
since they are not artistic creations but rather physical remains.
But the way relics are treated is not unlike the way (other) icons
can be an aid to one's devotional life.

Some people call icons "the poor man's Bible," and to a certain extent this is true. Icons could include vignettes that were
suggestive of biblical stories, reminding the faithful of what they
heard in the liturgy. Especially when most people were illiterate,
or could not afford their own copies of Christian texts, the icons
could help teach them what the Church believes. But this still
raises the question: are icons prohibited by the commandment
against making "graven images"?[618]

The truth is that the commandment does not prohibit images,
per se, but rather *idols*. What's the difference between an image
(or icon) and an idol? In part, the difference is how they're treated,
and we'll get to that in a moment, but for now it is important to

note that in the Old Testament, God shows approval of icons. Just five chapters after he receives the commandments, Moses is told to make two golden statues of cherubs for the top of the Ark of the Covenant.[619] Later, Moses is instructed to make an image of a serpent that, when looked at, would heal snake bites.[620] (When the early Church Fathers read this passage, they saw the serpent mounted on a pole as a foreshadowing of the cross of Christ—both having healing power.)[621] Both the cherubs and the serpent are kinds of icons, but not idols.

It is true that there was some concern in the early Church about icons and the danger of idolatry. The Synod of Elvira, in about the year 305, declared that churches should not have "pictures" in them.[622] However, this was a local synod, and did not express the opinion of the majority of early Church Fathers. Also, there may have been a fear that during a time of persecution, paintings on the walls of a church building might give away that it was a house of worship. In any case, the fact that the synod mentions icons means that they were a part of early Christian art and devotion. The Council of Trullo, in the year 692, forbade the depiction of Christ as a lamb (a staple of ancient church mosaics), on the grounds that people might take the image too literally and fall into some form of lamb worship, thus obscuring Jesus' true humanity.[623] Others felt that images of Jesus might emphasize his humanity too much, to the detriment of his divinity.

In the eighth century, an Eastern emperor issued an edict forbidding the creation or use of icons. This may have had something to do with the Eastern empire's contact with Islam, which strictly forbade sacred images, but there were also political motivations. The emperor wanted to control the Eastern monks, who were fighting for autonomy from the government, and the monasteries, which were receiving a lot of money from religious pilgrimages, yet without paying taxes. The emperor ordered an image of Christ to be destroyed, and the people rioted.

The pope protested the imperial edict, and it became an empire-wide controversy, with the iconoclasts (those against the use of icons) mainly in the East. Southern Italy, which had a high concentration of Greek immigrants, even had some violence and rioting. The Christian faithful were put in the position of having to choose between their emperor and their pope. Eventually, at the Second Council of Nicaea (the seventh ecumenical council), in 787, the bishops clarified what is appropriate with regard to icons. The council concluded that it is acceptable to *venerate* icons, but not to *worship* them. Although this was not the last word on the subject, and the controversy would erupt again in the ninth century before it was settled, this was the final determination.

So what's the difference between veneration and worship? To venerate is to treat with reverence, which can be appropriate for icons, saints, and holy places. However, worship (service and submission) is for God alone. To venerate an icon is to use it as a means for worshipping God; the icon is never the end in itself. Worship, on the other hand, is directed toward God, who alone is to be treated as an end in himself. So icons (and relics) are not the object of worship—they are windows into the spiritual realm. In fact, they encourage Christians to follow the example of the saints, which is always to direct our attention to Christ. If they ever become the object of worship, as the bronze serpent did for the Israelites (whereupon God commanded that it be destroyed),[624] they have ceased to be icons and become idols.

The concept of veneration of saints and icons is the same kind of reverence that God demands in the commandment to honor one's father and mother.[625] When we venerate the saints or their images in icons and statues, we are honoring our ancestors in the Faith. Just to be on the safe side, Eastern Christianity developed a tradition of limiting icons to two-dimensional images, and using a strictly defined style to prevent them from becoming too realistic. In addition, certain standard conventions of iconography are meant to teach important lessons. For example, icons of Jesus always have his hair parted in the middle, the two sides of his hair representing his two natures: human and divine. Also, Mary is never depicted alone. She is always with Jesus, and usually pointing toward him, to direct the viewer's devotion to him.

Christians use icons as part of the devotional life, looking
through them to the spiritual reality that they represent. However, icons are not one-way devotional aids. They are a window
into the spiritual realm, but they can also be a means of communicating grace to the one who contemplates them. We can *give*
through them, as we express our devotion to God, and we can
receive through them, as God blesses us with his grace. Because of
the Incarnation (itself an "icon" in which Jesus is the image of the
Father), we know that the physical can mediate God's grace. And
when we create artistic representations of Christ and the saints,
we are imitating our Creator by being creators ourselves—and
these created things can bring us into closer communion with our
Creator. So whether one venerates relics at a holy shrine, or uses
icons or statues as devotional aids; whether one learns Bible stories
from stained glass windows, or from a painting of Noah's Ark on
a church nursery wall; whether one enjoys a painting of Jesus or
sets up a nativity scene at Christmas time; or even whether one
wears a t-shirt with a Christian slogan or puts a fish on the bum-
per of a car; we all have icons as part of the practice of our faith.

$\sim$

We have explored the role of the saints, including Mary, as well
as relics and icons, in the historic Church. We have seen that
none of these are meant to obscure our relationship with God
in Christ. In fact, they enhance that relationship, by providing
windows into the heavenly realm. The reverence, or veneration, of these windows into the spiritual is an ancient part of
the Christian faith. The reality of sacred space and the belief in
the proximity of the saints—both to God through their death
in Christ, and to humanity through their remains—was an affirmation of the Christian doctrine of resurrection. In other
words, the Church rejected the philosophers' view of an afterlife
as a disembodied spirit, in favor of a doctrine of resurrection that
acknowledged physical creation as good and as something that
will be redeemed.

Protestants tend to see the afterlife as intimate fellowship
with God, but wholly removed from the world of the living.

Catholics, on the other hand, see the fellowship of the saints extending across the boundary line between life and afterlife. When we pray to the saints, we are really praying *with* the saints—taking part in a network of intercessory relationships that unites the Body of Christ.

There are inscriptions in the catacombs—graffiti, actually—that date back at least to the third century, or probably earlier. Near the tombs of the martyrs, early Christians scrawled their prayers to the saints. These are prayers asking for intercession, and are often as simple as, "Peter and Paul, pray for me." These early witnesses— graffiti, martyr documents, the earliest histories of the Church—all show that the belief in the intercession of the saints and the reverence of their relics is as old as Christianity itself. Therefore, if you wanted to find the most ancient expression of Christianity, or somehow get back to an "original" version of the Faith, it would have to include prayer to the saints, pilgrimages to holy sites, the veneration of saints and icons, and even the Marian doctrines. Having these made the early Church (and makes the Catholic Church today) rich and robust, and those who would desire to strip away these ancient expressions of the Faith must ask themselves if by doing so they are really diminishing it.

Featured Father

Augustine of Hippo: Sinner and Saint

Augustine is perhaps one of the most famous saints, even outside of the Catholic Church. His fame is well deserved because he is known as the first person in history to write an honest autobiography, in which he even tells the reader all the things he's embarrassed about. The book is his *Confessions*, and it became a best seller even while Augustine was still alive.

Born in the year 354, in North Africa, Augustine avoided the Church for a long time, until he became a professor of rhetoric in Milan and there encountered the bishop Ambrose. His mother's prayers were answered when Augustine was finally baptized in 386, just a few years after Christianity was made the official religion of the empire. Incidentally, Augustine's mother is now known to the Church as St. Monica, and she is the patron saint of mothers who pray for their wayward sons.

After his conversion to the Faith, Augustine returned to North Africa with his entourage, and formed a monastic community. He was eventually ordained a priest, and then chosen to be the bishop of the town of Hippo. There he preached, wrote theological documents, and lived the life of a monk. His community became the foundation of what is now known as Augustinian monasticism—in fact Martin Luther was an Augustinian friar.

Reading the *Confessions*, we learn about Augustine's disappointments—specifically his disappointment with his own ability to exercise self-control. This led him to a skepticism about human free will, and a strong doctrine of original sin. He was also a staunch supporter of the Council of Nicaea and its conclusions. In fact, Augustine wrote so much that it would be nearly impossible to study it all. He wrote important documents on theology that explain and clarify the doctrine of the Trinity, and he also wrote important documents on the interpretation of Scripture.

Although the Church ultimately did not accept all of Augustine's teachings, he was extremely influential for Western Christianity. In fact, he helped the West clarify its own understanding of the Church. In his confrontations with a schismatic group known as the Donatists, he rejected their view of the Church (that people who had stumbled in their faith should be excommunicated), and instead he advocated a view of the Church that said all people must be welcome. He argued that the Church is like a hospital for sinners, the clergy are like its doctors, and the sacraments are its medicine.

In the year 429, barbarian Vandals laid siege to the city of Hippo, and the isolated citizens ran out of clean water. Malaria broke out, and in 430, Augustine was taken ill, and died.

6

The Papacy

For those denominations that do not have bishops, it can be hard to understand how the hierarchy serves the unity of the Church, and how one bishop who is at the top of the hierarchy can be the point person for, and symbol of, that unity. But even those congregational and non-denominational congregations and "megachurches" that might criticize the Catholic Church for having a pope must necessarily have their own highest authority when it comes to matters of doctrine and the interpretation of Scripture. In other words, they all have their own "pope" (usually their founding pastor) who speaks for the whole group and settles disputes. If they didn't have this, they would soon split over differences of opinion. Many of them do anyway. The pope speaks for the Church that is headquartered at Rome, but with the authority of 2,000 years of Tradition behind him. The pope, and the city of Rome, stand for both orthodoxy and unity.

We have already explored the origins of the office of bishop. We saw that, since the late first century, bishops have always been the overseers of the Church's teaching (doctrine), sacraments (discipline), and the distribution of resources to the needy. We also saw that the bishops were—and remain—the guarantors of the unity of the Church, and the power they hold is exercised for the sake of that unity. In another chapter we explored the concept of apostolic succession. When we put it all together, and when we understand the relationship between apostolic succession and the bishops, two things become clear.

First of all, Christianity (like Judaism) is a religion founded on revelation. In other words, we do not believe one can find enlightenment simply by looking within oneself—we need God to reveal himself and his truth to us. We also do not believe that human beings are capable of saving themselves from their own sinfulness. This means we cannot be reconciled to God without his divine grace. So we need revelation and grace to be reconciled to God and receive salvation. And these are not things we can discover or create for ourselves—they must come to us from somewhere. They come first from God, but most of us receive them from those to whom they had already been given. This means that there is a necessary relationship of teacher and student between those who have already received and those who are receiving. This relationship is the basis for the hierarchy of the Church.[626]

Second, when Jesus Christ knew his earthly ministry was coming to an end, he entrusted the movement he founded, which he called his *church*, to the apostles he had chosen. He gave them his authority to continue his mission.[627] They, in turn, chose their own disciples, and granted this same authority to them—and it was these disciples who were first called bishops.[628] As the apostles' successors, bishops hold an office instituted by Christ for the sake of the continuation of his ministry—and he must have intended for the apostolic office to continue, since that is the only way the *Church* would continue.[629]

Therefore, just as we say that the bishops are the successors of the apostles, it can also be said that the apostles were the first bishops, since they fulfilled the role of overseers, with authority granted to them by Christ to teach the message they heard from him, to preside over the sacraments he instituted, and to lead the Church in caring for the poor, as he did. All of this they passed on to their disciples, who passed it on to their disciples, and this is how we receive the Faith. We receive the teachings that originated in divine revelation, and we receive grace through the sacraments, all presided over by the bishops, who today hold an office that is modeled after the apostles and receives its authority from them.[630]

Therefore, the hierarchy of the Church is patterned after the teacher-student relationship. It is more than simply a system for ranking people of more or less power, it is a network of relationships of discipleship. Teachers naturally have more authority than their students, and those who have been in the Faith and are more spiritually matured have more authority than those who are newer to the Faith. Furthermore, disputes are naturally settled by someone who is of a higher authority than those who are in disagreement, which means that there must be someone at the top of the hierarchy, someone who takes responsibility for the whole Church and who can arbitrate questions at the highest levels of authority. Both Scripture and Tradition acknowledge that the apostle Peter was the Church's first highest authority after Christ himself, effectively making him the first pope.

Was Peter the First Pope?

It's clear from the New Testament that Peter was the leader of the apostles.[631] In the lists of apostles, Peter is always named first.[632] He is also the first of Jesus' "inner circle" of three apostles (along with John and James). When John arrived at the empty tomb first, he deferred to Peter and allowed him to enter before himself.[633] When Peter correctly answered Jesus' question, "Who do you say that I am?" Jesus gave him the name Peter, which means "Rock," and he told Peter that upon this rock he would build his Church.[634] Later, Jesus charged Peter with strengthening the other apostles, and caring for the sheep of his flock.[635] Thus Peter is the first shepherd, or pastor, of the Church after Jesus himself.[636]

Furthermore, Jesus gave to Peter the "keys to the kingdom of heaven," and the authority to "bind" and "loose."[637] As the holder of the keys, Peter is the steward of the household of God.[638] This means that Jesus gave to Peter (and through him, to all the apostles) the authority to retain (bind) or forgive (loose, that is, release) sins in his name.[639] The authority that the bishops and priests now have to grant absolution and reconciliation comes from this authority that Jesus gave to Peter. Finally, we can see in the book of Acts that Peter spoke for the apostles by preaching the first Christian sermon, and speaking at the first Christian council in Jerusalem.[640] Therefore, no one can doubt that Jesus made Peter the leader of the apostles.

But was Peter the first bishop of Rome? As we noted in our discussion of apostolic succession, those cities where the local congregation was founded by an apostle could claim that the succession of bishops went back to that particular apostle. This assumes that after the apostles went their separate ways to spread the gospel throughout the world, each of them brought the Church to a different major city or part of the world. But we also know that there were "travelers from Rome" among the first converts after Pentecost.[641]

According to tradition, Peter arrived in Rome for the first time in the forties of the first century, or about ten years after that Pentecost when he had preached to a crowd that included Romans. This means that by the time he arrived in Rome, there were probably already Christians there, but without an apostolic leader. No doubt some of these Christians were converted by his preaching in Jerusalem a decade earlier. So as soon as he arrived, he would have been the highest Christian authority in the city. We also know that Peter left Rome at some point, because he was back in Jerusalem for the apostolic council in about the year 50, and Paul's letter to the Romans, written in A.D. 57 (before Paul had ever been to Rome), does not mention Peter. But by the time Peter wrote his first letter in the New Testament, he was back in Rome.[642] In the early sixties, both Peter and Paul were in Rome, where they were eventually martyred, sometime in the mid-sixties.

So although we cannot claim with certainty that Peter founded the church in Rome, we can say with confidence that he was its first apostolic authority: its first bishop. The early Fathers are unanimous in their assumption that Peter was in Rome, and that the apostolic succession of the church there goes back to Peter. They also all agree that Peter (along with Paul) was martyred in Rome, and that the location of his tomb was a well-known pilgrimage site. To this day, Peter's tomb is directly under the altar of St. Peter's Basilica in the Vatican— that is, the headquarters of the Church marks the holy ground where Peter is buried.

How Did the Bishop of Rome Get to Be the Pope?

So if we can call Peter the first bishop of Rome, then we can also call Peter the first pope, because the pope is always the bishop of Rome. But that raises the question: how did the bishop of Rome become the head of the Church? Why Rome, and not the bishop of some other city, like Jerusalem, for example? Or why, for that matter, does there have to be one bishop, a "pope," with more authority than the others? To answer these questions we have to go back to the early Church.

Since the bishops are the successors of the apostles, and since the first bishop of Rome, Peter, was the leader of the apostles, the successors of Peter are the leaders of all the other bishops.[643] Therefore, the Church Fathers believed that just as no priest has authority to teach or preside without it being granted by the local bishop, no bishop has any authority, or in fact could even be considered in communion with the Church of the apostles, if he is not in connection with the bishop of Rome.[644] In other words, just as the office of bishop in general is the guarantor of the unity of the Church in his local area, so the office of the papacy is the guarantor of unity on a global scale. The consensus of the first bishops, combined with actual experience over time, determined that there must be one person at the top of the hierarchy, otherwise unity would be threatened.

In the time of the early Church, the bishops of other cities were not always happy about submitting to the authority of the bishop of Rome—but they did admit that they should agree with him on doctrinal matters. When it came to theology and the interpretation of Scripture, the early consensus of the Church was that everyone must agree with what was being taught at Rome.[645]

Even on matters not directly related to doctrine, Rome emerged as the primary city. The early ecumenical councils of the Church designated seven *metropolitan* cities—rather like saying seven archbishoprics. In the east, they were Jerusalem, Caesarea, Antioch, Alexandria, and Constantinople; in the west, Rome and Carthage. The five eastern cities tended to jockey for position, whereas in the west Rome was by far the most important city. At the Council of Constantinople, in the year 381, it was clarified that Rome was the first city of the Church, with Constantinople (the new capital of the empire) in second place. Thus Rome emerged as the metropolitan of metropolitans, and the bishop of Rome as the archbishop of archbishops. In addition, Rome solidified its position by always being on the orthodox side of any theological debate, with no major heresies to embarrass it.[646]

And finally, the office of the bishop of Rome could boast some of the most important Church Fathers, as well as other strong personalities not matched anywhere else, who could enforce both the doctrine and the discipline of the Church, and who could act as negotiators and judges in disputes between other bishops. Let us look at some of the most important popes in the first millennium of the Church and the impact they had on the development of the papacy. The dates in parentheses are the years that they were the bishop of Rome.

Clement I (88–97)

We have already met Clement of Rome, but it bears reiterating that he wrote his letter to the Corinthians (*I Clement*) on the basis of authority derived from Peter. Some say that he was an actual disciple of Peter, and may have been ordained by Peter.[647] But even if that's not true (or especially if it's not true), his letter to the Corinthian Christians demonstrates the ability of the bishop of Rome—already by the end of the first century—to mediate a dispute in the church of another city. In this case, that city was all the way in Greece, and it was even one of Paul's churches!

Stephen I (254–257)

In the midst of a prolonged persecution of the Church by Roman authorities, a dispute emerged over whether a person who had been baptized by someone who denied the Faith to save

his life needed to be baptized again.[648] Cyprian, the bishop of
Carthage, at first advocated rebaptism of anyone whose baptism
was questioned. But Stephen confronted him, and defended the
earlier tradition of not rebaptizing. Stephen argued that rebaptism was in fact an offense against God because it is really God
who baptizes, and to rebaptize is to negate the work of God
in the original baptism. Stephen then took it upon himself to
reinstate clergy who were removed from their offices by Cyprian. This was an extremely important moment in the history of
the Church, since Stephen was able to exercise his authority as
bishop of Rome to confront the bishop of another metropolitan city who was advocating a practice inconsistent with the
Church's teaching and tradition.

The theological point at stake was also crucial. The Church
believes that God is active in every baptism, and to say that a
baptism is invalid simply because of sin in the life of the presider
amounts to saying that God was not faithful in that baptism.
Furthermore, if the Church were to accept Cyprian's point of
view, then one could never know if *any* sacraments were valid,
since one could never know the state of the minister's soul. If
grave sin in the life of a priest or bishop later came to light, it
would call into question the validity of every sacrament over
which that person had ever presided.

Miltiades (311–314)

Miltiades was the bishop of Rome when Constantine liberated
Rome from the tyrant Maxentius in the year 312, and he was
probably in Constantine's entourage when the new emperor
marched into the city in triumph. He was also the bishop of
Rome the following year when Constantine issued the Edict of
Milan, granting freedom of worship to all religions. Constantine gave Miltiades the Lateran palace, which would be rebuilt
into the cathedral of Rome, St. John Lateran, and the first papal
apartments. The emperor also decreed that all Church property
confiscated or destroyed in the persecutions must be returned

to the Church or paid for. Constantine granted to all Christian bishops the power of civil judges, so that they could decide disputes between Christians, allowing Christians to go to their bishop to decide a case rather than a secular judge. Miltiades advised Constantine with regard to the Donatists, a schismatic group that held a view of the sacraments similar to Cyprian's in the controversy over baptism. Once again, the Roman understanding of the sacraments held sway, mostly because that view of the sacraments was more consistent with prior Tradition and Church teaching, but also because of the authority of the bishop of Rome.

Sylvester I (314–335)

There are several legends about Sylvester of Rome, including that he baptized Emperor Constantine, and that Constantine granted to him huge tracts of land in Italy (the so-called *Donation of Constantine*). However, none of these legends are true. What is true, however, is that Sylvester was the bishop of Rome when the emperor paid for the building of the first basilica churches in Rome, including St. John Lateran as well as the Church of the Holy Cross in Jerusalem and the original St. Peter's. No doubt Sylvester supervised the building of these first basilicas as well as shrines constructed over the tombs of the martyrs, which later became the sites of important churches as well.

Sylvester was the bishop of Rome at the time of the first ecumenical council, the Council of Nicaea in 325, though he himself did not attend. However, he was represented at the council by delegates, and the council decreed that all churches should follow the lead of Rome when calculating the date for Easter. Even though this was not followed or enforced in the east, the council made the point that Rome was the center of the Church's unity on matters such as the dates of holy celebrations.[649]

What is equally significant is that Sylvester was the bishop of Rome when Constantine moved the capital of the empire out of Rome and took it to the East, to a city of his own creation,

Constantinople. With the emperor out of Rome, this left Sylvester and his successors as the most powerful men in the city, in effect giving the impression that the emperor had left Rome in the hands of the Christian bishop there. As time went on, it would be the bishop of Rome, and not the Roman government, who would lead the people of Rome during times of plague and famine, who would take charge of feeding the hungry, and who would even protect the city from invading barbarians. All that the Roman government could no longer do, as the West became increasingly isolated from the East (where the emperor now lived), the bishops of Rome would do.

Julius I (337–352)

After the Council of Nicaea, leaders of the heretical Arian factions continued to try to gain power in the East. Bishops Athanasius of Alexandria and Marcellus of Ancyra were forcibly removed and sent into exile. They both appealed to Pope Julius, who held a council in Rome to examine the matter. There it was determined that both of these bishops should be reinstated. Julius declared them reinstated, on the authority of the apostle Peter. This led to a regional council, the Council of Sardica, in the year 343, to which Julius sent delegates. Not only did the Council of Sardica affirm the earlier decision of the Roman council to reinstate Athanasius and Marcellus, but it also decreed that any deposed bishops may appeal to the bishop of Rome, affirming that the bishop of Rome is the "last court of appeals" in any conflict between bishops.

Damasus (366–384)

Pope Damasus was a fierce supporter of the Council of Nicaea and Nicene orthodoxy. His was a turbulent time, filled with controversy. But Emperor Gratian supported him in his efforts to remove a pagan altar from the senate house, and the emperor eventually acknowledged that he effectively ruled Rome.[650] In the year

380, Emperor Theodosius issued the Edict of Thessalonica, which made Christianity the official religion of the Roman Empire, and confirmed that the orthodox faith was the Catholic faith—that which "Peter delivered to the Romans." This edict re-affirmed Rome as the primary church in terms of theology—the one with which all other churches must agree in order to be correct.

Celestine I (422–432)

Like Julius before him, Celestine acted as arbiter in Eastern disputes over doctrine, most notably in the controversy between Cyril of Alexandria and Nestorius of Constantinople. Nestorius had questioned the tradition of calling Mary the Mother of God (in Greek: *Theotokos*), on the basis of his view that the two natures of Jesus Christ should be kept separate, and that only the human nature (not the divine) was held within the womb of Mary. Celestine supported Cyril in his investigation, and subsequent condemnation, of Nestorius, who was declared a heretic at the ecumenical Council of Ephesus in 431. Celestine did not attend that council himself, but Cyril acted on the authority of Celestine, and so Nestorius was confronted and Mary's title of Mother of God was confirmed as orthodox practice. The title Mother of God says as much about Jesus Christ as it does about Mary, since it affirms the union of the two natures (human and divine) in the person of Christ, and that union is what makes humanity's reconciliation with God possible. This was an extremely important affirmation for orthodox Christology, and it set the stage for the next ecumenical council at Chalcedon in 451.

Leo I (the Great, 440–461)

During the time of Celestine, the bishop of Alexandria was defending orthodox Christology against the bishop of Constantinople. But during the time of Leo, that situation was reversed, and the bishop of Constantinople (Flavian) was defending orthodoxy against the bishop of Alexandria, one Dioscorus. Leo supported

Flavian, and wrote a letter clarifying the Church's teaching on the two natures of Christ. This letter, known as Leo's *Tome*, was read and accepted as definitive at the fourth ecumenical Council of Chalcedon in the year 451. Leo claimed the authority of Peter himself, an authority that gave him the right to speak for the whole Church, even to other metropolitans, and to settle disputes between them. Thus, the bishop of Rome had the authority to settle controversies in the East, without even being there.

Leo also protected Rome from Attila the Hun, who threatened to attack the city, in about the same year as the Council of Chalcedon. Leo was able to persuade Attila to leave Rome alone, thus doing what the Roman government could not do. Still, it should be noted that up until the time of Leo any bishop, and certainly any metropolitan, could be called *papa*, or pope. Leo may have been the first bishop of Rome to truly be called *"the* pope."

Gregory I (the Great, 590–604)

By the end of the sixth century, the barbarians were a constant threat in Italy. Many of them had actually been trained by the Roman legions, and had served as auxiliaries to the legions, meant to guard the borders of the empire. With the withdrawal of the legions, some of these nomadic tribes from northern and eastern Europe began moving south and west, sacking cities and pillaging as they went along their way.

Gregory the Great had been the urban prefect of Rome, something like the chief of police, when he made the commitment to leave his secular job to become a monk. He was eventually ordained a deacon, then became the assistant to the bishop, and then was elected to succeed him as pope. In 595, Gregory negotiated with the Lombards, a barbarian tribe that had recently entered Italy, and convinced them to stay out of Rome. He eventually converted them to Christianity, and baptized the son of the chieftain.

During a time of plague, Gregory rallied the faithful of Rome to pray for an end to the sickness. He organized a procession through the streets of Rome, and was granted a vision of the angel of death putting away the sword of judgment. Today, this vision is commemorated with a statue of the angel sheathing his sword on the top of the Castel Sant'Angelo in Rome. Gregory also created deacon stations in Rome for the distribution of food to the poor, so that, once again, what the government could no longer do, the bishop of Rome did for the people.

Gregory enforced the claim of Roman authority, and when the patriarch of Constantinople took for himself the title of "ecumenical (worldwide) bishop," Gregory reprimanded him, and counseled humility. It is the bishop of Rome, Gregory said, who is responsible for governing the whole universal Church, and on that basis, Gregory wrote many letters to bishops all over the world, solidifying his authority over them. He also consolidated the Western monasteries under his control, and used them as headquarters and hubs to send out missionaries all over Europe. Because of his efforts, the last holdouts of paganism in northern Europe would eventually be converted to the Faith.

Zacharias (741–752)

In spite of the conversion of the leaders of the Lombards, they continued to be a problem for the Italians. Pope Zacharias (also known as Zachary) called upon the king of the Franks, Childeric III, but he refused to help. So the pope made a deal with the "Mayor of the Palace" of the Frankish court. This was Pepin the Short, son of Charles Martel, who functioned as a kind of viceroy. On Zacharias's authority, Childeric was deposed and Pepin was crowned in his place, beginning a new dynasty of Frankish royalty.

This is significant because it was clear to everyone that Pepin owed his crown to the pope. By deposing one king and crowning another, Zacharias had demonstrated that the bishop of Rome had the power to make or break a king, and even to create a new royal dynasty. King Pepin kept his promise to the pope and defeated the Lombards, and then he gave Zacharias the lands formerly held by them.[651] The bishop of Rome now controlled the land known as the "Papal States," which it would hold until the unification of Italy in 1870. Thus the papacy was elevated to the status of a kingdom, with lands to defend, but more importantly, it rose above secular kings on the social hierarchy. Now, not only bishops, but also kings, will appeal to the popes for arbitration of their disputes.

Leo III (795–816)

Pepin's son was Charles, known to the world as Charles the Great, or Charlemagne. He became king of the Franks in 768, and king of Italy in 774. On Christmas Day in the year 800, Charles went to Rome to worship in St. Peter's basilica, and when he knelt down before the altar, Pope Leo placed a crown on his head, crowning him emperor and effectively beginning what would come to be known as the Holy Roman Empire.

Although this action would alienate the Eastern emperors, it now became clear that the pope could create an emperor (not to mention an empire), meaning that he was even above emperors in the social hierarchy of the West. Of course, this was not the case in the East, and this would be one cause of the later schism and separation of East and West into two ecclesial bodies. The Eastern churches, always in the shadow of the emperor in Constantinople, would have to submit to secular authorities—the state ruled over the Church. But the West was the opposite—the Church ruled over the state. This elevated the authority of the bishop of Rome in the West, but it increased the resentment held toward the pope by the metropolitans of the East.

Charlemagne saw himself as both the protector of the Church and also its most prolific evangelist. He saw himself as the new Constantine, God's soldier, and to this day statues of Constantine and Charlemagne stand by the two entrances to the cathedral of Rome, St. John Lateran. Charlemagne gathered most of Europe together into one empire (in fact the word europa comes from this time), and then he set about bringing a kind of standardization to the Church in his empire. He wanted all of the churches to be on the same page, as it were, with regard to

liturgy, the creeds, and clergy education.⁶⁵² Charlemagne instituted what is often referred to as the Carolingian Renaissance,
and during the papacy of Leo III there was reform among the
clergy and the monasteries, there was an increase in literacy, and
classical writings were preserved and copied.

Even though Charlemagne's empire broke up in civil war after his death (paving the way for the modern national borders of
the countries of Europe), he did leave a legacy of securing the
pope's place at the top of the social hierarchy. And even when
later emperors would challenge the pope's authority, the reality
of that authority was proven by the struggle of challenging it.

The final split of mutual excommunication between the Eastern and Western halves of the Church came in the year 1054. All
of the popes after that time would not have been recognized as
authorities in the East. Nevertheless, the authority and influence
of the papacy continued to grow throughout the Middle Ages.⁶⁵³

The development of papal authority was the result of the convergence of two realities. One was the theological reality of the
priority of Peter and the line of his successors through apostolic
succession. It is a historical fact that the bishops of Rome were
never burdened with heresy, and faithfully transmitted the teaching of the apostles and the interpretations of Tradition down
through the generations. The other reality was that in actual
practice, the bishops of Rome became the arbiters of disputes
among the other bishops.⁶⁵⁴ Even a pagan emperor, in the year
272, understood that the Christians all the way in the city of
Antioch must be in communion with Rome to be authentically
part of the Church.⁶⁵⁵ Thus, to be Catholic is to be connected to
Rome, and to the bishop of Rome as the head of the Church.⁶⁵⁶

What Did the Church Fathers Say About the Pope?

Even before the bishop of Rome became the only bishop to
be called *papa*, the Church Fathers recognized that he was the
successor of Peter, and therefore was the leader of all the
successors of the apostles, the bishops. Of course, we wouldn't be

surprised if those Church Fathers who actually *were* the bishop of Rome spoke in favor of the pope's authority, since they would be reinforcing their own position. We have already seen what Clement of Rome and others contributed to papal authority. But the early bishops of other cities, even those reluctant to submit to the bishop of Rome on matters of ecclesial order, acknowledged that on matters of doctrine or the interpretation of Scripture, one could not be considered within the true Church without agreeing with the bishop of Rome. Let's take a look at a few of the things that bishops of other cities, and other Church Fathers, had to say about the authority of the pope.

Ignatius of Antioch (c. A.D. 110)

Ignatius was under arrest, and being transported to Rome for execution shortly after the turn of the second century, when he wrote the letters that are now available to us. In his letter to the Christians in Rome, written to prepare them to witness his martyrdom, he begins with a greeting to the church, "which also presides in the place of the district of the Romans."[657] At the very least, this salutation recognized Rome as a metropolitan see with jurisdiction over the other sees in its geographical area. But Ignatius goes on to say, "You have never envied anyone; you have taught others. And my wish is that those instructions that you issue when teaching disciples will remain in force."[658]

This is his acknowledgment that the church of Rome is the teacher of other churches, and the universal Church's authority over doctrine. Unlike in his other letters, Ignatius does not give advice or instructions to the Romans. He says, "I do not give you orders like Peter and Paul: they were apostles, I am a convict."[659] So even though Ignatius himself is the bishop of a metropolitan church, he defers to the church of Rome. Finally, he commends his own church of Antioch, and indeed the whole metropolitan area in Syria, to the love of the Roman church, which he says will be the bishop of Syria (along with Jesus Christ) after he is gone.[660]

Irenaeus of Lyons (c. A.D. 185)

Irenaeus had been in Rome for a council when his own bishop of Lyons was martyred, and he was elected the successor. But Irenaeus was no mere Roman yes-man. He was originally from the East, and his mentor was the famous bishop Polycarp of Smyrna. Polycarp had sent him to the West into Gaul (France) as a missionary to assist the previous bishop of Lyons. So Irenaeus lived in that time so early in the history of the Church when a Church Father could not be easily categorized as Eastern or Western. They were all well-traveled, and they all had read every Christian document ever written. And when Irenaeus wrote his extensive document of refutation against the various early Christian heresies, he described the correct teaching of the Church as

> that Tradition derived from the apostles, of the very great, the very ancient, and universally known Church founded and organized at Rome by the two most glorious apostles, Peter and Paul; as also the Faith preached to men, which comes down to our time by means of the successions of the bishops. For it is a matter of necessity that every Church should agree with this Church, on account of its pre-eminent authority, that is, the faithful everywhere, inasmuch as the apostolic Tradition has been preserved continuously by those who exist everywhere.[661]

Here Irenaeus clarifies the consensus of the Church with regard to the primacy of Rome. All churches must agree with the theology being taught at the church of Rome to be considered part of the universal Church.

Tertullian (c. 200–210)

Tertullian was not a bishop, and was probably not ordained at all. There is some evidence that he may have been a priest at one time, perhaps even in Rome, but by the time he wrote his theological documents he was back in his native North Africa. He had apparently had a falling out with the leadership in Rome, so he was not a supporter of the popes. Nevertheless, he still referred to the bishop of Rome as the "bishop of bishops."[672] He also said of the Roman church, "You have Rome, from which there comes even into our own hands the very authority [of the apostles themselves]. How happy is its church, on which apostles poured forth all their doctrine along with their blood, and where Peter endured a passion like his Lord's."[663] Tertullian's point is that the authority of the apostles resides in the church of Rome, and when heretics contradict orthodoxy theology, they are opposing Rome herself.

Cyprian of Carthage (c. 250)

Even though Cyprian battled with Stephen of Rome over the issue of baptism, he still acknowledged the authority of Rome, and he did eventually submit to it. On several occasions, he wrote that the unity of the universal Church depended on the primacy of the bishop of Rome as the Petrine origin of apostolic authority.[664]

Augustine of Hippo (c. 417)

In a sermon, Augustine commented on the controversy over the heretic Pelagius. Although Pelagius had at one time been cleared by a council in the East, eventually his true teachings came to light and he was confronted by councils in North Africa and Rome. To try to bring some closure to the matter, Augustine played the trump card: "Rome has spoken, the case is concluded."[665] In other words, the North African council(s) may have balanced out the earlier Eastern council, but the church of Rome had the final word on the subject. It was the authority of the Roman council that mattered.

The consensus of the Church Fathers, both from the East and the West, assumed and affirmed the primacy of Peter, the authority of Peter's successors, the bishops of Rome, and the necessity of the "chair of Peter" for the unity of the Church. In general, they were in agreement with the statement of Irenaeus when he said, "It is a matter of necessity that every Church should agree with this Church [Rome], on account of its pre-eminent authority."[666]

Having said that, it is important to note that it is the "chair of Peter" that carries the authority, and whoever occupies that chair—the bishop of Rome—only holds authority by virtue of the office. The popes are the popes precisely because they stand in the line of succession from Peter himself. It is not something in themselves, but the Tradition they have received, that gives them primacy. Therefore, when we speak of the pope's author-ity, we are speaking of the authority of the office. This is espe-cially the case when we say that the pope is infallible.

How Is the Pope Infallible?

In Luke 22, Jesus predicted that Peter would deny him, but he also prayed that after Peter turned back, his faith would not fail and he would strengthen the other disciples. And as we have seen, in Matthew 16 Jesus promised that the Church to be built on the rock of Peter would not be overcome by the "gates of hell." On the basis of these prayers and promises of Jesus, the Church believes that the successor of Peter could never lead the Church astray. Even in those times when the popes were cor-rupt, they did not proclaim that any heresy was a valid doctrine or change the nature of the Church in any way. So on the one hand, we cannot claim that all popes were perfect or even cho-sen by God, but on the other hand, even the worst of them could not damage the office of the papacy, since God has protected it—and in doing so, he has protected the Church.[667]

The point is that the doctrine of papal infallibility is really a doctrine of the infallibility of the Church itself, and the office of the bishop of Rome, not a doctrine of the personal perfection of whoever occupies that office.[668] We do not believe that the pope is without sin, or is somehow omniscient. As I like to tell my students, if the pope had to guess how many jelly beans were in a jar, he could very well guess wrong. Therefore, to say that the pope is infallible, is to say that he is protected from destructive error when he speaks for the Church dogmatically on matters of faith or morals.

At the First Vatican Council in 1870, Pope Pius IX affirmed the authority of the papacy, which was seen as especially necessary at a time when the bishop of Rome was losing secular power in the unification of Italy. At this time, the designation *ex cathedra*, meaning "from the chair [of Peter]" was defined.[669] To be infallible, a papal pronouncement must be made *ex cathedra*, or "from the chair"—in other words, the pope must be speaking on behalf of the Church and by virtue of his office. In a way this is a limitation on the pope, since it clarified that not everything he says is to be considered infallible. He can't just say whatever he wants and be correct—but when he is leading the Church, God's Holy Spirit will prevent him from forcing something on the Church that would take it into error on matters of faith or morals. It is important to note that there was no major opposition to this doctrine when the Church affirmed it in 1870—it was perceived that the Church was simply clarifying what had always been assumed.

The First Vatican Council's Dogmatic Constitution, *Pastor Aeternus*, clarifies the doctrine of papal infallibility:

> For the Holy Spirit was promised to the successors of Peter, not so that they might, by his revelation, make known some new doctrine, but that, by his assistance, they might religiously guard and faithfully expound the revelation or deposit of faith transmitted by the apostles.
>
> [W]e teach and define as a divinely revealed dogma that when the Roman Pontiff speaks ex cathedra, that is, when, in the exercise of his office as shepherd and teacher of all Christians, in virtue of his supreme apostolic authority, he defines a doctrine concerning faith or morals to be held by the whole Church, he possesses, by the divine assistance promised to him in blessed Peter, that infallibility which the divine Redeemer willed his Church to enjoy in defining doctrine concerning faith or morals. Therefore, such definitions of the

Roman Pontiff are of themselves, and not by the consent of
the Church, irreformable.[670]

Notice the document says "a doctrine concerning faith or morals to be held by the whole Church." This means that the papal
prerogative of *ex cathedra* is not something that could be used to
force something new on the Church—rather, it is used when a
pope wants to affirm something that the Church already believes
by consensus. So this is actually something by which a pope recognized the *sensus fidelium*, the consensus of the faithful in the whole
Church throughout its whole history. A Vatican official once explained it to me like this: If we imagine that the Church is like a
train, the pope is not the engine, pulling the train along from the
front. The pope is more like the caboose, bringing up the rear, and
affirming that the whole Church has arrived at some conclusion.

The truth is, the only time a pope has ever made an *ex cathedra* pronouncement was in 1950, to affirm the doctrine of
the Assumption of Mary.[671] It is ironic that some have criticized
this doctrine of infallibility as a "top-down" implement of au-
tocracy, when in fact the only time it has ever been used was
to affirm that the hierarchy had accepted a doctrine that came
from the grass roots of the Church—the Marian doctrines being
examples of "bottom-up" acceptance.

In actual practice, the pope never speaks only his own mind.
Whatever he says comes as a statement of the *magisterium* of the
Church, that is, the authoritative teaching office.[672] So it could be
said that in reality everything the pope says or writes is treated as
though it is infallible, but at the same time we have to remember
that he never says or writes anything without the consultation of
his colleagues, the other bishops. It is not that he speaks for the
Church because he is infallible, but that he is infallible because
he speaks for the Church. The pope is the "bishop of bishops,"
or the "pastor of pastors," but he is also the "servant of servants."

~

We have seen that the Church's hierarchy exists for the sake of
unity, and for passing on the teachings that come from divine

revelation. We have also seen that the apostle Peter was the first shepherd of the Church after Jesus, and could be called the first bishop of Rome. Since Peter was the leader of the apostles, his successors in Rome were seen as the leaders of the successors of the other apostles and thus the universal Church. The Church Fathers (many of them also bishops themselves) acknowledged that all bishops, and all churches, must agree with Rome to be considered part of that universal Church. To this day, we affirm that the pope is not only the guarantor of the unity of the Catholic Church, he is the "sign and servant" of that unity.[673]

Furthermore, the Church Fathers believed that there could be no unity without the Church's hierarchy, and they believed that the hierarchy would necessarily need one person at the top to be the final arbiter of disputes, the last court of appeals, and the chief authority. They believed that schism was the worst thing that could happen to the Church, and they tried to avoid it at all costs. For many of them, to cause division in the Church was the worst sin a person could commit.

It should be clear by now that the pope is not just a man, but he represents something much greater. We have seen how certain strong popes have contributed to the authority of the office: but does the man make the office, or does the office make the man? Remember that all the sacraments effect a change in the person who receives them, and that includes Holy Orders. The one who receives ordination is changed by it, so that God's Holy Spirit fills him with the gifts he will need to fulfill his office. It's the same with those who are then consecrated as bishops, and elevated to the office of the "bishop of bishops." We trust God to fill in the gaps and raise the man to the office.

Of course we cannot say that God will guarantee that every pope is a holy man. History shows us that this is not the case: in the Middle Ages and renaissance when corrupt rulers fixed the papal elections and chose men for all the wrong reasons, they got just what they wanted—corrupt popes. But God protected the Church in spite of those popes, and Jesus' promise that "the gates of hell will not prevail against it" remains in force.

Featured Father

Leo the Great: Theologian and Pope

Leo of Rome was an Italian, and was ordained a deacon under Pope Celestine (422–432), who had intervened in the Nestorian controversy and supported Cyril of Alexandria. It appears that during this time, Leo himself weighed in on the theological implications of the controversy. Leo would then serve as an ambassador for the next pope, Sixtus III (432–440). He also was responsible for writing a beautiful and elaborate inscription for the baptistery of St. John Lateran, the cathedral of Rome. A portion of that inscription reads as follows:

> *Here a people is consecrated*
> *To be born a heavenly city from a budding seed*
> *Established by waters made fruitful by the Spirit*
> *Plunge in, oh sinner, to be cleansed by the sacred flow . . .*

> *Whether you are burdened by ancestral sin or your own*
> *This is the fountain of life, which has cleansed the whole world*
> *Taking its origin from Christ's wound*
> *Hope for the heavenly kingdom*

Leo was elected as the next bishop of Rome when Sixtus died in August of 440. During his pontificate, Leo worked to confront the heresies of Pelagianism as well as the gnostic Manichees and Priscillianists. As the Christological controversies were carried on in the East, Leo weighed in there, too. He wrote his famous *Tome*, the letter in support of Flavian of Constantinople, in which he clarified for the Church the language that was to be used to describe the person of Christ. Leo wrote that Christ is "one person in both natures," meaning that Jesus Christ is fully human and fully divine, and that these two natures were not diminished in any way by their union, and yet they are not to be thought of as separate. Thus Leo finished what Celestine had started, clarifying and supporting orthodox Christology throughout the controversies in the East. The fourth ecumenical Council of Chalcedon, in 451, affirmed Leo's *Tome* as having come from the successor of Peter, and as expressing true doctrine.

Leo wrote many other letters to bishops across the world, confronting heresy and enforcing the Church's discipline. He did all this for the sake of the Church's unity, and to prevent schism. He was an eloquent preacher, and many of his sermons survive.

Shortly after the Council of Chalcedon received and affirmed Leo's *Tome*, Leo himself met with Attila the Hun, who was pillaging his way through Italy, and persuaded him not to attack the city of Rome. A few years later, he negotiated a peace treaty with the barbarian tribe known as the Vandals, and persuaded them to leave Rome.

7

Finding Common Ground in the Early Church

All of us who believe in Jesus Christ as the divine Son of God and savior are of the same religion. Whether we're Catholic, Orthodox, or Protestant, Christianity is our religion and common faith. We Catholics believe the Catholic Church to be the true Church because of its direct connection to Jesus Christ through apostolic succession.[674] We acknowledge that Christianity is divided in ways that prevent us from sharing a common Eucharistic table, and that in the past this division has led to misunderstandings and even animosity between us. One purpose of this book has been to address those misunderstandings by demonstrating, for Catholics and non-Catholics alike, that Catholicism is both rational and ancient.

The Second Vatican Council's Decree on Ecumenism says that the Church accepts non-Catholic Christians "with respect and affection as brothers . . . all who have been justified by faith in baptism are incorporated into Christ; they therefore have a right to be called Christians, and with good reason are accepted as brothers by the children of the Catholic Church."[675] Thus non-Catholics are still in communion with the Catholic Church by our common baptism, though that communion is imperfect.[676] And although we cannot share the sacrament of the Eucharist, our common baptism unites us in the communion of the saints.[677] Non-Catholic Christians have the means of grace, and access to salvation.[678] Since the Second Vatican Council, the Catholic Church has made a serious effort to reach out to other Christian churches for the purpose of dialogue, and with the priority of reconciliation with our "separated brethren."[679]

So we respect the faith of anyone who sincerely identifies with Jesus Christ as Lord and savior, who is baptized in the name of the Father, Son, and Holy Spirit, and who accepts the

227

doctrines outlined in the Nicene Creed. We believe we are still connected to our non-Catholic brothers and sisters in the one universal Church that Jesus founded.[680] Therefore, let us end this book on common ground, by emphasizing that the place for dialogue to begin is with the beliefs that we hold together.

Preliminary Points for Dialogue

As Catholics, we must not pretend that the Church didn't need reform in the times of people like John Wycliffe and Martin Luther. We admit that there was a time when the office of the papacy was ruled by secular princes and overrun with corruption. Ecclesiastical offices were bought and sold, and therefore ministry was neglected. Reconciliation, in the form of indulgences, became a fundraising campaign. We also admit that sometimes even ancient traditions such as prayer to the saints and the veneration of relics and icons could be abused and fall into superstition—not as a matter of official policy, but in actual popular practice. And by the late Middle Ages, homilies sometimes focused more on the saints than on Jesus Christ. All of this we must acknowledge.

At the same time, Protestants must acknowledge that Jesus keeps all his promises, including his promise that the gates of hell will not prevail against the Church.[681] This means that we cannot begin any dialogue with the assumption of an apostate Church, as though at some point the Church "went off the rails" and ceased to be the Church that Christ and the apostles founded. We have to remember that it is within the Church where the Holy Spirit is experienced most powerfully and profoundly, and so we have to take into consideration the ways in which the Spirit has been guiding the Church from the beginning and all throughout its history—or if not, then we are saying that the Spirit has not been guiding the Church.

If we see the Protestant Reformation as an attempt at reforming the Church that unfortunately led to schism, then we can all agree that reform was needed—and in many ways has been made within the Church. But if it is proposed that the Reformation was meant to recapture a pristine Church, from a time before it apostatized, then we can't agree. As we have seen in this book, the traditions rejected by many Protestants are so ancient that it would be impossible to get back to a Church that existed before them.

Therefore, true reformation is not about rejecting manmade traditions that were later added to Christianity—scraping off the barnacles, as it were, from the ship of the Church—but rather it should be the attempt to curb and eradicate *abuses* of those traditions. On this both Protestants and Catholics must be able to agree, if the ultimate goal of our dialogue is to be unity rather than more division.

Therefore, in the spirit of Jesus' prayer "that they may all be one" (John 17), we must be about the business of healing the divisions in the Body of Christ.[682] When we speak of "ecumenical dialogue," we are using the same word that was used of the early general councils of the Church. An ecumenical council was a *worldwide* council of the Church—where all the bishops of the world were invited, and the decisions were binding on all the local churches of the world. So the word, "ecumenical," as it is used today, refers to inter-denominational relations with the one religion of Christianity.[683] Ecumenical dialogue is Christians talking with other Christians across the boundaries of denomination.

ANCIENT ECUMENICAL LESSONS

It may seem anachronistic to look for guidance in ecumenical relations in the early Church, given that during the time of most of the Fathers the Church was essentially one. However, there are two cases of schism in the early Church that have historical significance for the discussion at hand.

As we have already seen, in the middle of the third century a wave of persecution led to a controversy over the validity of the sacraments. At the heart of the matter was the issue of the "lapsed"—those Christians who had denied the Faith to save their lives.[684] Would a baptism performed by a lapsed priest (or an ordination performed by a lapsed bishop) be valid? But in more general terms, the persecution also forced the question of what to do when a lapsed layperson wanted to return to the Church and the Eucharist. Should he be refused, and excommunicated permanently? Should he be reconciled to the Church without any consequences? While the majority of the Church chose a middle way (the sacrament of penance), there was a "rigorist" faction that made few allowances for the lapsed to be reconciled. Eventually, that faction coalesced under the leadership of the theologian-priest Novatian, and when he lost the election for bishop of Rome in the year 251, his followers consecrated him as a bishop anyway—making him an "anti-pope," or a rival bishop of Rome. This created a schism that lasted for a few centuries before the Novatianists eventually were folded back into the Catholic Church.

Novatian was called a heretic by his contemporaries because he split the Church. But in reality, Novatian's theology was thoroughly orthodox—in fact, he wrote a document on the Trinity that helped define orthodoxy for the third century, and laid the groundwork for the fourth-century refutation of Arianism and for the Nicene Creed. Later, at the Council of Nicaea, the Novatianists were represented by one of their bishops, who had been invited to the council. At that first ecumenical council, the Novatianists' theology was accepted as orthodox (because their bishop signed the creed), and the validity of their clergy was even recognized to the point that if any Novatianist clergy wanted to come into the Catholic Church, their ordination would be accepted. Yet by saying this, it was acknowledged that they were not part of the Catholic Church. For the first time in history, in the year 325 and at an ecumenical council no less, it was acknowledged that a group could be *Christian, but not Catholic.* They were accepted as orthodox, but not connected to the rest of the Body of Christ because they did not submit to the authority of the bishop of Rome.

If we allow a bit of anachronism, we could call the Novatianist movement the first "Protestant denomination," because
it rejected the Church's hierarchy—specifically, it believed
that the majority of the bishops were being too lenient toward
those who had committed apostasy. And although we should
applaud the mainstream (Catholic) Church for discerning that
it is better to err on the side of mercy and reconciliation, we
can at least respect the zeal of the rigorists, who believed that
reconciling someone who had denied the Faith to save his life
was a slap in the face to the martyrs. In reality, some leaders
of the Catholic Church gave in to the temptation to use their
power to persecute the Novatianists, but the official decision
of the Council of Nicaea was that they were not heretics and
that theirs was an expression of Christianity in which a person
could hope for salvation. If we choose to, we can see this as
a precedent for the way we now recognize the validity of the
Protestant denominations.

In the fifth century, the fourth ecumenical council, at Chalcedon, was a watershed for the Church. There, in spite of all of
the Church's efforts to maintain its unity, the universal Church
was divided permanently. The year 451 marks the first time a
schism split the Church into separated ecclesial bodies that still
exist to this day. The debates over how to understand the union
of Jesus' two natures (humanity and divinity) led to difficult
misunderstandings exacerbated by differences in the Greek and
Latin languages, as well as by the political ambitions of certain
metropolitan bishops. In the end, two groups were declared heretical, but these two groups were large enough to stand their
ground, separate from the mainstream Church, and continue on
as distinct "denominations."

The movement led by the followers of Nestorius of
Constantinople, which was perceived as proposing too much
separation between the two natures of Christ, split and became
what is known today as the Assyrian Church of the East. The
movement led by Dioscorus of Alexandria and the followers
of the monk Eutyches, which was perceived as proposing too

little distinction between the two natures of Christ, split and
became what is known today as the Oriental Orthodox (or
Coptic) Church. In both of these cases, the mainstream Church
(that is, the majority of bishops) declared that these groups had
not described the person of Christ with the proper balance of
distinction and unity of the two natures. And in both of these
cases, the schismatic groups could not see that the mainstream
Church had found the middle ground. Each perceived the
middle as being too close to the other extreme.[685]

The good news is that in the twentieth century the Catholic
Church reconciled with these two groups, and although they
are still considered "non-Chalcedonian" churches, we recognize
them (and they recognize us) as validly Christian and not heretical. We also now admit that a lot of what led to the condemna-
tions of heresy was the result of misunderstanding and the problems of translating theological terms back and forth between
Latin and Greek. Back then, people were using different Greek
words to talk about the same concepts, or the same Greek words
to talk about different concepts. But we now see that the way
these groups describe the person of Christ is within the bounds
of orthodoxy, even though it may be slightly different from the
way we do it.

Although this reconciliation didn't happen until the twentieth century, and so was not something the Church Fathers could
have anticipated, it demonstrates the Catholic Church's desire
for unity and willingness to see past the problems of ancient
politics and language issues. This is not to say that all the heresies
of the early Church fall into this category. Heresies such as Arianism and Gnosticism were not a matter of misunderstanding,
and their teachings about Christ were unacceptable because the
Christ they preached was not the Christ of the Gospels. So we
have to be clear that we are not saying all schism can be overcome simply by waving it off as a matter of semantics. But in
cases where the division is not a matter of real theological differences, we can live with some diversity in the ways we describe
our theology and worship our common Lord.

ARE WE STILL SPEAKING TWO DIFFERENT LANGUAGES?

One could argue that in the dialogue between Catholics and Protestants, we are still talking past each other. And nowhere is this more true than when the conversation gets around to the topic of conversion. The word *conversion* means different things to Catholics and Protestants, in part because it has meant different things throughout the history of the Church.

In the first few centuries of the Church, when the Roman Empire was pagan and Christianity was persecuted, conversion meant a change from pagan (or Jewish) to Christian. It was a change from one religion to another, and it took a significant commitment (sometimes even life-threatening) and a willingness to change one's entire lifestyle and personal relationships. This means that conversion often included a decision point, but it also required catechesis and ongoing formation. The catechesis came both before and after baptism, so the concept of conversion was never separated from the ongoing formation—people who decided to *be* a Christian needed to grow in their understanding of how to *live as* a Christian.

When Christianity was legalized and eventually became the official religion of the Roman Empire, almost everyone became Christian, and many of them for reasons other than faith commitment or spiritual convictions. So from the fourth century on, conversion took on the meaning of a change from a nominal, going-through-the-motions kind of Christianity, to a serious kind of Christianity that many believed required an austere lifestyle that set one apart from the masses. This kind of conversion was embodied in the hermits and monks, but the idea that there were different levels of spiritual commitment permeated the whole Church. This ultimately enhanced the notion that the Christian life was not simply about a one-time decision (since so many people had made that decision for social reasons, or had not made it for themselves), but in fact the Christian life was about ongoing spiritual growth. Conversion was, more than ever, a way of life.

By the late Middle Ages, some people perceived that the Church had once again become complacent, partly due to the fact that pretty much everyone in Europe was Christian. So when the Protestant Reformation came along, it defined conversion in a new way. For the Reformers, conversion meant a rejection of certain aspects of the Church—including its leaders—and pledging loyalty to teachers who had separated themselves from the hierarchy. This required a personal decision, but the role of ongoing formation was diminished in favor of an emphasis on simply being on the right side of the divide. It was as if the meaning of conversion had gone back to a pre-Constantinian definition, but one where the lifestyle could be assumed. In actual fact, some of the Reformers treated the Catholic Church as though it were a different (non-Christian) religion. And as we know, this way of understanding conversion also led some of the later Reformers to reject infant baptism in favor of a baptism that only admits those who could make a personal decision for themselves.

Therefore, the Protestant tradition is built on a definition of conversion that is based on a personal decision, which is to a large extent an intellectual conversion, which means that Protestant preaching was originally more concerned with convincing people to come over to their side. Catholic preaching, on the other hand, was based more on a tradition of exhortation to spiritual growth and encouraging people to improve their behavior.[686] Catholic preaching did not need to convince, only to empower.

Today, conversion for Protestants often focuses on a one-time decision to identify with Christ as Lord and savior, and to commit one's life to him. For many Protestants, that means they see their conversion as a past event. It is done once, and generally not repeated. To Catholics, conversion is a lifelong process that (for most of us) began at our baptism before we were conscious of the Faith or able to choose it for ourselves. It is not an individual decision, strictly speaking, because it begins in community, and is sustained in community—that is, in the Church, and through the sacraments. As Pope St. John Paul II wrote, "In this life, conversion is a goal which is never fully attained . . . conversion is a life-long task . . . it is not an end in itself but a journey towards God."[687]

For most Catholics, our conversion is not something we can point to in the past as a moment in our lives to be remembered by a date. This is a good thing, because it usually means that we were born into a Christian home and brought to baptism by Christian parents and sponsors who took their own faith seriously. And because growth in the Faith begins and is nurtured in the Church, we allow for the vicarious faith of parents and sponsors to set a person on the journey even before he is aware of it. This also means that as Catholics we believe that we may have multiple conversion experiences—what some might call "mountain top" experiences—that energize us and motivate us to continue on the journey of spiritual maturity. We may actually rededicate ourselves to Christ many times throughout our lives.

Furthermore, many Protestants tend to break up the Christian life and salvation into categories such as justification and sanctification, which leads them to categorize different kinds of grace, such as prevenient grace, justifying grace, and sanctifying grace. There is nothing inherently wrong with this; it is a sincere attempt to understand the work of God in the salvation of the faithful. But for Catholics, the whole process is more of a mystery, and we don't normally draw strict lines between different kinds of grace or different stages in the journey toward salvation. We can talk about the different works of God that we call grace, but we don't tend to turn them into a linear (or chronological) progression.

Nevertheless, if we listen to each other, we can understand each other. What the Catholic calls conversion, the Protestant understands as the whole process that includes justification and sanctification. What the Protestant calls conversion is, for the Catholic, simply the beginning of the journey. Where and how that journey begins can vary from person to person, and as long as no one makes his particular experience of conversion a normative requirement for all Christians, then we can agree that all of us who are on the journey are in fact "born again."[688] But we also have to admit that spiritual rebirth is not a one-time thing. It may begin with an awakening, but salvation is not complete without ongoing renewal. The good news is, we are not limited to one second chance in life.

Therefore, what we can learn from the history of the Church, and from the Church Fathers, is this. First of all it is possible to be separated from our brothers and sisters in Christ, and yet for them to truly be our brothers and sisters. In other words, it is possible to be *Christian*, even though one is not *Catholic*. This is the situation in which we find ourselves with the Church today, and with our "separated brethren" in the Protestant denominations. Second, it is possible that in some ways our division is over old problems that no longer exist, or over misunderstandings that come from using the same words in different ways. This is not to say that all of our disagreements can be overcome easily, but some of them can be reduced to an acceptable diversity of expression if we talk them through and understand each other. In other words, discussion about what we mean when we talk about our faith is a good place to start to find common ground.

Church Unity in Light of the Early Fathers

We will conclude our study with seven specific areas in which the Church Fathers can help us find common ground. What follows is my proposed list of seven essentials, based on Scripture and Tradition, and on the witness of the Church Fathers.[689] In each case, the Church Fathers that we have surveyed in the preceding chapters, along with ongoing ecumenical dialogue, inform our conclusions about the essential aspects of the Faith.

1. The Authority of the Scriptures and the Importance of Tradition

We can agree that the scriptures contained in the Christian Bible, and especially the New Testament, are collectively to be taken as the inspired word of God. We can also agree that this revelation from God is necessary because we as humans are not able to come to ultimate truths simply through discovery or self-examination. Truth does not come from within us, and it does not evolve over time.[690] Truth has a source, and that source is outside of us—the source of truth is the divine *Logos*, the eternal and living Word of God, who was the agent of creation, who inspired and spoke through the scriptures, and who was incarnate in the person of Jesus Christ. The scriptures that the *Logos* inspired are infallible and authoritative for humanity, and normative for the Church. And although we may have different ways to speak of "inerrancy," we can agree that we are not the masters over Sacred Scripture, but must submit ourselves to it.

We also have to admit that Scripture doesn't interpret itself, and that attention to Sacred Tradition is necessary for correct interpretation (and for avoiding the interpretive mistakes of the past) and for coming to consensus on the meaning of difficult passages. We should agree that a strict application of *sola scriptura* is impossible, since even those who claim to espouse it do not really limit themselves to only what is named in the pages of the Bible. Instead, we must take seriously both the authority of Scripture as a guide for Tradition and the necessity of apostolic Tradition in the formation of the scriptural canon and its interpretation.

The word of God has a certain primacy over Tradition because the words of Scripture are inspired, which is why we read Scripture in worship, and not the Church Fathers.[691] On the other hand, Tradition helps us interpret Scripture, and Christians of many denominations do say one of the historic creeds of the Church, usually the Nicene Creed. As the Anglican bishop N. T. Wright wrote, "the phrase, 'authority of Scripture' can make Christian sense only if it is a shorthand for 'the authority of the Triune God, exercised somehow *through* Scripture.'"[692] The Catholic Church would add that the authority of God is also exercised through the Church, which is founded on the writings and interpretations of the early Church Fathers. Remember that the Word of God (capital "W") is Jesus Christ, the Living Word, and his person and his works are the primary revelation of God.[693]

In Scripture, then, "the words, for their part, proclaim the works, and bring to light the mystery they contain. The most intimate truth which this revelation gives us about God and the salvation of man shines forth in Christ, who is himself both the mediator and the sum total of Revelation."[694] So we must be careful that we don't become devoted to the written word over the Living Word, Jesus Christ. It is important for us to be clear that Scripture and Tradition do not oppose each other; they are complementary. In fact, the Councils of Nicaea and Constantinople, which gave us the Nicene Creed, demonstrated that a strict adherence to *sola scriptura* actually leads to heresy and division. The truth is, all heresy is the result of someone interpreting Scripture apart from Tradition—thinking they know better than all those who have come before them.[695]

Correct biblical interpretation strives for a balance that recognizes the importance of grounding the text of Scripture in history, but does not ignore a deeper spiritual meaning. According to the Pontifical Biblical Commission document, *The Interpretation of the Bible in the Church*, "Historical-critical exegesis has too often tended to limit the meaning of texts by tying it too rigidly to precise historical circumstances."[696] On the other hand, "one must reject as unauthentic every interpretation alien to the meaning expressed by the human authors in their written text. To admit the possibility of such alien meanings would be the equivalent of cutting off the biblical message from its root, which is the word of God in its historical communication; it would also mean opening the door to interpretations of a wildly subjective nature."[697] The point is to find a middle way between the extremes of a literalistic approach to Scripture and an overly spiritualized approach.[698] This means interpreting each text in light of the whole witness of Scripture, and taking into account the ways that the Church has historically interpreted the passage(s) in question.

We can also agree on the value of studying Scripture, since the written word of God is a tangible witness to the Living Word of God. We can appreciate the value of studying Scripture using critical methods, as long as the method doesn't become the authority instead of the text. We recognize together that when we study Scripture, we are confronted with our own failures and imperfections, and we are made to acknowledge our sin and the consequence of alienation from God. Whether we speak of original sin or personal sin, we all realize that we are left in a state of need, facing God's justice, hoping for God's mercy. The scriptures leave no uncertainty that on our own we are condemned by our sin, and we need a savior.

2. Salvation Through Jesus Christ

We can agree that Jesus Christ is our savior, and the solution to the problem of human sin. He is the only mediator between God and humanity, and he is the incarnation of the divine *Logos*. As a human, he is unique among humanity; he was born of a miraculous virginal conception, and he remained fully divine in his life among us. We can agree on the historical reality of his miracles, which demonstrate his divine authority and agency, and also on the historical reality of his bodily Resurrection.

We can agree that salvation is not earned by human works but is made possible by divine intervention in the incarnation of Jesus Christ, which includes his ministry, his Passion and death, and his Resurrection. The voluntary sacrifice of his life was an atonement that is both a satisfaction of God's justice and an expression of God's mercy. Salvation is made effective for individuals through the Church—by the invitation of God's grace that comes through the Church's preaching and sacraments, and through the response to that invitation that is corporate and individual faith. This should be the foundation and motivation for the good works that characterize the life of faith.[699] We are all called to ongoing spiritual growth, and whether we call that a process of conversion or sanctification, the expectation is that the journey of faith continues throughout all of life. The emphasis must not be on some conversion experience in the past, but on the present and the future, in which we live a life of continually identifying with Jesus Christ as Lord and responding to God's invitations of grace. There will be significant strides, found in periodic mountaintop experiences, as well as minor victories, realized every time we resist temptation. But when we fail, we can be confident that Christ offers forgiveness and reconciliation.

3. The Institution of the Church

We can agree on the necessity of the Church, since salvation does not happen in isolation, but in community.[700] The universal Church, in spite of denominational divisions, is still the one Body of Christ. The Church is one, holy (instituted by Christ himself and inspired by God), catholic (worldwide), and apostolic (connected to the apostles and founded on their teachings). It is the instrument of the kingdom of God on earth, and it will continue unadulterated until Christ returns at the end of the Church age. We must also acknowledge that to a certain extent God protects the universal Church from serious error, so that there was never a time since its founding when there was no authentic expression of Christianity on the earth.

We should agree that all local expressions of the universal Church need to be connected to it in some way. In other words, no local congregation can be completely autonomous and still call itself a part of the Body of Christ. The one Church is not something we hope for, it is something that already exists, and all Christians are already brothers and sisters in the same Lord Jesus Christ, indwelt by the same Holy Spirit of God, and united in the communion of saints. Therefore, the unity we hope for is a unity that would demonstrate to the world the deeper unity that already exists.

4. The Sacrament of Baptism and the Priesthood of All Believers

We can agree on the importance of baptism as initiation into the Church, and as adoption into the family of God. As a sacrament and a means of grace, baptism is a rite in which God is powerfully active, and the recipient is permanently changed. All Christian baptisms[701] conducted in the name of the Father, Son, and Holy Spirit, with the element of water, are valid and should be recognized as such. Because the universal Church is one, there is only one baptism, and we are baptized into the universal Church, not into one denomination or another.[702] This is extremely important because, objectively speaking, to reject or repeat a valid baptism (including infant baptism) is an act of schism, and an offense against the Body of Christ. In fact, the greatest barrier to unity is the rejection of infant baptism and the rebaptism of those validly baptized in another denomination. Those denominations and congregations that practice rebaptism must reconsider this position for the sake of Jesus' prayer, that we all might be one.[703] In addition, those congregations that baptize in alternative formulas (other than "Father, Son, and Holy Spirit") must realize that by doing so they imply heresy and call into question which God one is being baptized into. [704]

We can also agree that all Christians are, by virtue of their baptism, commissioned for ministry (the "priesthood of all believers").[705] Not only should all Christians read and study the scriptures, they should also know the historic creeds and ancient prayers. And all Christians should participate in the life and ministry of the Church, including regular attendance at worship.[706] Therefore, Catholics and Protestants can agree that, on the one hand, Christianity is not a spectator sport, and all Christians are expected to participate in the general ministry of the Church; and on the other hand, it is necessary that there are some who are called to be set apart for special (ordained) ministry and leadership within the Church.

5. The Sacrament of the Eucharist and the Communion of Saints

Although we may have different beliefs about what happens on the Eucharistic altar/table, we can agree that we are following Jesus' command when we regularly participate in the Lord's Supper and receive Holy Communion.[707] We can agree that the sacrament unites us with Christ, and with each other, in the communion of the saints that spans across time and across the boundary between life and afterlife. Even those Protestant denominations that choose not to call their ordinances "sacraments" can still acknowledge that the table of Communion is a defining and unifying factor in the Church. We should also agree that the sacrament of the Eucharist is a necessary sign of membership in the Church, along with baptism. The celebration of the Eucharist is a powerful proclamation of the gospel, and it reiterates the promise of the heavenly banquet. Finally, although we may differ on how we understand the presence of Christ in the sacrament of the Eucharist, we can agree that the Lord Jesus Christ is more powerfully present there than in any other expression of Christian gathering or worship.

6. The Responsibility of Outreach Beyond the Church

We can agree that there is no such thing as a private Christianity, and that Christianity cannot exist only in the privacy of an individual's prayer life. As Christians, we are not followers of Christ if we do not reach out in love toward our fellow humans and in care for the poor, the sick, and the marginalized. The Church is to be an instrument of extending God's love and compassion to others, including those outside of the Church. In addition, Christians have a responsibility to participate in the works of God in the world, and by doing so, we participate in the process of our own conversion/sanctification, and we "work out our salvation."[708] Thus the Christian life is not prayer alone, or even prayer and worship alone—but is rather characterized by the "spiritual tripod" of private devotion, corporate worship, and social responsibility.[709]

7. The Nicene Creed

Finally, we can agree that the Nicene Creed summarizes the heart of the gospel and provides an authoritative interpretation of New Testament theology. In principle, we should also agree on the Chalcedonian Definition, though we can allow the non-Chalcedonian churches the freedom to express their Christology in other complementary ways. The doctrine of the Trinity is not only the most important Christian doctrine—it defines Christianity itself, and therefore to reject it, or to opt for an alternative understanding of God, is to be something other than Christian.

The historic creeds, and especially the Nicene Creed, are both normative and authoritative for the Church. As Philip Turner wrote in the introduction to *Nicene Christianity: The Future for a New Ecumenism*:

> The creeds thus served, and I believe continue to serve, as tokens or badges of Christian identity. They provided and continue to provide a norm both for reading the Scriptures and for evangelization and instruction. They provide a means of recognition for God's people, scattered as they are among the peoples of the earth. They have served both as a means of identity and as a basis for unity. Perhaps most of all, they contain the basic confession of Christians—a summary of their witness about the truth of God in Christ Jesus. Creeds are outlines of instruction, but they are also forms of witness . . . In a positive sense, they have served as a guide to a correct reading of Scripture and an adequate expression of belief and identity. Negatively, they have served to rule out certain false readings and expressions.[710]

With these seven essentials, we can join with our fellow Christians in cooperating with God's grace and doing God's will in the world. These are the very things, without which Christianity would cease to be Christian. We can use these areas of agreement as a springboard for common mission, and also for continued dialogue.[711] But ecumenical dialogue is more than simply focusing on areas of agreement. It must also recognize that each side of the conversation has gifts to give the other. The Second Vatican Council's document on ecumenism states, "Catholics must gladly acknowledge and esteem the truly Christian endowments from our common heritage which are to be found among our separated brethren."[712]

∾

All Christians have accepted Christ as their savior, simply by being willing to identify with him. By being baptized and belonging to the universal Church, and by being confirmed in the Faith, by reciting the creeds, and by participating in the Eucharist, we say we are his people.[713] We are regenerated, but not as a past event, rather we are all in the process of regeneration and redemption.[7014]This is not entirely a matter of personal decision, but it is partly a gift of God and partly a gift of the Christian community in which we find ourselves.[715] For Catholics, the Eucharist itself is the primary proclamation of the gospel, and so the Mass is an invitation to respond—in other words, every Mass is an altar call—and when Catholics respond to the invitation by coming forward to receive the body and blood of Christ, we accept him as our savior, and we identify ourselves as his followers.[716] If and when we Catholics are confronted by a Protestant who asks us if we have accepted Jesus Christ as our (personal) savior, our answer should be: Yes! Every week! Every time we cross ourselves, say the creed, and receive Holy Communion.

To be ecumenical, therefore, is to recognize the validity of each other's experiences of conversion, and not to discount or exclude a fellow Christian just because he doesn't have a single point of personal decision. To be ecumenical is to admit that none of us are entirely sanctified, and we are all on a journey in which God's Holy Spirit is working on us, and in us, to grow us into the people God wants us to be.

The purpose of this book has been to explain the Catholic Faith, so that Catholics would be able to understand it and share it, and so that non-Catholics would see where we Catholics are coming from. It may not satisfy every Protestant objection, especially for those who refuse to accept the authority of Tradition we find in the Church Fathers. Nevertheless, this book has demonstrated that for the most part, the Catholic Church of today remains consistent with the Church of the apostles and early Fathers. Therefore, if one wanted to find an expression of Christianity that was most like the early Church, it would have to include those Catholic doctrines and practices rejected by many of the Protestant Reformers and in the end it would look very much like the Catholic Church.

Having said that, we as Catholics do recognize the validity of other Christian denominations and the diversity of experiences of conversion in Jesus Christ. We recognize that those who accept the essentials listed above—and especially who affirm the Nicene Creed (for whatever is not Trinitarian is not Christian)—they are our brothers and sisters in Christ, indwelt by the same Holy Spirit and initiated into the same Body of Christ and communion of saints. Part of my hope is that this book will lead to mutual understanding, and eventually allow Catholics and Protestants to work together to spread the gospel and care for the needy.

Finally, it is hoped that all Christians will stand together to support and protect our brothers and sisters who are still being persecuted in those countries that do not have religious freedom.

Featured Father

Novatian: Theologian and Anti-Pope

Novatian was a priest in the city of Rome in the middle of the third century. He was probably born around the year 200, and ordained by about 240. At some time in the 240's, he distinguished himself as a premier theologian by writing a document that we refer to as *On the Trinity*. In this document, Novatian summarized the orthodoxy of his time, and he also anticipated the decisions of later ecumenical councils. In fact, he was the first theologian to clarify the doctrine of *eternal generation*, which is now expressed in the creed in the line, "born of the Father before all ages." This was important because it allowed the fourth-century bishops to refute Arianism, the major heresy that led to the Council of Nicaea in 325.

In the year 250, the Roman emperor Decius issued a proclamation requiring all inhabitants of the empire to make a pagan sacrifice as a test of loyalty to the state. For Christians, making the sacrifice meant denying Christ and swearing that they were not members of the Church. But refusal to make the required sacrifice meant arrest, torture, and probably execution. One of the first to be executed was the bishop of Rome, Fabian. All of this led to the problem of reconciling those Christians who gave in and made the sacrifice to save their lives (or their livelihoods). How could they be allowed to return to the Church?

Novatian was a "rigorist," which means that he advocated excommunicating everyone who had denied the Faith. His position as a top theologian had even made him a kind of "acting bishop" of Rome after the death of Fabian. But when the Church was able to elect a new bishop in the year 251, Novatian lost the election to Cornelius, who advocated using the sacrament of penance to reconcile the lapsed. At this point, the rigorist faction rallied around Novatian and made him their bishop, calling him the bishop of Rome in opposition to Cornelius. This created a schism—a split of the Church—that lasted for several centuries. This faction was called Novatianists, or Purists, and they existed alongside the Catholic Church, but separate from it.

At least one Novatianist bishop was present at the Council of Nicaea in 325. He signed the creed written at the council, and so he was accepted as orthodox—that is, he was accepted as validly Christian by virtue of his theology, but it was also acknowledged that he was not within the Catholic Church. Therefore, the Council of Nicaea recognized for the first time that it was possible to be Christian, but not Catholic. So it could be said that Novatian was the first "Protestant" and the Novatianists were the first non-Catholic "denomination."

The point of highlighting Novatian is not to glorify dissent or justify the rejection of legitimately elected popes. For in spite of the fact that Novatian was a brilliant and orthodox theologian, and a martyr, he is not considered a saint because he split the Church—and the majority of the Church Fathers would come to the conclusion that splitting the Church was about the worst sin anyone could commit. But this episode in the Church's history does demonstrate the ongoing struggle for both the integrity and the unity of the Church. And it anticipates our contemporary situation in which we view our "separated brethren" as Christian, even though they are not Catholic.

Appendix I

Timeline of Early Church Fathers and Events

Lived	Name	Years as Bishop	Known For
30–100	Clement of Rome	88–97	I Clement
50–110	Ignatius of Antioch	uncertain	Letters to churches
69–156	Polycarp of Smyrna	uncertain	Martyrdom
112–165	Justin Martyr		Apologies, martyrdom
110–172	Tatian		Tried to harmonize Gospels
† 180	Melito of Sardis	uncertain	Easter homily
133–190	Athenagoras		Apology
115–188	Theophilus of Antioch	168–188	Letters to Autolychus
155–215	Clement of Alexandria		Catechetical treatises
125–202	Irenaeus of Lyons	177–202	Anti-heresy writings
145–225	Tertullian (Lay teacher of Carthage)		Father of Latin theology
170–236	Hippolytus	uncertain	Anti-heresy writings
186–254	Origen		Controversial catechist
200–258	Novatian		Theologian, anti-pope
† 257	Stephen of Rome	254–257	Baptism controversy
† 258	Cyprian of Carthage	248–258	Baptism controversy
† 311	Methodius of Olympus	uncertain	Opposed Origen

Lived	Name	Years as Bishop	Known For
240–320	Lactantius (Lay teacher of N. Africa)		Tutor of Constantine's son
313	Edict of Milan		Granted freedom of religion
325	COUNCIL OF NICAEA		Confronted Arius
296–373	Athanasius of Alexandria	326–373	Opposed Arianism
263–339	Eusebius of Caesarea	314–339	First Church historian
300–368	Hilary of Poitiers	350–368	Wrote on the Trinity
313–386	Cyril of Jerusalem	350–386	Catechetical treatises
313–398	Didymus the Blind		Catechetical treatises
380	Edict of Thessalonica		Paganism illegal
381	COUNCIL OF CONSTANTINOPLE		Confronted Apollinarius
304–384	Damasus of Rome	366–384	Catacomb inscriptions
310–391	Pacian of Barcelona	365–391	Letters against Novatianists
330–379	Basil of Caesarea	370–379	Wrote on the Holy Spirit
330–390	Gregory of Nazianzus	379–381	Wrote on the Holy Spirit
335–394	Gregory of Nyssa	372–376	Wrote on the Holy Spirit
340–397	Ambrose of Milan	374–397	Wrote on the sacraments
334–399	Siricius of Rome	384–399	Opposed heresy in Rome
315–403	Epiphanius of Salamis	366–403	Anti-heresy writings

Lived	Name	Years as Bishop	Known For
347–407	John Chrysostom	398–407	Eloquent homilies
† 417	Innocent I of Rome	410–417	
347–420	Jerome		Translated Scripture
354–430	Augustine of Hippo	396–430	*Confessions*, theology
360–435	John Cassian		
431	COUNCIL OF EPHESUS		Confronted Nestorius
† 445	Vincent of Lerins		Vincentian Canon
400–461	Leo the Great of Rome	440–461	*The Tome*
451	COUNCIL OF CHALCEDON		Confronted Eutyches
540–604	Gregory the Great of Rome	590–604	Authority of the papacy
676–749	John of Damascus		Assumption of Mary
† 860	Paschasius Radbertus		Wrote on the Eucharist
1020–85	Gregory VII of Rome (Hildebrand)	1073–1085	*Dictatus Papae*
1010–89	Lanfranc of Canterbury	1070–1089	Wrote on the Eucharist
1215	FOURTH LATERAN COUNCIL		Affirmed transubstantiation

Appendix II

Seven Essentials on Which Catholics and Protestants Can Agree

1. The Authority of Scripture and the Importance of Tradition
   - Sacred Scripture is the inspired word of God.
   - Scripture is infallible and authoritative.
   - Revelation is necessary because truth does not come from within.
   - Tradition is necessary for the interpretation of Scripture.
   - All believers should study Scripture.

2. Salvation through Jesus Christ
   - Jesus Christ is our savior and the solution to the problem of human sin.
   - He was born of a miraculous virginal conception.
   - He is fully human and fully divine.
   - His miracles demonstrate his divine authority.
   - After his death on the cross, he was raised bodily.
   - Salvation is not earned by works but is made possible by the atonement.
   - Those in the family of God are expected to participate in good works.
   - Conversion (or sanctification) is an ongoing process of spiritual growth.

3. The Institution of the Church
   - The Church is necessary, since salvation does not happen in isolation.
   - There is only one universal Church, which is the Body of Christ.

- The Church is the instrument of the kingdom of God on earth.
- God protects the universal Church from losing its identity
- No local congregation can be completely autonomous.

4. The Sacrament of Baptism and the Priesthood of All Believers
   - All baptisms in the name of the Father, Son, and Holy Spirit are valid.
   - Christians are baptized into the Body of Christ, not into one denomination.
   - There is only one baptism, and baptisms are not to be repeated.
   - Rebaptism is an act of schism and an offense against the Body of Christ.
   - All Christians are, by virtue of their baptism, commissioned for ministry.

5. The Sacrament of the Eucharist and the Communion of Saints
   - We are following Jesus' command when we receive Holy Communion.
   - The sacrament unites us with the communion of the saints.
   - The table of Communion is a defining and unifying factor in the Church.
   - The Eucharist is a necessary sign of membership in the Church.
   - The celebration of the Eucharist is a powerful proclamation of the gospel.
   - The Eucharist reiterates the promise of the heavenly banquet.

6. The Responsibility of Outreach Beyond the Church
   - There is no such thing as a private Christianity.
   - The Church is an instrument of extending God's love and compassion.
   - Christians have a responsibility to participate in the works of God.

- We participate in the process of our own conversion/sanctification.

7. The Nicene Creed
   - The Nicene Creed provides an authoritative interpretation of Scripture.
   - The doctrine of the Trinity defines Christianity itself.
   - The Nicene Creed is both normative and authoritative for the Church.

Notes

1   See Matt. 16:15–19.

2   Gal. 1:18, 1 Cor. 15:3–11. See also 1 Cor. 11:23–26. Even though Paul says he received the tradition of the institution of the Eucharist "from the Lord," he is quoting liturgy here, and must have received it from the Lord through the other apostles.

3   CCC 857.

4   Note that the name "Peter" that Jesus gives to Simon means "rock" in both Aramaic (*kephas*) and Greek (*petros*).

5   See CCC 8.

6   The Greek word for "bishop," *episkopos*, literally means "overseer."

7   See also CCC 861–862.

8   Cf. the Parable of the Wicked Tenants, Matt. 21:33–46, Mark 12:1–12, Luke 20:9–19.

9   1 Clement 42, 44.

10 1 Clement 63.

11 Letter to the Magnesians 6–7.

12 Letter to the Trallians 3.

13 Letter to the Philadelphians 3–4.

14 Letter to the Smyrnaeans 8. See also St. Augustine of Hippo, *Against the Letter of Mani Called "Fundamental"* 4.5.

15 For an explanation of gnosticism, see my book, *Reading the Early Church Fathers*, pp. 58–77.

16 *Against Heresies* 2.9.1. See also 3.1.1.

17 *Against Heresies* 3.3.1–2.

18 *Against Heresies* 3.4.

19 Irenaeus of Lyons, *Against Heresies* 4.1.

20 Tertullian is often not considered a Father of the Church, but he was undoubtedly an influential early Christian writer and teacher.

21 *Prescription Against the Heretics* 19–21. See also 32.

22 Ibid., 28.

23 Ibid., 36–37.

24 In Colossians, Paul is actually concerned about *syncretism*, the combining of elements of various religions into a kind of New Age philosophy that we refer to as docetism. Docetism was the precursor to gnosticism.

25 *Dei Verbum* 11. See also CCC 102–105.

26 Ibid., 19.

27 Ibid., 24.

28 Compare Matt. 6:19–21 with Sirach 29:10–12; Matt. 7:12 with Tobit 4:15; Matt. 7:16–20 with Sirach 27:6; Matt. 9:36 with Judith 11:19; and Matt. 24:15–16 with I Macc., chapters 1–2 (note especially verses 1:54 and 2:28). Also, the Pharisees' hypothetical test of Jesus in Matt. 22:23–33 seems to be based on a story in Tobit, chapters 3 and 7.

29 The development of the New Testament canon is described in Papandrea, *Reading the Early Church Fathers*, chapter 6, "The New Testament Canon."

30 See, for example, Williams, D. H. *Tradition, Scripture, and Interpretation: A Sourcebook of the Ancient Church* (Grand Rapids: Baker Academic, 2006), 22.

31 See Papandrea, James L., *Trinity 101: Father, Son, Holy Spirit* (Liguori, MO: Liguori Publications, 2012), 17-50.

32 See John 14:25–26, 16:12–15.

33 *Dei Verbum* 8. Cf. 2 Thess. 2:15, Jude 3.

34 Ibid., 8 (see also 10).

35 *Dignitatis Humanae* 1. See also Vincent of Lerins, *Commonitorium* 23:54–58.

36 Deut. 19:14, 27:17, Proverbs 22:28, 23:10.

37 The concept is called *progressive revelation*. See my book, *Reading the Early Church Fathers*, 126–127.

38 CCC 78.

39 CCC 83.

40 *Dei Verbum* 10.

41 Tertullian, *The Chaplet* 3. This is not to imply that in all cases we must interpret Scripture passages in the same way that the early Fathers did. However, where there is consensus on doctrinal issues, and especially where their interpretations were ratified by ecumenical councils, we cannot ignore their conclusions.

42 *Dei Verbum* 12.

43 This was about the same time that the Church was coming to a consensus on which books should make up the New Testament, though it is not true that the Council of Nicaea discussed the issue, or that the emperor Constantine had anything to do with the formation of the canon.

44 Even the great St. Augustine proposed a view of divine election (predestination) which was eventually rejected by the Church; however,

it was taken up again by some of the Protestant Reformers.

45 *Epistle to Diognetus* 11. The passage is quoted, somewhat modified, in Williams, 48.

46 Irenaeus of Lyons, *Against Heresies* 1.10.2–3.

47 Tertullian, *Prescription Against the Heretics* 14.

48 Cyril of Jerusalem, *Catechetical Lectures* 5.12. The passage is quoted, somewhat modified, in Williams, 16.

49 Augustine of Hippo, *Sermon* 212.2, quoted in Williams, 27.

50 Augustine of Hippo, *On Christian Doctrine* 3.2.

51 Vincent of Lerins, *Commonitorium* 2.4–3.8.

52 Gregory of Rome, *Epistle* 1.25.

53 CCC 1030–1031.

54 See Matt. 5:22, 29–30, 10:28, 18:9. For a discussion of the "lake of fire" in the book of Revelation, see my book, *The Wedding of the Lamb: A Historical Approach to the Book of* Rev., 57–59 (especially note 38), 180–187.

55 Dan. 12:10, Mal. 3:1–3. See also John the Baptist's words in Matt. 3:11/Luke 3:16.

56 Prov. 17:3, Isa. 1:25, Mal. 3:3, Wis. 3:1–7, Sir. 2:5. The idea is that the precious metal is heated until it melts, and the impurities would rise to the top of the molten metal, allowing the smith to skim off the impurities, leaving a purified metal.

57 See 1 Pet. 1:7, Rev. 21:27.

58 This was a general consensus among the early Church Fathers. For example, see *Martyrdom of Polycarp* 2, Hermas, *The Shepherd* 24, and *II Clement* 20.

59 See 2 Macc. 12; note especially verses 43–45.

60 CCC 1030–1032

61 Tertullian, *On Monogamy* 10.

62 Tertullian, *The Chaplet* 3, *On the Soul* 35.

63 Cyprian of Carthage, *Epistle* 51.20.

64 St. Augustine went so far as to say that it was wrong to pray for the martyrs; *Sermon* 159.1.

65 Lactantius, *Divine Institutes* 7.21.

66 Cyril of Jerusalem, *Catechetical Lectures* 23.9.

67 Gregory of Nyssa, *Sermon on the Dead*.

68 Augustine of Hippo, *City of God* 21.13. See also Caesarius of Arles, *Sermon* 179.

69 Benedict XVI, *Spe Salvi* 47.

70 N.T. Wright, *The Last Word: Beyond the Bible Wars to a New Understand-*

ing of the Authority of Scripture (San Francisco: HarperCollins, 2005), 67.

71 Wright, 73.

72 See, for example, Williams 16–17.

73 As a case in point, the Catholic Church had already condemned slavery on the basis of both Scripture and Tradition, while many Protestant leaders were continuing to use "Scripture alone" to justify it. In 1435, Pope Eugene IV condemned slavery, on threat of excommunication. In 1537, Pope Paul III condemned the justification for slavery that claimed dark–skinned people were inferior to light skinned people. Some Protestants used Genesis 9:18–27 as a biblical "proof" that dark-skinned people (thought to be the descendants of Ham/Canaan) were ordained by God to be enslaved. For more in this, see Stark, Rodney, The Victory of Reason (New York: Random House, 2006), 26–31.

74 For an example, notice that the doctrine of *sola scriptura* would leave the Church with no way to rule out polygamy. (1 Tim. 3:2, that bishops must be "the husband of one wife" is not about polygamy, but it means that a bishop should not be divorced and remarried. Even if it was a prohibition against polygamy, it would only apply to clergy.) And some Protestants would go on to justify slavery by citing Scripture.

75 See 2 Pet. 3:15–16.

76 This is based on my own experience as a former Protestant pastor, and as one who has spent a significant amount of time in the evangelical Protestant world, as well as having attended "megachurch" services. A Catholic service will have fifteen minutes of Scripture readings before a ten-minute interpretation (a homily that is consistent with the Tradition that has stood the test of time), while many of the so-called megachurches will have just a few minutes of Scripture before a forty-five minute interpretation (which may be a very good Bible study, but it's still the interpretation of one man who is not accountable to any higher, or more time-honored, authority).

77 See 2 Pet. 1:20.

78 Williams, 27.

79 *Dei Verbum* 9–10.

80 CCC 84.

81 CCC 133.

82 See John 1:1–18.

83 *Dei Verbum* 2.

84 See Gal. 1:6–9.

85 See Gal. 2:21, 5:2–4.

86 See Luke 10:38–42.

87 Papandrea, James L., *Spiritual Blueprint: How We Live, Work, Love, Play, and Pray* (Liguori, MO: Liguori Publications, 2010), 89-90.

88 For a detailed treatment of these heresies of the early Church, see my book, *Reading the Early Church Fathers: From the Didache to Nicaea*, 58–82.

89 See 1 John 2:19–23, 4:1–6.

90 See 1 John 2:3–11, 3:14–24.

91 See 1 Cor. 13, Rom. 1:5 (note the expression, "the obedience of faith"), 2:5–16, 1 Thess. 1:3 (note the phrase, "your work of faith"), 2 Thess. 1:11.

92 See Phil. 2:13, John 15:1–5.

93 See Matt. 6:14–15.

94 Papandrea, *Spiritual Blueprint*, vii-xi.

95 See, for example, Justin Martyr, *I Apology* 43, *II Apology* 7, *Dialogue with Trypho* 141 (Justin says that angels also have free will, evidenced by the rebellion of those angels who would become demons, implying that free will is not limited to humanity nor to the *imago dei*), Tatian, *Address to the Greeks* 7, Theophilus of Antioch, *To Autolychus* 2.27, Irenaeus of Lyons, *Against Heresies* 4.37.1–4 (note that Irenaeus here says that free will is part of the image of God).

96 See, for example, Justin Martyr, *I Apology* 44 (quoting Plato, *Republic* 10), Tatian, *Address to the Greeks* 11, Theophilus of Antioch, *To Autolychus* 2.17, 2.25, Clement of Alexandria, *Exhortation to the Greeks* 6 (Clement is also quoting Plato, and affirms that God is only the cause of good things), Hippolytus, *Refutation of All Heresies* 1.16.

97 See, for example, Justin Martyr, *I Apology* 43, Irenaeus of Lyons, *Against Heresies* 4.37.2.

98 See, for example, Justin Martyr, *I Apology* 44, *Dialogue with Trypho* 141, Irenaeus of Lyons, *Against Heresies* 4.29.2, 4.39.4.

99 See John 3:1–8, 1 Pet. 1:22–23. See also CCC 683, 1215, 1266, 1992.

100 See, for example, Hermas, *The Shepherd* 11.5, 93.2, Clement of Alexandria, *Exhortation to the Greeks* 10, *The Instructor* 1.6, Irenaeus of Lyons, *Against Heresies* 1.21.1, *Demonstration of the Apostolic Preaching* 3, 7, Hippolytus, *On the Holy Theophany* 8–10, Cyprian of Carthage, *Epistle* 62.8, 73.7, 75.1, 10–15, Novatian, *De Trinitate* 10.9, *On Purity* 2, and the anonymous, *On Rebaptism* 10.

101 See Hermas, *The Shepherd* 32.4, Irenaeus of Lyons, *Demonstration of the Apostolic Preaching* 3, 42, and the document known as *II Clement* 6.

102 Irenaeus of Lyons, *Demonstration of the Apostolic Preaching* 3, 42

103 See also CCC 978, 1263–1264, 2520.

104 Justin Martyr, *I Apology* 61, Cyprian of Carthage, *Epistle* 54.13, 75.16, *On the Unity of the Catholic Church* 20–21, the *Didascalia Apostolorum* 5, 20, and the anonymous *On Rebaptism* 12.

105 CCC 405, 978, 1263–1264, 2520.

106 See, for example, Hermas, *The Shepherd* 7.1, 33.3, 41, 72.3, Clement of Alexandria, *Who Is the Rich Man That Shall Be Saved?* 39, Irenaeus of Lyons, *Demonstration of the Apostolic Preaching* 42, and the *Didascalia Apostolorum* 5, 20. Baptism was considered the "seal" of the Faith (cf. Rev. 7:3–8), and post-baptismal sin could break the seal, and "evict" the Holy Spirit from one's life. Just as early baptism was preceded by an exorcism to free the baptizand from any demonic presence, post-baptismal sin was thought to "exorcise" the Holy Spirit, leaving the person spiritually void and susceptible to demonic possession (cf. Matt. 12:43–45/Luke 11:24–26). However, this did not mean that the change effected in a Christian by baptism was completely undone, since the Church taught that it was never appropriate to rebaptize. See CCC 1265, 1272, 1274, 1280, 1446. The concept of "deadly" or mortal sin comes from 1 John 5:16–17.

107 Some early Church Fathers, in the time before the formalization of the sacrament of reconciliation, taught that a Christian was only allowed one post-baptismal sin, and after that, the person should be excommunicated. See, for example, Hermas, *The Shepherd* 29.8, 31.6, Clement of Alexandria, *Who Is the Rich Man That Shall Be Saved?* 39, *Miscellanies* 2.13. Although this very rigorist position would not ultimately be accepted by the Church, their point was that a continual pattern of sin and repentance is not much better than having no faith at all, based on Heb. 6:4–6.

108 See Cyprian of Carthage, *Epistle* 51.27. For the early Church Fathers, the worst sins one could commit were teaching heresy or creating schism, adultery, and murder, in that order. Schism came to be considered the worst because it was an offense against Christ's prayer for unity (John 17:20–21), and ironically it was precisely over the issue of how to deal with post-baptismal sin that a schism was created in the third century. Those who split from the majority Church did so over the issue of reconciling sinners, and they were subsequently considered hypocrites for committing the even worse sin of splitting the Church. Adultery is probably considered second only because it was happening more often in the Church than murder, so it was a more present issue.

109 CCC 1861.

110 See, for example, Irenaeus of Lyons, *Against Heresies* 4.15.1, Tertullian did have a list of seven sins that he considered "graver and destructive" (murder, idolatry, fraud, apostasy, blasphemy, adultery, and fornication); however, at other times he indicated that the worst sins were those which broke one of the Ten Commandments. He also seemed to think that the worst sins could not be forgiven, but this was probably due to his Montanist rigorism. See Tertullian, *On Modesty* 19. See also Cyprian of Carthage, *Epistle* 51. Pacian of Barcelona, *Epistle* 3.34, 44–47, defined mortal sins as those sins not yet repented. See the *Catechism of the Catholic Church* 1858.

111 See, for example, Hermas, *The Shepherd* 74.4, 96.1, 103. The sin of apostasy was of immediate concern in times of persecution, when Christians could be required to participate in idolatry, deny the Faith, or even curse Christ to save their lives. However, the Church would eventually conclude that even this sin could be forgiven.

112 Often the persecutors would require participation in pagan sacrifice as proof that a person has rejected Christianity. For a description of persecution in the early Church, see my book, *Reading the Early Church Fathers* 10–17, 156–183.

113 See, for an early example, Hermas, *The Shepherd* 72. That teaching a heresy is a mortal sin was a universal assumption among the early Church Fathers, and so it would be impossible to cite them all here.

114 See 1 John 5:16.

115 See 1 Cor. 5:13. See also the *Didache* 15.3.

116 *Didascalia Apostolorum* 10–11, 23, *On Rebaptism* 13.

117 See, for example, Justin Martyr, *I Apology* 16. Cf. also Matt. 12:31–32/Mark 3:28–29 (the blasphemy of the Holy Spirit), Luke 8:13, 22:32 (Peter's faith could, and did, fail), Rom. 11:22 (a person can be "cut off"), 1 Cor. 9:27, 10:11–12, 15:1–2 (even Paul worried that he could be disqualified), Gal. 5:4, Heb. 10:26–31, 1 Pet. 2:20–21. Some even wondered, on the basis of Heb. 6:4–6, whether the Christian who committed a mortal sin should be reconciled at all.

118 Polycarp of Smyrna, Letter to the Philippians 11; Ignatius of Antioch, Letter to the Philadelphians 3–4, 7. Since the authority to excommunicate rested with the bishop, the authority to reconcile also rested with the bishop.

119 Ignatius of Antioch, Letter to the Philadelphians 3.

120 CCC 1430.

HANDED DOWN

121 CCC 980, 1426.

122 Polycarp of Smyrna, Letter to the Philippians 10.2.

123 *Epistle of Barnabas* 19.10. As in the New Testament, the word "ransom" is used in the sense of freedom, or manumission. It does not imply a ransom theory of atonement in which humanity is held captive by Satan.

124 Clement of Alexandria, *The Instructor* 3.12. Clement says he is quoting Scripture here, but it is unclear what passage he has in mind.

125 Irenaeus of Lyons, *Against Heresies* 4.12.5.

126 For example, see Hermas, *The Shepherd* 66.4–5.

127 *II Clement* 16.4.

128 Ibid., Cf. Cyprian of Carthage, *On the Lapsed* 35. Some advocated combining fasting with almsgiving. The money saved on food from fasting should be given to the hungry. Hermas, *The Shepherd* 56, *Didascalia Apostolorum* 19.

129 See also Prov. 10:12, which Peter may be quoting.

130 See, for example, Hermas, *The Shepherd* 50–51. Also, see Helen Rhee's excellent book, *Loving the Poor, Saving the Rich: Wealth, Poverty, and Early Christian Formation.*

131 See Matt. 19:24–26.

132 Clement of Alexandria, *Who Is the Rich Man That Shall Be Saved?* 13–14, 26.

133 Clement of Alexandria, *The Instructor* 2.3, 3.6, *Who Is the Rich Man That Shall Be Saved?* 31. See also the *Didache* 4.8, which says that everything we have is a gift from God, and ultimately belongs to God.

134 Clement of Alexandria, *Who Is the Rich Man That Shall Be Saved?* 33. See also Hermas, *The Shepherd* 27.4. However, the *Didascalia Apostolorum* 4 does say that the lazy and drunken do not deserve to receive alms, but this document seems to be in the minority on that point. To avoid scandal and abuse, the *Didascalia Apostolorum* 9, 14, also advised that alms were to be given to the Church (to the bishop) for fair distribution. This did, in fact, become the standard practice in the early Church.

135 See Cyprian of Carthage, *Epistle* 51.22. Cf. CCC 1426.

136 See Matt. 10:22, 24:13. Jesus' comments here are in the context of his prediction of coming persecution of Christians.

137 Clement of Alexandria, *Who Is the Rich Man That Shall Be Saved?* 1, 3.

138 See CCC 1437, 1446, 1468–1469.

139 Justin Martyr, *I Apology* 12, 16. Clement of Alexandria wrote that salvation may be bought back with "love and living faith." Clement

of Alexandria, *Exhortation to the Greeks* 9. Irenaeus of Lyons said that while everyone is a child of God by nature, not everyone is a child of God "with respect to obedience and doctrine," meaning that belief alone is not enough to make one a child of God. Irenaeus of Lyons, *Against Heresies* 4.41.2. See also Cyprian of Carthage, *Epistle* 54.13, *On the Lapsed* 17, 19, and the anonymous, *Against Novatian* 10, 14, 18. Note that suffering could also be a form of penance under the right circumstances. *II Clement* 20.1–2. Cf. 1 Pet. 4:12–19.

140 Cyprian of Carthage, *Epistle* 58.1. See CCC 1437, 1446, 1468–1469.

141 Pacian of Barcelona, *Epistle* 3.18.

142 Clement of Alexandria, *Who Is the Rich Man That Shall Be Saved?* 8. Many of the early writers believed that pre–Christian Jews who followed the law would be saved, but not by the law itself, rather through Christ, because they put their hope in their future Messiah. On this, see, Justin Martyr, *Dialogue with Trypho* 45, and Irenaeus of Lyons, *Against Heresies* 4.22.2, 4.27.2, 4.33.1.

143 For a detailed treatment of the persecutions and its effects on the Church, see my books *Novatian of Rome and the Culmination of Pre-Nicene Orthodoxy*, 47–70, and, *Reading the Early Church Fathers*, 10–17, 156–183.

144 See CCC 1459. Penance can "make satisfaction" for sin, in the sense of repairing the damage done by the sin. For example, if one steals, it is not enough to confess the sin of theft, one must also give back whatever was stolen.

145 Augustine of Hippo, *On the Spirit and the Letter* 7, 60.

146 Ibid., 4, 25, 52, 54.

147 Ibid., 5.

148 Ibid., 38. For Augustine, grace is irresistible because it is the offer that can't be refused. In a version of the Roman patron-client system, God becomes the patron offering a gift (salvation) which the clients (elect humans) cannot refuse. However, this creates another problem, in that if anyone is thought to be among the elect, but then is finally not saved (perhaps a Church member who becomes an apostate and never repents), the only explanation is the awkward argument that the person must not have been truly among the elect in the first place. Election, then, becomes defined by perseverance. All the elect must persevere, but if someone does not persevere, he must not have been among the elect after all.

149 John Cassian, *Conferences* 13.16–17.

150 Ibid., 13.7.

151 CCC 154–155. Cf. Matt. 22:1–14, the Parable of the Wedding Banquet.

See also Rom. 10:9, John 1:11–13. All are invited, but the invitation requires a response, an RSVP. See Papandrea, *Spiritual Blueprint*, 95.

152 CCC 1033.

153 Cf. Matt. 8:5–13.

154 Although Augustine wrote favorably about free will early in his career, the controversy with Pelagius pushed him to all but deny it in his later works. His conclusions on election and perseverance were finally rejected by the Church at the Council of Orange in 529.

155 The charge is sometimes leveled against Protestants who presume that a conversion experience guarantees perseverance, and that they will be saved no matter what they do. This is a form of cheap grace based on the "once saved always saved" doctrine of perseverance, or as it is sometimes called, "altar call and that's all." However, Catholics exhibit their own version of cheap grace if they believe that their salvation is guaranteed by their baptism and they can just go through the motions. In this sense, they have bought into the misunderstanding of baptismal regeneration that includes perseverance. Both versions of cheap grace do not take into account the reality of post-baptismal sin and the possibility of the loss of salvation.

156 CCC 1033, 1816.

157 Happily, the 1999 *Joint Declaration on the Doctrine of Justification,* by the Lutheran World Federation and the Catholic Church, shows how far Catholics and many Protestants (not limited to Lutherans) have come toward agreement on many important points related to faith and works. Here are a few excerpts:

Together we confess: By grace alone, in faith in Christ's saving work and not because of any merit on our part, we are accepted by God and receive the Holy Spirit, who renews our hearts while equipping and calling us to good works.

Faith is itself God's gift through the Holy Spirit who works through word and sacrament in the community of believers and who, at the same time, leads believers into that renewal of life which God will bring to completion in eternal life.

We confess together that good works—a Christian life lived in faith, hope, and love—follow justification and are its fruits.

158 Tertullian, *On Idolatry* 19, where Tertullian says, "There is no agreement between the divine and human sacrament, the standard of Christ, and the standard of the devil, the camp of light and the camp of darkness." His point is to contrast the sacraments of the Church

with the "sacred oaths" of the pagan cults, including those associated with military service.

159 For example, see Tertullian, *On the Military Crown* (*De Corona*) 11.

160 Irenaeus of Lyons, *Demonstration of the Apostolic Preaching* 100. Irenaeus calls the three persons of the Trinity in the Trinitarian formula, the "three articles of our seal."

161 See Rev. 7:1–8. See also Papandrea, James L., *The Wedding of the Lamb: A Historical Approach to the Book of Revelation* (Eugene, OR: Pickwick Publications, 2011), chapter 10, "Jesus Saw it Coming – The Gospels and Revelation."

162 Novatian, *On the Trinity* 19.12. See also 19.16–20, where Novatian says that the crossing of Jacob's arms in his blessing was a sacred mystery that foreshadowed the cross of Christ. Novatian said that the Old Testament prophecies that were fulfilled by Jesus Christ were sacred mysteries, and called their fulfillment "incarnate truth" (*corporatae veritatis*). *On the Trinity* 9.2.

163 Ibid., 1.13.

164 *Sacrosanctum Concilium* 3.59.

165 For example, see Ignatius of Antioch, Letter to the Ephesians 20.2, where Ignatius refers to the sacrament as the "medicine of eternal life."

166 See 2 Cor. 12:9–10.

167 See Ignatius of Antioch, Letter to the Smyrnaeans 9. Also note that Church discipline was connected to the sacraments, so that *excommunication* meant to be *excluded* from *communion*, as well as the other sacraments. The bishops also had to oversee Church discipline because, in order to maintain unity, a person excommunicated by one bishop could not simply go to another bishop to receive the sacraments. Such a practice would inevitably lead to division in the Church.

168 CCC 1671–1674, 1680–1690.

169 CCC 1670. See also *Sacrosanctum Concilium* 3.60.

170 See Matt. 9:6, 16:19, John 20:23.

171 See John 2:1–11. Cf. also Matt. 19:4–6.

172 See Matt. 26:6–13/Mark 14:3–9/John 12:1–8.

173 Cyprian of Carthage, *Epistle* 71.1. Cf. Acts 10:47, 19:2. See also John 3:5–6. Some early Church Fathers interpreted the phrase "water and the Spirit" to refer to the two parts of baptism, or baptism and confirmation.

174 Tertullian, *On Baptism* 6–8, excerpts. See also 9–10.

175 CCC 1290. In the Eastern Orthodox churches, baptism and confirmation are still one rite, and even infants who are baptized are im-

268   HANDED DOWN

mediately confirmed.

176 *Didache* 14.1, italics added for emphasis. See also *Didache* 4.

177 All seven sacraments are affirmed by the medieval scholastic Peter Lombard, in the twelfth century. See Peter Lombard, *Sentences*, Book 4. Then they were all affirmed by the Church councils of Florence (in 1439) and Trent (1545–1563).

178 See, for example, Tertullian, *On Baptism* 8.

179 Cyprian of Carthage, *Epistle* 75.15. See also CCC 1219, 1221.

180 Matt. 28:19, Acts 2:37–41. Acts 16:30 does not mention baptism, though it is clearly assumed as the next step after belief. See also CCC 1223.

181 *Didache* 7, Justin Martyr, *I Apology* 61, Irenaeus of Lyons, *Demonstration of the Apostolic Preaching* 100, Tertullian, *On Baptism* 15. Alternative formulas such as, "Creator, Redeemer, Sustainer," are invalid and do not constitute a baptism. According to the Congregation for the Doctrine of the Faith, February 2008, alternative baptismal formulas (including Mormon baptism, which uses the right words but with a different intended meaning) are not valid. The issue is important because anyone wishing to come into the Catholic Church from a denomination that baptizes using alternative formulae would be considered not to have been baptized, and would have to be baptized as part of their initiation. See Papandrea, James L., *Trinity 101: Father, Son, Holy Spirit* (Liguori, MO: Liguori Publications, 2012), 88–90.

182 *Didache* 7.1–3. See also Tertullian, *On Baptism* 4.

183 See Clement of Alexandria, *Exhortation to the Greeks* 10, Cyprian of Carthage, *Epistle* 75.12.

184 *Apostolic Constitutions* 1, 7, CCC 1241–1242. On anointing associated with baptism, see Tertullian, *On Baptism* 7, Basil of Caesarea, *On the Holy Spirit* 12.28, John Chrysostom, *Baptismal Instructions* 2, and the anonymous *Didascalia Apostolorum* 16, and *Apostolic Constitutions* 7.

185 Tatian, *To the Greeks* 19, Tertullian, *On the Military Crown (De Corona)* 23, (Pseudo) Hippolytus, *Apostolic Tradition* 20–21, *Didascalia Apostolorum* 26, John Chrysostom, *Baptismal Instructions* 2. Cf. Matt. 13:43–45.

186 *Didache* 7.4, Justin Martyr, *I Apology* 61, Tertullian, *On Baptism* 20, (Pseudo) Hippolytus, *Apostolic Tradition* 20, and the anonymous *Apostolic Constitutions* 7.2.22.

187 When a woman was baptized, a deaconess would assist her as she went through the water naked, while the bishop waited on the other side of a curtain.

188 Tertullian, *On Baptism* 8, *Apostolic Tradition* 19, 21, John Chrysostom, *Baptismal Instructions* 2.

189 *Apostolic Tradition* 21.

190 For example, see Tertullian, *On Baptism* 4–7. For the anointing, see the *Didascalia Apostolorum* 16.

191 See Titus 3:5, CCC 1215.

192 CCC 1293.

193 Cyprian of Carthage, *Epistle* 58.4.

194 See Eph. 4:4–6, Irenaeus of Lyons, *Demonstration of the Apostolic Preaching* 24.

195 CCC 1271, italics from the original.

196 See 1 Pet. 2:5, 9, Rev. 1:6. CCC 1268.

197 See 1 Cor. 6:19.

198 See John 1:12–13, 2 Cor. 5:17, Novatian, *On the Trinity* 10.9, CCC 1265.

199 See Rom. 6:3–4, Hermas, *The Shepherd* 93, Augustine of Hippo, *Handbook on Faith, Hope, and Love* 42. See also CCC 1214.

200 *II Clement* 7–8, Hermas, *The Shepherd* 72, 93, Melito of Sardis, *Homily on the Passover* 16–17, Clement of Alexandria, *Exhortation to the Greeks* 11, Irenaeus of Lyons, *Demonstration of the Apostolic Preaching* 3, 24, 100, Cyprian of Carthage, *Epistle* 72.9, Eusebius of Caesarea, *Ecclesiastical History* 6.5. See also CCC 1272, 1274.

201 *Apostolic Tradition* 20, 42. To cross oneself in the early Church probably meant making the sign of the cross on the forehead with the thumb of the right hand.

202 *Apostolic Tradition* 42. If the exorcism before a baptism cleans the house of the soul, the baptism itself seals the soul against the return of any demons, cf. Matt. 13:43–45.

203 For example, Cyprian of Carthage, *On the Unity of the Catholic Church* 18. See Deut. 6:4–9, 11:18. Cf. Matt. 23:5.

204 Tertullian, *On Baptism* 18. Tertullian went on to say, "If any understand the weighty import of baptism, they will fear its reception more than its delay."

205 *Apostolic Tradition* 17. Eventually, the catechumenate was divided into two phases: the first phase when the candidates for baptism were called auditors (*audientes*), consisting of an examination of one's life and readiness, which could take years; and the second phase when the candidates were called catechumens (*competentes*), which began with an enrollment at the beginning of Lent, and continued up to the baptism at the Easter Vigil. On this enrollment, or "election," see

Apostolic Tradition 20.

206 Normally, baptism is considered necessary for salvation; however, in cases where baptism is not possible, the desire for baptism counts. See CCC 1257–1259. This is because God is merciful and does not wish to see anyone excluded from salvation due to circumstances beyond his control (see 1 Pet. 3:9). In fact, the CCC states, "Every man who is ignorant of the gospel of Christ and of his Church, but seeks the truth and does the will of God in accordance with his understanding of it, can be saved. It may be supposed that such persons would have *desired baptism explicitly* if they had known its necessity" (1260, italics in the original). Note that infants who die without baptism are also entrusted to God's mercy (1261). This is because baptism, as well as every other sacrament, is a work of God, not a work of humans. So as long as a baptism is done in the name of the *right* God, that is the Tri-une God—Father, Son, and Holy Spirit—with valid matter (water), other factors cannot invalidate the baptism, not even grave sin or lack of faith on the part of the presider. In fact, in an emergency situation, anyone can perform a valid baptism—it doesn't have to be clergy, and technically speaking, it doesn't even have to be a Christian, as long as the person performing the baptism uses the correct formula, and has the right intentions (CCC 1256).

207 Cyprian of Carthage, *Epistle* 64.2.

208 See Matt. 9:18–26/Mark 5:21–43/Luke 8:40–56. See also the similar story of the centurion's servant, Matt.8:5–13/Luke 7:1–10, as well as Matt. 15:22–28/Mark 7:24–30, Matt. 17:14–21/Mark 9:14–29/Luke 9:37–43.

209 See Acts 16:25–34.

210 See Acts 16:33.

211 See Tertullian, *On Baptism* 18. Tertullian is concerned that baptizing a person who is not ready (and then who could potentially fall back into sin) could have negative implications for the salvation of the sponsors, who have pledged their faith for the person who was baptized.

212 Augustine of Hippo, *On Baptism Against the Donatists* 4.24.31.

213 Cyprian of Carthage, *On the Lapsed* 9.

214 Cyprian of Carthage, *Epistle* 58.6.

215 CCC 1231, 1298. On pre-baptismal catechesis, see *Didache* 7, *Apostolic Tradition* 17–18.

216 Part of the reason that baptism is considered necessary for salvation is

that it removes original sin. While it is beyond the scope of the present book to enter into a detailed discussion of original sin, suffice it to say that original sin is a concept held by the Church Fathers long before St. Augustine (who is often credited with—or blamed for—inventing it). See CCC 1250. Baptism is not technically required for salvation, if the lack of baptism was beyond a person's control, or not due to a rejection or postponement of baptism. Like the "good thief," who had faith and the right intention, those who died without the chance for baptism (such as martyrs) were considered still within God's grace. See Cyprian of Carthage, *Epistle* 72.22.

217 CCC 1266.

218 Cyprian of Carthage, *Epistle* 58.5–6.

219 See the *Didascalia Apostolorum* 10, 24, 26. The author(s) of the *Didascalia* worried that rebaptism could undo the original baptism, leaving the person, not baptized twice, but rather not baptized at all. Although this is not the teaching of the Church today (because baptism cannot be undone), it is still considered heretical and an act of schism to rebaptize. See also CCC 1280. For more on this controversy, see Papandrea, *Reading the Early Church Fathers*, 168-175, and *Trinity 101*, 88-90.

220 See CCC 1288–1289.

221 Ambrose of Milan, *On the Mysteries* 7.42. CCC 1302.

222 *On Rebaptism* 3, 12, 17, Cyprian of Carthage, *Epistle* 71.1, 73.7, 75.1, 10, 15. Cyprian went so far as to imply that the Holy Spirit was not received by the person in baptism, but in confirmation. See also Tertullian, *On Baptism* 6–10.

223 Innocent I of Rome, *Epistle to Victricius* 9.

224 *On Rebaptism* 3, Cyprian of Carthage, *Epistle* 72.9.

225 Tertullian, *Prescription Against Heretics* 36, and cf. 40, where Tertullian uses the phrase, "the administrations of Christ's sacraments." See CCC 1295.

226 See John 3:5, *On Rebaptism* 17.

227 Cyprian of Carthage, *Epistle* 71.1, 72.21, 75.1, 10, 15. Cyprian refers to baptism and confirmation as the "dual sacrament," which shows that to a certain extent they were still thought of as two parts of one initiation. Confirmation itself is not required for salvation, as evidenced by cases in which people were baptized as infants, but died before their confirmation. See *On Rebaptism* 4, 11.

228 CCC 1322.

229 CCC 1304.

230 See Gen. 14:18, Exod. 16–17.

231 For example, see Cyprian of Carthage, *Epistle* 62. Cf. Matt. 14:13–21/Mark 6:30–44/Luke 9:10–17, Matt. 15:32–39/Mark 8:1–10, John 2:1–11.

232 See John 6.

233 Ignatius of Antioch, Letter to the Ephesians 20.

234 Clement of Alexandria, *Instructor* 2.1–2.

235 CCC 1424.

236 *Didache* 14.1, Cyprian of Carthage, *Epistle* 9.2, 10.1. For Cyprian, to receive the Eucharist "unworthily" (1 Cor. 11:27–28) meant receiving without an examination of conscience and confession of sins.

237 Tertullian, *On Baptism* 19.

238 Ignatius of Antioch, Letter to the Philadelphians 3, 8. See also CCC 1469.

239 Jas. 5:15–16.

240 See 2 Cor. 5:18–20. See also CCC 1442.

241 CCC 1443.

242 See Irenaeus of Lyons, *Against Heresies* 1.13.5, Tertullian, *On Baptism* 19, Cyprian of Carthage, *Epistle* 45.2.

243 *Didascalia Apostolorum* 7, 10. Cyprian of Carthage, *Epistle* 9.2, 11.2.

244 CCC 1430.

245 CCC 1490.

246 Ambrose of Milan, *Epistle* 41.12.

247 *Didascalia Apostolorum* 6–7.

248 CCC 1423.

249 Phil. 2:12. CCC 1431, 1435.

250 CCC 1459.

251 CCC 1435, 1460.

252 Cyprian of Carthage, *On the Lapsed* 35. See also Polycarp, Letter to the Philippians 10, *II Clement* 16, and the *Didascalia Apostolorum* 19. On almsgiving as a penance, cf. Tobit 4:10, 1 Pet. 4:8.

253 See Matt. 16:19, John 20:22–23. CCC 1445, 1448.

254 CCC 1441–1442, 1461.

255 *Didascalia Apostolorum* 6. Origen, *Homily on Leviticus, Against Celsus* 6.

256 Pacian of Barcelona, *Epistle* 1.11–14, 3.17.

257 CCC 1436–1437.

258 Novatian, *Epistle* 1.7. Eventually, the western (Catholic) Church would follow the lead of Celtic priests who were using penitentials: books that outlined standardized penance for a wide variety of sins. This was an attempt to bring consistency (the same sin got the same

penance every time) and fairness (a priest could not play favorites and give his friends a lighter penance).

259 Cyprian of Carthage, *Epistle* 58.1, 71.2. See also *Lumen Gentium* 2.4.

260 See 1 John 1:8–10.

261 See John 21:15–19.

262 *Against Novatian* 8. See also Pacian of Barcelona, *Epistle* 3.24–25. See also CCC 1429.

263 Cyprian of Carthage, *Epistle* 54.13, *On the Lapsed* 15. See also Eusebius of Caesarea, *Ecclesiastical History* 6.42.

264 CCC 1447.

265 CCC 1603.

266 See also CCC 1605.

267 See John 2:1–11, CCC 1601, 1613.

268 See Eph. 5:25–32. Cf. Clement of Alexandria, *The Instructor* 1.4.

269 Hugh of St. Victor, *On the Sacraments of the Christian Faith* 13.

270 CCC 1601, 1613.

271 There were Roman laws against adultery, but this was an attempt to curb a decline in the number of "legitimate" children that the aristocratic classes were producing. The laws were neither followed nor enforced, except as a way to persecute one's enemies.

272 Judith Evans Grubbs, "'Pagan' and 'Christian' Marriage: The State of the Question," in *Early Christian Studies* 2 (1994), 365, 375.

273 CCC 1626, 1628. See also Lactantius, *Divine Institutes* 6.23.23–30, quoted in Grubbs, 397–398.

274 Christians were discouraged from marrying non-Christians. See Hermas, *The Shepherd* 29 (Mandate/Commandment 4.1), and Tertullian, *To His Wife* 2. Nevertheless, such mixed marriages were probably common; Grubbs, 403.

275 Ignatius of Antioch, Letter to Polycarp 5. See also Clement of Alexandria, *The Instructor* 3.63.1, and Tertullian, *On Monogamy* 11.1.

276 Hunter, David, G., "Augustine and the Making of Marriage in Roman North Africa," in *Journal of Early Christian Studies* 11:1 (2003), 71. The Church father in question is Tertullian, who wrote of the Church affirming a marriage, though it is not clear what he means by "affirming." The word is variously translated as "cementing," "arranging," "contracting," or "sealing." Based on the evidence we have, it seems unlikely that the Church arranged marriages, though it is possible that Christian clergy facilitated the unions of couples who desired to be married.

277 Tertullian, *On Modesty* 4. Here Tertullian criticizes secret affairs (relationships not announced in the Church) as the same as adultery.

278 For example, see Tertullian, *On Idolatry* 16.3, *On the Military Crown* (*De Corona*) 13.4, and canons 53–54 of the Council of Laodicea (363/364). Cf. Grubbs 389.

279 John Chrysostom, *Homily 12 on* Col. *4:18* in *St. John Chrysostom: On Marriage and Family Life*, trans. Catharine P. Roth and David Anderson, (Crestwood, NY: St Vladimir's Seminary Press, 1986), pp. 79–80.

280 Hunter, 63, 69. Emperor Constantine instituted laws to make divorce more difficult, but he did not repeal the laws against marriage across social class lines; Grubbs 386–387.

281 Jesus himself had compared eternal life in the kingdom of God to a wedding reception. See the parable of the wedding banquet, Matt. 22:1–14.

282 Hunter, 73.

283 In the Western Church, the couple are the ordinary ministers of matrimony, conferring and receiving the sacrament themselves.

284 John Chrysostom, *Homilies on Col. 12*, Augustine of Hippo, *On Original Sin* 39, 42. Augustine calls matrimony the *connubii sacramentum*, the sacrament of marriage.

285 CCC 1614, 1640. Although an annulment is possible, the annulment, technically speaking, assumes that the conditions for a proper sacramental union were not met by the first marriage. CCC 1629.

286 The early Church Fathers discouraged second marriages, even for widows and widowers. See Justin Martyr, *I Apology* 1.15, Athenagoras, *A Plea for the Christians* 33, Hermas, *The Shepherd* 32 (Mandate/Commandment 4.4), Clement of Alexandria, *The Miscellanies* 1.82, and Tertullian, *To His Wife*. Some bishops allowed second marriages for lay people but not for clergy (cf. 1 Tim. 3:2), while others held even lay people to this standard. Some bishops allowed divorced people to remarry, while others called remarriage after divorce a form of adultery (cf. Matt. 5:31–32). See also my *Spiritual Blueprint*, 56–65.

287 CCC 1609.

288 Matrimony also participates in creation by being open to new life. It is only within marriage that God's command to "be fruitful and multiply" can be fulfilled (Gen. 1:28). CCC 1643, 1652. Beginning with Clement of Alexandria, Christian teachers have said that sex, even within marriage, was for procreation only. See Clement of Alexandria, *The Instructor* 2.10. This was in response to gnostic groups who celebrated sex in any context, but taught that procreation was

to be avoided. Not all early Christians took this strict approach, for example, see Lactantius, *Divine Institutes* 6.23.25–26. Still, the early Church Fathers were unanimous that the union of marriage exists primarily for having children. See Athenagoras, *A Plea for the Christians* 33, and the anonymous *Apostolic Constitutions* 6.5 (6.28). Thus the Church has concluded that the marital union must be open to life or it is diminished, and Lactantius went so far as to say that if a couple cannot afford another child, they should remain celibate. This was to prevent the possibility that a child might be aborted, discarded (exposed), or sold into slavery. It should go without saying that the Church has always taught that sex is only appropriate within the context of marriage (1 Cor. 6:15–20). The requirement that a union must be at least potentially procreative is part of the rationale behind the Church's insistence that matrimony must be between a man and a woman.

289 In the early Church, the vocation of matrimony was sometimes held to be a lesser calling than the celibate life. For example, see Novatian, *On Purity* 7. Cf. 1 Cor. 7:5–9. However, John Chrysostom described matrimony as a pleasure without a downside. See John Chrysostom, *Homilies on* Matt. 37.9. Cf. 1 Cor. 7:5. Eventually, the Catholic Church has acknowledged that the vocation of matrimony is not less important than, or any kind of concession from, the vocation of celibacy or ordination. Both vocations are equally valid, and equally spiritual. Both vocations contribute equally (though differently) to the spiritual growth of Christians, to the mission of the Church, and to the well-being of the world.

290 John Chrysostom, *Homilies on* Eph. 20. Note that when Chrysostom says, "our life together," he is not referring to the home life of husband and wife (since he was celibate), but to the life of the Christian community.

291 Acts 1:21–26, 6:3–6, 13:2–3, 14:23, 1 Cor. 4:17, 1 Thess. 3:2.

292 Acts 13:2–3, Titus 1:5f. Cf. CCC 1590. Note that at this early stage, the words for priest (*presbyter*) and bishop (*episkopos*, or "overseer") are interchangeable. While the apostles were still alive, they served the function that we now associate with bishops (overseers of churches in certain regions), and the local pastors were under their authority. It is acknowledged that the authorship of the pastoral epistles is a matter of perennial debate; however, it must also be acknowledged that it was not a matter of debate in the early Church. Those who

lived in close chronological proximity to the letters themselves did not question their Pauline authorship.

293 See Num. 8:10, 27:15–23, 1 Sam. 16:11–13, Acts 13:2–3.

294 Augustine of Hippo, *Answers to the Letters of Petilian the Donatist* 2.30 (69), *On the Gospel of John* 5.15.

295 CCC 1538, 1592.

296 *Apostolic Tradition* 4, Bradshaw, 22–24, 30–32.

297 *Apostolic Tradition* 10, 28.

298 CCC 1582–1583.

299 *Apostolic Tradition* 2. At first, the priests of a city elected their bishop, by choosing one of their own to represent and lead them; later the bishops of neighboring cities elected their colleague, by choosing one of the local priests to join their ranks. Since the bishops held the authority to determine who could preside (authority delegated to the priests) it was considered more appropriate that the ones who had that authority should elect who would be given the authority. In some places, the election was ratified by the laity, when the newly elected bishop was announced and acclaimed in a special liturgy. See Cyprian of Carthage, *Epistle* 40.2, 51.8, 54.5–6, and the *Apostolic Church Order* 16.

300 This is the letter known as *I Clement*.

301 Ignatius of Antioch, Letter to the Ephesians 5–6, Translation in Holmes, 187. Cf. also 2, 20. See Papandrea, *Reading the Early Church Fathers*, 24–27.

302 Ignatius of Antioch, Letter to the Smyrnaeans 8–9, Translation in Holmes, 255–257 (slightly modified for clarity). See also Letter to the Magnesians 3, 6–7, *Letter to the Trallians* 2–3, 7, Letter to the Philadelphians 4, 7, Letter to Polycarp 6.

303 See Phil. 1:1, 1 Tim. 3:1–13. 1 Timothy 5:17 demonstrates that the terms bishop and priest were interchangeable, as it mentions "priests who preside." There were also deaconesses, whose ministry it was to assist women in baptism and to visit in homes where there were no chaperones. 1 Timothy 3:11 probably refers to deaconesses.

304 See, for example, Ignatius of Antioch, Letter to the Trallians 3, Letter to Polycarp 6. By the end of the second century, Irenaeus of Lyons could refer to the "order of presbyters," or priesthood. See Irenaeus of Lyons, Against Heresies 4.26.1. CCC 1536.

305 Justin Martyr, *I Apology* 67.

306 Tertullian, *Prescription Against the Heretics* 41.

307 On the difference between vocation and occupation, see my *Spiritual*

Blueprint, 1–6.

308 The early Church Fathers did not use the word "clergy," which is of course an English word. The term has the same root as the word "clerk," and it comes from a more recent time when it was assumed that the clergy were often the only people in town who could read and write. In the early Church, by contrast, it was possible that a bishop or priest might not be literate. In that case, a designated lector would read the scriptures in worship, and a secretary would take dictation for correspondence. To the early Church Fathers, it was more important that a bishop not be divorced and remarried. See the *Didascalia Apostolorum* 4. Eventually, of course, it would be considered important that clergy be educated in a special way, which becomes somewhat formalized in the Middle Ages.

309 Bradshaw, Paul F. *Ordination Rites of the Ancient Churches of East and West* (New York: Pueblo, 1990), 18.

310 CCC 1534.

311 CCC 1558.

312 For the early Church Fathers, to oppose the bishop was the very definition of schism. See Ignatius of Antioch, Letter to the Magnesians 7.1, Letter to the Trallians 2.2, 3.1, Letter to the Ephesians 5.2–3, Letter to the Philadelphians 2.2, 7.2, Letter to the Smyrnaeans 8.1–2, 9.1. Eventually, they would face the problem of disputes between bishops, but as that problem arose, so did the authority of the bishop of Rome as the "bishop of bishops."

313 Ignatius of Antioch, Letter to the Magnesians 6.2, Letter to the Ephesians 5.3, 6.1, Letter to the Philadelphians 8.1.

314 CCC 1555, 1576. In the early Church, it was possible for a deacon to be elected bishop, "skipping over" the level of priest. In that case, the deacon would then be ordained priest and consecrated bishop all at once.

315 Jerome, *Epistle* 146.1.1–6.

316 CCC 1564.

317 Irenaeus of Lyons, *Against Heresies* 4.32.

318 See 1 Pet. 1:20. See also Polycarp, Letter to the Philippians 7, where he urges his audience to trust what was handed down to them rather than risk heresy.

319 See John Chrysostom, *Homily on Pentecost* 1.

320 CCC 1548–1550. Because the bishop or priest takes on the role of Bridegroom to the Church as Bride, this is one of the reasons that Catholic ordination is reserved for men. CCC 1577. It is also impor-

tant to note that the early Christian tradition of a male-only priesthood was in part a reaction against schismatic or heretical groups
who did allow women to preside in their liturgies. One such situation is described by Irenaeus of Lyons, *Against Heresies* 1.13.2. In
that case, certain gnostics used women as assistants in a ritual that
mimicked Christian Eucharist, but made it seem like a magic trick.

321 CCC 1515.

322 CCC 1554.

323 CCC 1570–1571.

324 See 1 Pet. 2:5, 9, Rev. 1:6.

325 CCC 1535, 1538.

326 CCC 1580. Note that even in the east, a priest who is unmarried
when he is ordained cannot marry later but must remain celibate.

327 See 1 Cor. 7:7–9.

328 Siricius of Rome, at a Synod of Rome, A.D. 386 (the same year as St.
Augustine's conversion to Christianity).

329 Nevertheless, it is true that the inheritances of clergy children created
problems for the Church (and the nobility) in the Middle Ages, resulting in a renewed effort to enforce the expectation of clergy celibacy.

330 See 1 Cor. 4:15, Philem. 10.

331 See Jas. 5:14–15, CCC 1503, 1506–1510.

332 CCC 1531.

333 Origen, *Homilies on Leviticus* 2.4, *Sacramentary of Serapion* 29.1.

334 John Chrysostom, *On the Priesthood* 3.6.

335 Anointing is considered a sacrament at the Second Council of Constantinople, in 553. It was affirmed along with the other sacraments
at the councils of Florence (1439) and Trent.

336 Matt. 26:6–13/Mark 14:3–9/John 12:1–8.

337 CCC 1517, 1524, 1532.

338 CCC 1514–1515. See also *Sacrosanctum Concilium* 3.73–74.

339 CCC 1521, 1532.

340 CCC 1520.

341 See *Sacrosanctum Concilium* 3.61.

342 CCC 1211, quoting Thomas Aquinas.

343 See Rom. 12:4–5, 1 Cor. 12:12–26, Eph. 1:22–23, 5:29–32, Col.
1:18, 3:15.

344 CCC 1396.

345 CCC 1329, see also Matt. 26:26–29/Mark 14:22–25/Luke 22:15–20,
and 1 Cor. 11:23–30.

346 Matt. 26:29, Mark 14:22–25, Luke 22:15–20.
347 1 Cor. 10:16–17, see also CCC 1334.
348 Luke 22:19, 1 Cor. 11:23–26.
349 Num. 10:10.
350 Acts 2:46.
351 See also CCC 1341–1342.
352 See Matt. 22:1–14.
353 CCC 1326, 1329, 1335, 1402–1403.
354 CCC 1392.
355 CCC 1331.
356 See also Matt. 25:1–13, Eph. 5:23–32.
357 See 1 Cor. 10:16–17, 1 John 4:13. See also Lanfranc of Canterbury, *On the Body and Blood of the Lord* 17.
358 Heb. 12:1–2. Note that the Mass can be offered for those who have passed away, *Didascalia Apostolorum* 26, CCC 1371, 1414.
359 CCC 1354.
360 CCC 1328.
361 Jesus "took bread, and after he had given thanks, broke it and said, 'This is my body that is for you. Do this in remembrance of me.' In the same way also the cup, after supper, saying, 'This cup is the new covenant in my blood. Do this, as often as you drink it, in remembrance of me'" (1 Cor. 11:23–25).
362 The church order document known as the *Apostolic Tradition* also mentions the presence of cheese, olives, and even flowers on the table. *Apostolic Tradition* 5, 32.
363 *Didascalia Apostolorum* 26.6.22. Although the Church did not make a practice of having regular worship services in the catacombs, it is probably the case that the Eucharist was offered either in the catacombs or aboveground over the graves of the martyrs. Families who gathered at a grave site to honor their beloved dead with a meal could invite a priest or bishop to preside over the Eucharist for their guests. In addition, funeral services in the catacombs would have included the Eucharist as well.
364 Perhaps the problems that Paul is addressing in 1 Corinthians 11:17–22 can give us a clue as to why the sacrament was eventually separated from the meal. See also Clement of Alexandria, *Instructor* 2.1.
365 See 1 Cor. 11:17–34.
366 Clement of Alexandria, *The Instructor* 2.1.
367 Justin Martyr, *I Apology* 67.

368 *Apostolic Tradition* 25–27. The division of morning sacrament and evening meal may also have had something to do with the logistical problems associated with offering the Eucharist to a growing number of Christians in any given city. As the Church grew, the bishops alone (one bishop per city) could not serve all the Christians, so the authority of presiding over the Eucharist was delegated to the priests. Also note that the role of the deacon in the early Church was to assist the presider in the distribution of the Eucharistic elements, even taking them to those who could not be at the liturgy. Justin Martyr, *I Apology* 67, Cyprian of Carthage, *On the Lapsed* 25.

369 Cyprian of Carthage, *Epistle* 62.16. See also *Apostolic Tradition* 25–27.

370 *Didascalia Apostolorum* 26.

371 See 1 Cor. 11:26. See also CCC 1324, 1325.

372 Justin Martyr, *I Apology* 65, Clement of Alexandria, *The Instructor* 2.2.19–20. Cyprian of Carthage, *Epistle* 62.9–13, also says that the wine with water represent Christ and his Church, the head and the body.

373 CCC 1332.

374 See John 6:53–56.

375 In other words, he was not saying that his body *symbolized* food or that his blood *symbolized* drink—such an idea would reduce the statement to meaninglessness, since it would really have to mean that the bread symbolized his body, and the wine symbolized his blood, not the other way around.

376 See John 6:60–61, 66. For those who might argue that in fact Jesus never said these words, and that this saying is an invention of the early Church placed into the mouth of Jesus by the author of the gospel, the presence in the story of disciples who left Jesus over this issue would still demonstrate that the prevailing view in early Christianity was that the elements of the Eucharist are more than mere metaphors for the body and blood of Christ. While I do believe that this teaching originated with Jesus, even if it could be proven that the Bread of Life Discourse reflects a context of division in the Johannine communities over Eucharistic theology, it would still demonstrate that the majority (and apostolic) understanding of the Eucharist assumed a real (non-metaphorical) interpretation of this passage. Also, if this teaching of Jesus was fabricated for the writing of the gospel, it does not seem likely that the author would also invent a scenario where so many people rejected Jesus' teaching.

377 See Mic. 3:3. For those who left Jesus, the idea of eating his body and drinking his blood sounded absurd, and to hold to such a belief in Hebrew culture would seem profoundly disrespectful, or even sacrilegious. On the other hand, this does not imply that Jesus was promoting a literalistic (annihilationist) view of the Eucharist. As St. Cyril of Jerusalem pointed out, if that's what the crowd thought he meant, then they misunderstood him. See Cyril of Jerusalem, *On the Mysteries* 4:3–7 (Lecture 22 of his catechetical lectures, *On the Body and Blood of Christ* 3–7).

378 This is an important theme in the other Gospels as well, and is sometimes presented as a contrast with those who rejected Christ.

379 See John 1:10–13.

380 See John 6:48–51, CCC 1334. Some have objected that John 6:63, "the flesh is of no avail," should be interpreted to indicate that Jesus' other statements should be taken metaphorically. However, if this were the case, Jesus would be contradicting himself, since he said in John 6:51 that his flesh is given for the life of the world. Rather than ascribe such a contradiction to Jesus, it is clear that the word, "flesh" in 6:63 is not a reference to Jesus' flesh, but to the carnal nature of those who were walking away from Jesus. They could not accept Jesus' teaching because they were trusting in the flesh, rather than trusting in God.

381 See 1 Cor. 11:23.

382 See 1 Cor. 11:23–26, see also Acts 2:46.

383 See 1 Cor. 11:27–30.

384 See 1 Cor. 11:17–22.

385 *Didache* 9.5, 14.1, Justin Martyr, *I Apology* 66. See also the *Didascalia Apostolorum* 11, which says that the Eucharist is ineffective if the recipient holds malice against anyone (cf. Matt. 5:23–24). Finally, note Paul's emphasis on self-examination in 1 Cor. 11.

386 1 John 4:1–3.

387 Ignatius of Antioch, Letter to Smyrna 6.

388 Ibid., 6. See also 3:1–3. It is clear that Ignatius did not mean this to be interpreted metaphorically, since then he would have no argument against the Docetics. To interpret his words metaphorically would be the interpretation of the Docetics themselves.

389 Ignatius of Antioch, Letter to Ephesus 20.

390 Ignatius of Antioch, Letter to Philadelphia 3–4.

391 See John 1:14.

392 Justin Martyr, *I Apology* 66.

393 CCC 1412–1414.

394 Irenaeus of Lyons, *Against Heresies* 4.18.5.

395 Irenaeus of Lyons, *Against Heresies* 5.2.3. See also *Against Heresies* 4.18.4–5, 4.33.2. Note that the "mingled cup" refers to the mixture of some water with the wine. Clement of Alexandria said that the wine and water represented the divinity and humanity of Christ, respectively. Clement of Alexandria, *Instructor* 2.2.

396 Tertullian, *Against Marcion* 3.19, 4.40. See also Novatian, *On the Trinity* 9.2, 10.5, 18.14, 19.2, 16–20, where it is clear that Novatian follows Tertullian in connecting the concept of a *type* with the term *figure*. Old Testament types that foreshadow New Testament realities are "sacraments" (sacred mysteries) in which the figure is the image, or appearance, of the type; but the fulfillment of the type (the *antitype*) is "incarnate truth" (*corporatae veritatis*), the very embodiment of truth. In other words, the figure is something that is the image of the reality, the substance is the reality (truth) itself. When applied to the Eucharistic elements, this means that the bread and wine are figures, but after the consecration, the Body and Blood are substances, which exist as the deeper reality.

397 Tertullian, *On the Resurrection of the Flesh* 8.

398 Tertullian, *Against Marcion* 4.40.

399 Tertullian, *On the Chaplet* 3.

400 Tertullian, *Against Marcion* 1.14.

401 See Tertullian, *Against Praxeas* 2.

402 Tertullian, *On Prayer* 6.

403 Hippolytus, *Commentary on Proverbs*.

404 Hippolytus, *Commentary on Proverbs*.

405 Cyprian of Carthage, *Letter* 62.8–11. Ironically, the heresy of adoptionism led some to the same practice as the opposite heresy, docetism. Both rejected the use of wine in the sacrament, a practice known as *aquarianism*. Others apparently rejected the sacrament altogether. Cyprian quoted the apostle Paul's words about the Judaizers, when he said that those who reject the wine preach "another gospel" (Gal. 1:8).

406 Cyprian of Carthage, *Letter* 62.15.

407 Cyprian of Carthage, *Letter* 62.15.

408 Cyprian of Carthage, *On the Lapsed* 16. Cf. 1 Cor. 11:27.

409 Cyprian famously remarked, "Whoever does not have the Church for a mother cannot have God for a Father."

410 Cyril of Jerusalem, *Catechetical Lecture* 19.7

411 Cyril of Jerusalem, *On the Mysteries* 4:2–3 (Lecture 22 of his catechetical lectures, *On the Body and Blood of Christ* 2–3). Cf. 1 Pet. 1:4. Note that Cyril, living in the east, was writing in Greek. Therefore, the word translated "figure" is not the same Latin word that Tertullian used, but is actually the Greek word *typos*, or "type."

412 Cyril of Jerusalem, *On the Mysteries* 4:6, 9 (Lecture 22 of his catechetical lectures, *On the Body and Blood of Christ* 6, 9).

413 Ambrose of Milan, *On the Mysteries* 4.14.

414 Ambrose of Milan, *On the Mysteries* 9.52–53. Cf. Psalm 33:9.

415 Ambrose of Milan, *On the Mysteries* 9.58.

416 See, for example, Augustine of Hippo, *On the Trinity* 5.9, and *On Christian Doctrine*, especially 3.5.

417 Augustine of Hippo, *Sermon* 227.

418 Augustine of Hippo, *Sermon* 272.

419 Note that for Augustine, what is true is real, so that what is more true (the deeper truth) is more real. See Augustine of Hippo, *On the Trinity* 8.1.2.

420 Clement of Alexandria and perhaps Origen, coming as they did from a tradition of always preferring the allegorical interpretation, did write in ways that could be interpreted as though they believed the Eucharistic elements to be merely symbolic. See, for example, Clement of Alexandria, *Instructor* 1.6. But we should hardly expect that there would be no diversity of thought (on any issue) in the early Church, and the fact that Clement and Origen may be the exception to the rule demonstrates that the vast majority of early Church Fathers were in agreement. Also, it must be pointed out that many aspects of Origen's theology were heretical, so he cannot be used as an authority when speaking of the consensus of the Church Fathers.

421 For the observation that "heresy forces orthodoxy to define itself," see Papandrea, James L., *Trinity 101: Father, Son, Holy Spirit* (Liguori, MO: Liguori Publications, 2012), 67-73.

422 In using the word "true/truly," Radbertus is making a reference to John 6:55.

423 Paschasius Radbertus, *On the Body and Blood of the Lord* 1.2–3.

424 Paschasius Radbertus, *On the Body and Blood of the Lord* 1.5.

425 Paschasius Radbertus, *On the Body and Blood of the Lord* 2.2.

426 Paschasius Radbertus, *On the Body and Blood of the Lord* 4.1.

427 Ratramnus, *On the Body and Blood of the Lord* 30, 69–89.

428 Ratramnus probably thought he was safeguarding the omnipresence
     of the divine nature. However, because the Church Fathers believed
     that the divine nature of Christ was contained, or *circumscribed*, within
     the womb of Mary (a doctrine confirmed at the third ecumenical
     Council of Ephesus in 431), most had no trouble with the belief
     that the divinity of Christ was also circumscribed in the Eucharistic
     elements. If Ratramnus can properly be called a heretic, it would
     be for a quasi-Nestorian Christology applied to the Eucharist. That
     the Church Fathers understood the connection between the real
     presence of Christ in the Eucharist and the circumscription of the
     divine *Logos* in the womb of Mary (*Theotokos*, or Mother of God), see
     Lanfranc of Canterbury, *On the Body and Blood of the Lord* 17.

429 Ratramnus, *On the Body and Blood of the Lord* 9.

430 Ratramnus, *On the Body and Blood of the Lord* 16.

431 Ratramnus, *On the Body and Blood of the Lord* 49.

432 In some ways, this difference could be chalked up to the difference
     between a Platonic and an Aristotelian approach to reality.

433 It was not until about two centuries later that Ratramnus would be
     condemned as a heretic, and centuries after that when his document
     would eventually be placed on the list of forbidden books.

434 At the time of the Protestant Reformation, some of the Reformers
     were concerned about the trend of people not receiving the elements.
     They were also concerned about the medieval practice of using the
     Eucharist as a private ceremony, which separated the sacrament from
     the gathering of the faithful, and lost an important part of its mean-
     ing as creating the Body of Christ, the Church. And although many
     of the Reformers did not question the traditional understanding of
     the Mass as transubstantiation, some reacted to these medieval prac-
     tices by diminishing or denying the miraculous nature of the sacra-
     ment. Some of the earliest Reformers, such as John Wycliffe, fol-
     lowed the lead of Berengar, and advocated consubstantiation. Martin
     Luther was originally accepting of the doctrine of transubstantiation,
     but eventually most Reformers opted for consubstantiation. Only
     the later Reformers went to the extreme of saying that the elements
     of bread and wine were never anything more than metaphors for the
     body and blood of Christ, and the sacrament was nothing more than
     a symbolic, memorial meal. This view, *memorialism*, was never held
     in the history of the Church before the Reformation. Some Catholics

at the time unfortunately overreacted against the reformers' rejection of transubstantiation by going to the other extreme, supposing that what happened in the Mass was actually a *transformation* (change of form) of the physical aspects of the elements as well as the substance of the elements. This view, called *annihilation*, assumed that even the accidents of bread and wine ceased to be bread and wine, but are transformed into the body and blood of Christ in such a way that recipients were thought to be literally chewing the flesh of Christ. This was exactly the understanding of the Eucharist that Ratramnus was attacking in his document, and it is also the description of the Eucharist used in Berengar's forced confession. To make matters worse, many non-Catholics still believe that this is the definition of transubstantiation. However, to truly understand transubstantiation is to realize that it is the middle way between a purely symbolic non-miraculous understanding of the Eucharist, and a grotesquely literalistic understanding of the Eucharist.

435 Lanfranc of Canterbury, *On the Body and Blood of the Lord* 9, 17.

436 Ambrose of Milan, *On the Mysteries* 9, quoted in Lanfranc of Canterbury, *On the Body and Blood of the Lord* 9.

437 Lanfranc of Canterbury, *On the Body and Blood of the Lord* 9.

438 Lanfranc of Canterbury, *On the Body and Blood of the Lord* 13.

439 Lanfranc of Canterbury, *On the Body and Blood of the Lord* 18.

440 CCC 1374, 1413.

441 Lanfranc of Canterbury, *On the Body and Blood of the Lord* 9, 14.

442 Lanfranc of Canterbury, *On the Body and Blood of the Lord* 17. Cf. the distinction that some of the Church Fathers made between *form* and *likeness* in Philippians 2:6–7. Here, *form* is equal to substance, and *likeness* is equal to appearance. In the incarnation, the divine nature of Christ was always the same *form* (divine substance) as the Father, but then he acquired both the *form* and the *likeness* of humanity (a full human nature). In the Eucharist, before the consecration, the elements are bread and wine in both their *form* and *likeness*. After the consecration, their *likeness* remains bread and wine, but their *form* has become the body and blood of Christ. The *form* changed, the *likeness* did not. Therefore just as, in the Incarnation, the *form* of divinity is hidden under the *likeness* of humanity, so also in the Eucharist, the *form* of the body and blood (and also the divinity) is hidden under the *likeness* of the material—the tangible aspects of bread and wine. However, this is not a perfect analogy, since in the Incarnation, the resulting person of Jesus Christ has two

natures (two underlying *forms*), humanity and divinity. Cf. Lanfranc of Canterbury, *On the Body and Blood of the Lord* 20.

443 See Matt. 26:26–28, Mark 14:22–24, Luke 22:19–10, 1 Cor. 11:24–25.

444 Lanfranc of Canterbury, *On the Body and Blood of the Lord* 18. Here Lanfranc is quoting Ambrose.

445 *Apostolic Tradition* 36–38.

446 For the earlier practice of placing the Eucharistic bread in the recipients' hands, see Cyprian of Carthage, *On the Lapsed* 26.

447 The Western Church was using unleavened bread, since Jesus would have shared unleavened bread at the Last Supper, which was a Passover meal. The Eastern Church, however, had developed the tradition of using leavened (risen) bread, as a reminder of the risen Christ. By the year 1000, the West was moving to uniform pressed wafers made by monks.

448 Clement of Alexandria, *Instructor* 1.6. See also Eusebius of Caesarea, *Ecclesiastical History* 6.44. Note that the doctrine of concomitance, as it is called, is not a medieval invention created to justify the withholding of the cup from the laity, but goes back to the early Church. CCC 1377, 1390. Today most Catholic churches offer both elements, but still may offer the bread only when logistical limitations, such as large crowds, dictate.

449 In addition, it is also the case that the smallest piece contains the whole presence, because of the fact that the body of Christ cannot be dissipated (broken into pieces), and because of the doctrine of divine simplicity, which says that divinity cannot be divided. Therefore, many pieces of Eucharistic host are still the one body, just as many Masses going on all over the world are still sharing the one body of Christ. Technically speaking, there is a sense in which the body of Christ remains in the heavenly realm where it ascended, though his body, blood, soul, and divinity are also present in the elements. The point is that the real presence of Christ, localized in the Eucharistic elements, does not diminish the omnipresence of Christ, just as the presence of the divine nature of Christ in the womb of Mary did not diminish the omnipresence of the Word of God. See Papandrea, Jas. L. *Trinity 101: Father, Son, Holy Spirit* (Liguori, MO: Liguori Publications, 2012), 109–111.

450 *Didache* 14.1, cf. *Didascalia Apostolorum* 11.

451 See 1 Cor. 11:27–32.

452 Cyprian of Carthage, *Epistle* 9.2, 10.1, *On the Lapsed* 15, 26.

453 CCC 1378.

454 Council of Trent, 1545–1563. Even St. Francis of Assisi preached encouragement for people to come back to the table and receive the sacrament.

455 CCC 1333.

456 CCC 1353.

457 CCC 1380, 1381.

458 CCC 1353, 1375.

459 Matt. 18:20. Note that this passage comes in the context of the apostles' authority to forgive sins and reconcile sinners.

460 See Exod. 13:21–22, 40:34–38.

461 See Matt. 18:20. Notice that in Matthew 25, Jesus also implies a kind of presence when he says that whenever we minister to others in his name, it is as though we are serving him.

462 CCC 1373. See Luke 24:13–35. Just as the disciples on the road to Emmaus discovered, Christ is recognized in the breaking of the bread.

463 See Heb. 9–10.

464 CCC 1366.

465 CCC 1364, 1367, italics in the original. The reference is to the Council of Trent (1562). Cf. Heb. 7:25–27.

466 Athenagoras, *A Plea for the Christians* 13, Eusebius of Caesarea, *Ecclesiastical History* 10.4–5.

467 Cyprian of Carthage, *Epistle* 62.9.

468 There are exceptional circumstances under which non-Catholics may licitly receive Communion, but ordinarily it is reserved for Catholics (see the Code of Canon Law, 844).

469 See 1 Cor. 11:29.

470 See 1 Cor. 11:28. See also *Didascalia Apostolorum* 11, as well as Cyprian of Carthage, *Epistle* 9.2, 10.1, *On the Lapsed* 15, 26.

471 For more on this, see Papandrea, *Reading the Early Church Fathers*, 58-75.

472 *Didache* 9.5 (based on Matt. 7:6, "Do not give what is holy to dogs"), Justin Martyr, *I Apology* 66.

473 *Apostolic Tradition* 36–38, *Didascalia Apostolorum* 10.

474 *Apostolic Tradition* 36–38, *Didascalia Apostolorum* 10. Cf. Novatian, *On the Spectacles* 5, where he criticizes Christians who don't go directly home after receiving the Eucharist, taking the body and blood of Christ with them to the pagan games and shows. Pope Paul VI referred to this passage in *Mysterium Fidei* (1965).

475 Justin Martyr, *I Apology* 66.

476 See 1 Cor. 5:1–5, 99–13, *Didascalia Apostolorum* 10. Note that divorce, by itself, does not exclude one from the Eucharist. It is when a person remarries outside the Church, or in some other way does not bring his relationship into compliance with the Church's teaching, that the Church asks that person to "regularize" his situation before returning to the table. A divorced person may receive the sacrament. But someone who is divorced would normally need an annulment before getting remarried in order for that second marriage to be a valid sacramental marriage. Since the bishops are in succession from the apostles, they hold the authority over the sacraments, so they are the ones who ultimately determine who will preside and who will receive.

477 CCC 1322, 1324.

478 See CCC 1399, 1401.

479 CCC 1373–1374. Cf. Matt. 18:20.

480 CCC 1391. Cf. John 6:56, 15:1–10.

481 CCC 1393–1395.

482 *Didascalia Apostolorum* 26, Cyril of Jerusalem, *On the Mysteries* 5.9–10 (Lecture 23 of his catechetical lectures, *On the Sacred Liturgy and Communion* 9–10), John Cassian, *Conferences* 9.11, 27. See also CCC 1371.

483 Ignatius of Antioch, Letter to the Philadelphians 3–4.

484 CCC 1396.

485 CCC 1324.

486 In fact, the early Christians understood that the Eucharist replaced Passover for the Church. See Cyprian of Carthage, *Epistle* 62.9. Baptism and Eucharist were the Christian parallels to circumcision and Passover. CCC 1334, 1340.

487 CCC 1354, 1364, 1366. The Greek word for "remembering" is *anamnesis*, which literally means, "not forgetting."

488 See, for example, Cyprian of Carthage, *Epistle* 62.9, and 62.17, where he says, "the Lord's Passion is the sacrifice that we offer." For early Christian writers like Cyprian, the Eucharist replaced the sacrifices of the Old Testament.

489 Athenagoras, *Plea for the Christians* 13, Eusebius of Caesarea, *Ecclesiastical History* 10.4–5, and *Life of Constantine*. Cf. Heb., chapter 9. CCC 1367.

490 See Heb. 13:15, 1 Pet. 2:5, CCC 1330.

491 CCC 1366.

492 CCC 1393–1395, 1414. Technically, the Eucharist forgives venial sins. Mortal sins also require the sacrament of confession/reconciliation.

493 Paschasius Radbertus, *On the Body and Blood of the Lord* 1.6, 6.1. CCC 1391, 1396.

494 CCC 1324, 1330, 1374, 1407.

495 See Matt. 18:20.

496 CCC 1383.

497 CCC 1382.

498 CCC 1332.

499 See, for example, Rom. 1:7, and 1 Cor. 1:2. The term is also used in the book of Acts to refer to Christian believers.

500 See Rom. 1:7, 1 Cor. 1:2.

501 See 1 Pet. 2:5.

502 See Sir. 11:28.

503 Augustine said it would be wrong to pray for the martyrs, as we pray for the other dead, since the martyrs do not need our prayers, their salvation is certain. Augustine of Hippo, *Sermon* 159.1.

504 Papandrea, *Reading the Early Church Fathers*, 15-17.

505 See Helen Rhee's excellent book, *Early Christian Literature: Christ and Culture in the Second and Third Centuries* (Routledge, 2005).

506 *Lumen Gentium* 50

507 See Matt. 25:1–13.

508 See 1 Cor. 6:19.

509 CCC 955, 962.

510 *Lumen Gentium* 49

511 See 1 Cor. 12:12–27, CCC 947, 961.

512 CCC 946.

513 *Lumen Gentium* 50. Also quoted in CCC 957.

514 CCC 950, 960.

515 CCC 950, 957, 960.

516 *Lumen Gentium* 50.

517 For more, see my book *The Wedding of the Lamb: A Historical Approach to the Book of Revelation*, 92–95.

518 Clement of Alexandria, *Miscellanies* 7:12.

519 *Lumen Gentium* 50.

520 See Exod. 20:1–5.

521 See Matt. 17:1–8/Mark 9:2–8/Luke 9:28–36.

522 *Lumen Gentium* 49

523 See Phil. 1:20–23. Cf. Jerome, *To Vigilantius* 6.

524 2 Tim. 2:12, See Augustine of Hippo, *City of God* 20.9. Cf. Council of Trent, *On the Invocation, Veneration, And Relics of the Saints, And on*

Sacred Images (1563).

525 See 1 Cor. 13:12. Cf. Luke 12:2–3.

526 See Luke 16:19–31. The text actually says that he went to "hades," which is not exactly the same as our popular conception of hell. However, it does say that he was "being tormented."

527 See 2 Macc. 15:12–14.

528 See 1 Tim. 2:5. Both the Council of Trent and the Second Vatican Council affirmed that Christ is the one and only mediator between God and humanity, and that the practice of prayer to the saints does not compromise that. See *Lumen Gentium* 51, 60, CCC 970.

529 Jerome, *To Vigilantius* 6.

530 See Jas. 5:16, Rev. 5:8, 8:3–5.

531 See 2 Macc. 12:46, CCC 956.

532 See Exod. 20:12.

533 *Lumen Gentium* 50. Cf. Rom. 13:7, Heb. 13:7.

534 See Matt. 25:21, Rev. 5:8, 8:3–5, *Lumen Gentium* 49, CCC 2683.

535 This is in the Catacombs of San Sebastiano, in Rome. See my book *Rome: A Pilgrim's Guide to the Eternal City* (Eugene, OR: Cascade Books, 2012), 74–75.

536 *Martyrdom of Polycarp* 17.2–3. See also CCC 957.

537 See Luke 2:22–38.

538 Methodius of Olympus, *Oration on Simeon and Anna* 14.

539 Athanasius of Alexandria, *On the Incarnation of the Word* 57.

540 Cyril of Jerusalem, *Catechetical Lectures* 23.9 (*On the Mysteries* 5: *On the Sacred Liturgy and Communion*).

541 Gregory of Nazianzus, *Orations* 18.4.

542 Augustine of Hippo, *Sermons on the Gospel of John* 84.1. See also *Sermon* 159.1, and *City of God* 20.9.

543 See Isa. 7:14, cf. Mic. 5:2–3. It is often pointed out that in Isaiah, the Hebrew term for *virgin* could simply mean a young, unmarried girl. However, it would be expected that a young, unmarried girl would be a virgin—rather like the older English use of the word, "maiden." But Matthew is not reading the Hebrew text, he is reading the Greek text of the Septuagint, where the meaning is more clearly that of *virgin* as we understand it. In any case, the issue remains that the Old Testament text, in its original context, is speaking of a normal human birth—the young girl was a virgin until she became pregnant. Nevertheless, the early Christians understood this passage as having a deeper meaning than Isaiah's present situation, and Matthew 1:22–23 interprets it as a prophecy

of Mary's miraculous conception of Jesus. The bottom line is that if one is unwilling to believe in the miraculous virgin birth of Jesus, the possibility of a prophecy will not convince that person. For those of us who are willing to believe, it is enough to say that the apostles believed it, and the gospels record it. See *Lumen Gentium* 55 and CCC 496–497.

544 See Matt. 1:22–23.

545 CCC 2617.

546 See Luke 1:37, cf. Matt. 19:26/Mark 10:27/Luke 18:27. CCC 273, 967.

547 See *Lumen Gentium* 56, CCC 488. See also Augustine of Hippo, *On Holy Virginity* 4.4.

548 CCC 144, 511.

549 Irenaeus of Lyons, *Against Heresies* 3.22.4. Quoted in *Lumen Gentium* 55–56 (in chapter 8, "Our Lady").

550 See Rom. 5:15–19, 1 Cor. 15:22, 45.

551 See Exod. 25:16–22, 40:34–35, cf. Heb. 9:5. CCC 697, 2676.

552 Wisdom is personified in biblical passages such as Proverbs 8:1–9:6 and Sirach 24. The living Wisdom of God is called the *Logos*, or "Word" of God in the Gospel of John. The Word of God was incarnate in and through Mary. CCC 721. On the *Logos*, see Papandrea, James L., *Trinity 101: Father, Son, Holy Spirit* (Liguori, MO: Liguori Publications, 2012), 50-54.

553 See Luke 1:43, CCC 495, 509. Around the turn of the fourth century, bishop Methodius of Olympus preached a homily in which he included an invocation to Mary as Mother of God, which demonstrates that it was an accepted, mainstream title. Methodius of Olympus, *Oration on Simeon and Anna* 14.

554 For more on this, see Papandrea, *Reading the Early Church Fathers*, 214-215.

555 Rev. 12:17. Cf. Micah 5:2, Rom. 8:29. See Papandrea, *The Wedding of the Lamb* 110–112.

556 John 19:26–27.

557 CCC 501, 963, 968.

558 *Lumen Gentium* 53. The section in italics is from Augustine of Hippo, *On Holy Virginity* 6.

559 See Eph. 5:25–32. *Lumen Gentium* 65 (in chapter 8, "Our Lady").

560 CCC 507, 773, 973, 2030. Because of Mary, it can also be said that the Church is our mother.

561 See Rom. 5:12–19.

562 CCC 491, 508.

563 *Lumen Gentium* 56.

564 CCC 411.

565 See Luke 1:48, *Lumen Gentium* 66 (in chapter 8, "Our Lady").

566 Third century, attributed to Hippolytus.

567 Ephraim the Syrian, *Nisibene Hymns* 27:8.

568 Ambrose of Milan, *Commentary on Psalm* 118:22–30.

569 CCC 489, 970.

570 Irenaeus of Lyons, *Against Heresies* 3.22.4. By "cause of salvation," Irenaeus does not mean that she is savior or mediator of salvation, rather he only means that she contributed to our salvation.

571 See Rom. 3:23. The Church has always believed that the "all" in this passage does not include Mary. Our Eastern Orthodox brothers and sisters also believed that Mary had no sin; CCC 493.

572 Pius IX, *Ineffabilis Deus* (December 8, 1854). This was not an *ex cathedra* pronouncement, since it was before the institution of such pronouncements, which occurred in 1870. However, it is still considered a dogma of the Church.

573 Eastern Orthodox Christians do believe that Mary was without sin; however, they do not officially accept the doctrine of the Immaculate Conception, mostly because they believe it is unnecessary, since they have a different view of original sin from the West. (It may also be partly due to the fact that the doctrine was affirmed by a Roman pope, after the split between East and West, and so to officially accept the doctrine would be to appear to acknowledge papal authority.) However, the Eastern Orthodox churches do not consider the doctrine a heresy, and eastern Christians are free to believe it if they choose to. Eastern Orthodox Christians also share the Catholic beliefs of the Perpetual Virginity and the Assumption of Mary.

574 Many people have believed that Mary felt no pain in childbirth, since the pain of childbirth is said to be a result of sin (Gen. 3:16). Therefore, since she was born without original sin, and had no personal sin, some have reasoned that she must not have experienced the pain of childbirth.

575 CCC 499, 510. Eventually, Mary's Perpetual Virginity would become an encouragement to female celibate vocations. In fact, since Mary is held up as an example for Christians (after only Jesus himself), many people reasoned that celibacy must be a higher calling than matrimony, and for a long time the Church did promote such a priority. However, it must be pointed out that although many people have connected her virginity with her sinlessness, her sinlessness is

not really a function of her virginity, since her sinlessness precedes her lifelong sexual continence. In any case, the doctrine of Mary's purity (the Immaculate Conception) is not dependent on the doctrine of Mary's continence (the Perpetual Virginity) in a way that implies that all sex is sinful or that matrimony is a lesser vocation than celibacy. Today the Church teaches that both matrimony and celibacy are equally valid vocations. Mary's situation is unique in the sense that, in a way, she was called to both.

576 Augustine of Hippo, *Sermon* 186.1. See also Leo of Rome, *Sermon* 22.2.

577 CCC 500. See Matt. 13:55–56, Mark 3:31–35, 6:3, John 7:5, Gal. 1:19. The Catholic Church teaches that the James and Joseph mentioned in Matthew 13:55 are the same James and Joseph mentioned in Matthew 27:56, and so are the sons of the "other Mary" of Matthew 27:1 and 28:1.

578 CCC 500.

579 Cf. 1 Cor. 9:5, and Augustine of Hippo, *On the Trinity* 8.8.

580 The exception to this is Jerome, who believed that Joseph had also committed himself to celibacy, and therefore had not been married before. So Jerome believed that the "brothers and sisters of the Lord" were cousins or other relatives. See Jerome, *The Perpetual Virginity of Blessed Mary*, 19, 21.

581 See Hilary, *Commentary on Matthew* 1.4, and Jerome, *The Perpetual Virginity of Blessed Mary*, 14–15.

582 In addition to the Church Fathers already referred to, see Didymus the Blind, *On the Trinity* 3.4, Ambrose of Milan, *Epistle* 63.111, Epiphanius of Salamis, *Panarion* 78.6, Athanasius, *Against the Arians* 2.70, Augustine of Hippo, *On Holy Virginity* 4.4, Leo I (the Great) of Rome, *Sermon* 22.2, *Epistle* 28.2 (The Tome). Also note that Jerome maintains that the doctrine was taught by Ignatius of Antioch, Polycarp of Smyrna, Justin Martyr, Irenaeus of Lyons, and many others. See Jerome, *The Perpetual Virginity of Blessed Mary*, 19, 21.

583 Athanasius of Alexandria, *Against the Arians*, 2:70.

584 In 1522, for example, Zwingli preached a sermon called *On the Perpetual Virginity of Mary*. For more, see Tim Staples, *Behold Your Mother* (San Diego: Catholic Answers Press, 2014), 169.

585 See Gen. 5:21–24, 2 Kgs. 2:11, Sir. 44:16, Heb. 11:5.

586 That Mary did die is affirmed in Pius X, *Munificentissimus Deus* (November 1, 1950).

587 See Gen. 3:17–19. Some people have believed that Mary's incorrupt-

ibility would mean that she could not die, arguing that death itself is the result of sin. This is one of the justifications for the belief that she never died. Others went so far as to claim that she could not have even grown old; however, it is clear that she did grow up from a child, which is part of the aging process. Nevertheless, a minority of people have maintained that Mary grew to an age of perfection and then never aged beyond that, and never died.

588 Cf. John 10:18. Although in some contexts the Ascension is described as the Son being taken up by the Father, the Son is still fully divine, and therefore is capable of ascending himself.

589 CCC 966, 974. Cf. 1 Cor. 15:36–58.

590 CCC 972.

591 CCC 966.

592 The primary sources for the dormition and Assumption of Mary include Ps. Melito of Sardis, *The Passing of the Blessed Mary*, Ps. John the Theologian, *The Dormition of the Holy Theotokos*, Ps. Cyril of Jerusalem, *Homily on the Dormition*, Theodosius of Alexandria, *Homily on the Dormition*, Ps. Evodius of Rome, *Homily on the Dormition*, Ps. Joseph of Arimathea, *The Passing of the Blessed Virgin Mary*, John of Damascus, *Sermons on the Assumption*, the anonymous *Palm of the Tree of Life*, *The Six Books*, *Obsequies of the Virgin*, and Jacobus de Voragine (13th c.), *The Golden Legend*.

593 2 Sam. 6:6–7.

594 This is the only time that the pope's prerogative of an infallible (*ex cathedra*) pronouncement has ever been exercised, other than the initial definition of the prerogative itself, in 1870. See the chapter on the papacy for more on infallibility.

595 CCC 487.

596 CCC 964.

597 Irenaeus of Lyons, *Against Heresies* 3.22.4. Quoted in *Lumen Gentium* 56.

598 Sometimes the Latin term *Mediatrix* is used, but this does not mean "mediator" in the sense of savior; it has the meaning of instrumental cause, in the sense of facilitator, or instrument. CCC 970.

599 CCC 971.

600 The Roman patron-client system was a system of mutual benefit, but even there the patron is in a position of power and authority over the client.

601 *Lumen Gentium* 58, 62, 69.

602 See John 2:1–11, CCC 2618.

603 CCC 969, 975.

604 See also *Lumen Gentium* 62, 65, 67.

605 See Luke 1:28.

606 See Luke 1:42.

607 The Greek word, properly translated "babble," comes from *battalogesete*, which means "to go on endlessly." It is often translated as "repetition," however the word is a verb, not a noun, and so it does not refer to recited prayers.

608 Cf. Luke 18:9–14, the parable of the Pharisee and the tax collector.

609 See Eph. 4:1–6.

610 See Rev. 6:9–11.

611 CCC 957.

612 *Martyrdom of Polycarp* 18.2–3. Translation in Michael W. Holmes, *The Apostolic Fathers: Greek Texts and English Translations* (Grand Rapids: Baker Academic, 2007), 327.

613 Eusebius of Caesarea, *Ecclesiastical History* 6.9.

614 Eusebius of Caesarea, *Life of Constantine* 3.42–43, Sozomen, *Ecclesiastical History* 1.17.

615 It has been popularly alleged that if one could put together all the pieces of the True Cross that are venerated in the world, it would make many crosses, implying that the pieces of wood circulating are forgeries. This is not really true, however, since all the relics of the True Cross are documented by the Church, and there are not that many of them.

616 In fact, these icons are not so much *Eastern* as *early*. The Byzantine Christians have simply retained what was a very early style of icon painting. If you look at the mosaics in the most ancient churches in Rome, for example, you will see a similar style, because those mosaics come from the early Church. So icons, and the use of icons in devotional practice, was never exclusively Eastern, it dates back to the early Church across the whole Roman Empire.

617 Tertullian, *Apology* 16. The sign of the cross seems to have been in use even before the image of a cross was used as a symbol in the Church. However, Tertullian, at the turn of the third century, mentions the cross as an object of veneration.

618 See Exod. 20:4–5.

619 See Exod. 25:18–20. Cf. also I Kings 6:29–32, 8:6–66, 2 Chronicles 3:7–14.

620 See Num. 21:8–9.

621 Justin Martyr, *Dialogue with Trypho* 94.

622 Synod of Elvira, Canon 36.

623 This rule is no longer followed, since modern (nineteenth and twentieth century) mosaics in Rome sometimes copy the early ones in depicting Christ as the Lamb of God. This is the case in the outdoor mosaic on the church of San Paolo Fuori le Mura (St. Paul Outside the Walls).

624 See 2 Kgs. 18:4.

625 See Exod. 20:12.

626 See CCC 875.

627 See Mark 3:14–15, Luke 22:29–30, CCC 551.

628 See CCC 935.

629 See CCC 861–862.

630 See CCC 877.

631 *Unitatis Redintegratio* 2.

632 See Mark 3:16/Luke 6:13–16. Cf. 1 Cor. 15:5.

633 See Mark 9:2, John 20:3–8.

634 See Matt. 16:17–19. Admittedly, this passage is not included in the gospel of Mark, which according to tradition was written from the testimony of Peter and for the church of Rome. This could be explained by the humility of Peter, who was Mark's source of information, while Matthew's Gospel, written by an eyewitness, records the conversation.

635 See Luke 22:31–32, John 21:15–17. Note that the Luke passage is in the context of Jesus' prediction of Peter's denial. Even though Peter denied him, Jesus not only forgave him but appointed him to lead the apostles.

636 CCC 816.

637 See Matt. 16:17–19. Jesus gave the keys of the kingdom to Peter but the authority that comes with the keys—the authority to bind (retain) and loose (forgive) sins is granted to the bishops, the successors of all of the apostles (John 20:23), and through them to the priests who hear confessions and grant absolution.

638 See CCC 553. Cf. Isaiah 22:20–22.

639 See CCC 881. See also *Lumen Gentium* 22.

640 See Acts 2:14–41, 15:6–11. Cf. CCC 552, 765.

641 See Acts 2:10.

642 1 Peter 5:13, for example, refers to "Babylon"—a code word for Rome.

643 *Lumen Gentium* 19, CCC 880.

644 CCC 883.

645 As we saw in an earlier chapter, apostolic succession assumes that the teaching of the Church is handed down from the apostles to the bishops, and from the early bishops to their successors in any given

city. But what happens when two bishops disagree on some aspect of interpretation? If and when two bishops disagree, the one with the more direct succession back to an apostle would theoretically have the higher authority. But it could still be unclear if both of the disputing bishops claim succession from one of Jesus' disciples. At that point, it becomes a question of which of the apostles had a higher authority. In the end, Peter always has the highest authority as the leader of the apostles. That means in any dispute between bishops, the successor of Peter (the bishop of Rome) trumps all others. If the bishop of Rome is not directly involved in the dispute, the "winner" is whoever can claim to be in agreement with the bishop of Rome. Therefore, on the question of doctrine and the interpretation of Scripture, the early consensus of the Church at large was that everyone must agree with what was being taught at Rome.

646 It has been argued that "orthodoxy" is a label which can only be applied after the debate is over, and therefore if Rome is always on the winning side, that may be evidence more of its power than its authenticity. However, one must keep in mind that orthodoxy is not defined simply as the majority position at any given time—orthodoxy is also the position that is most consistent with the orthodoxy of the previous generation and its conclusions. Therefore, when we assume the reality of apostolic succession, the connection of the bishops of Rome to Peter explains why the Roman church did not deviate from apostolic orthodoxy. By contrast, the see of the other metropolitans all had proponents of major heresies as their bishops at one time or another—bishops such as Paul of Samosata (bishop of Antioch), Eusebius of Caesarea (who was at one time an Arian), Nestorius of Constantinople, and Dioscorus of Alexandria (supporter of Eutyches the monophysite).

647 Tertullian, *Prescription Against the Heretics* 32.

648 For more on this controversy, see Papandrea, James L., *Reading the Early Church Fathers: From the Didache to Nicaea* (Mahwah, NJ: Paulist Press, 2012), 168-175.

649 Synodal Letter to the Egyptian churches.

650 Lewis Ayres. *Nicaea and its Legacy: An Approach to Fourth-Century Trinitarian Theology* (Oxford: Oxford University Press, 2004), 260–261.

651 Based on a forged document known as the *Donation of Constantine.*

652 It was probably at this time that the addition to the Nicene Creed known as the *filioque* clause ("and the Son") was made mandatory for

all the churches of the West.

653 Gregory VII (bishop 1073–1085) codified the existing expectations of papal authority in a document known as the *Dictatus Papae*. There he set down that only the bishop of Rome can be called the ecumenical (or universal) bishop. Also, the authority to depose or reinstate other bishops, transfer a bishop, or divide or create a new see (the bishop's area) rests only with the bishop of Rome. Only the bishop of Rome can call a general council of the Church, and he is the ultimate judge in all Church matters. A sentence passed by him cannot be reversed by anyone else, and he may be judged by no one, not even a king or emperor. The bishop of Rome may depose a king or an emperor, and may free a king's subjects from his reign. In short, whoever is not in the good graces of the bishop of Rome is not in the Church. Most of the *Dictatus Papae* was not new, but Gregory made it official. Of course all of this was meant to reinforce the pope's authority, and Gregory included some protocols that made the pope seem like royalty, including that secular kings must kiss the pope's feet. Although a lot of the *Dictatus Papae* is no longer followed, at the time the office of the papacy had become something of a royal court, complete with a bank, and lawyers, and ambassadors. The point, however, is that the *Dictatus Papae* put in writing what the popes had been claiming for some time, that they embodied the highest human authority on earth. The document stated, "that the Roman church has never erred, nor will it err to all eternity, the Scripture bearing witness." (Cf. the promise of Jesus in Matthew 16, when he said to Peter, "you are Peter, and upon this rock I will build my Church, and the gates of hell shall not prevail against it.") The point is that regardless of the lengths to which popes would go in claiming authority, the consensus of the Church was that Jesus had promised Peter that the Church would never go astray to such an extent that it would cease to be the Church. Should that happen, hell would win, and Jesus said that could never happen. So, as we will see below, the concept of papal infallibility is based on this premise, that Jesus made this promise to Peter, and to Peter's successors, the bishops of Rome.

654 *Unitatis Redintegratio* 14.

655 This was in the context of the removal of the heretic Paul of Samosata from the see of Antioch.

656 CCC 834.

657 Ignatius of Antioch, Letter to the Romans (salutation).

658 Ibid., 3.1.
659 Ibid., 4.3.
660 Ibid., 9.1.
661 Irenaeus of Lyons, *Against Heresies* 3.3.2.
662 Tertullian, *On Modesty* 1.
663 Tertullian, *Prescription Against the Heretics* 36.
664 Cyprian of Carthage, *On the Unity of the Catholic Church* 4–6, *Epistle* 39.5, 68.8.
665 Augustine of Hippo, *Sermon* 131.10.
666 *Against Heresies* 3.2.2.
667 See John 16:13.
668 See CCC 891.
669 The concept was not new, however. It was based on early Church precedent and on Gregory VII's *Dictatus Papae.*
670 *Pastor Aeternus* 6, 9.
671 Technically speaking, it could be said that there have actually been two *ex cathedra* pronouncements, the first one being the affirmation of papal infallibility itself in 1870.
672 See CCC 890–892.
673 See CCC 1369.
674 *Unitatis Redintegratio* 3. See also CCC 816.
675 Ibid., 3.
676 Ibid.
677 Ibid., 4, 22. See Eph. 4:1–6.
678 Ibid., 3.
679 Ibid., 1.
680 Ibid.
681 See Matt. 16:18.
682 See the 1995 encyclical of Pope John Paul II, *Ut Unum Sint.*
683 Conversation between Christianity and other religions, such as Islam, Buddhism, or Hinduism, is properly called "interfaith" dialogue. The Catholic Church treats Judaism as a special case, so while it is not considered a denomination within Christianity, it is also not considered a completely different religion.
684 On the Decian persecution and the schism of Novatian, see Papandrea, James L., *Novatian of Rome and the Culmination of Pre-Nicene Orthodoxy* (Eugene, OR: Pickwick Publications, 2011), 47-70, and *Reading the Early Church Fathers: From the Didache to Nicaea* (Mahwah, NJ: Paulist Press, 2012), 156-168.

685 For more information on this controversy and the resulting schism, see Papandrea, *Reading the Early Church Fathers*, 210-219.

686 Cf. Justin Martyr, *I Apology* 67. Writing in the middle of the second century, Justin says this of the homily, "When the reader has ceased, the presider verbally instructs, and exhorts to the imitation of these good things." In other words, the homily was not to convince people to become Christian, because it was assumed that only Christians were there to hear it.

687 John Paul II, *Ecclesia in America* 28–30.

688 Or, "born from above"; see John 3:3–8, 1 Pet. 1:3, 23.

689 I am not proposing a Catholic fundamentalism, if such a thing could even exist. If the seven essentials bear resemblance to some of the "fundamentals" it is simply because they are the marks of traditional, historic, and apostolic Christianity. However, other aspects of fundamentalism, such as its separationism, are to be avoided.

690 Aquilina, Mike, and James L. Papandrea, *Seven Revolutions: How Christianity Changed the World, and Can Change it Again* (New York: Image/Random House, 2015), 218-221.

691 Pontifical Biblical Commission, *The Interpretation of the Bible in the Church* (1994), 4.A.1. Notice that, in spite of some Protestant claims to be more attentive to Scripture, a Catholic service will have fifteen minutes of Scripture readings before a ten-minute homily, while many of the so-called megachurches will have just a few minutes of Scripture before a forty-five minute sermon (which may be a very good Bible study, but it's still more *interpretation* than Scripture).

692 Wright, 23–24 (the emphasis is Wright's own).

693 See John 1:1–18.

694 *Dei Verbum* 2.

695 To accept Scripture alone and not Tradition is to leave the Church with no way to discern what parts of Scripture apply to our lives, and in what way. We do not follow the dietary laws of ancient Hebrew religion, and we do not even follow all of the rules proposed by the New Testament, such as requiring that women be veiled in Church. So how do we know which *biblical* mandates are a product of another time and culture and may be set aside, and which ones are timeless and universally normative for Christians? The answer is Tradition.

696 *The Interpretation of the Bible in the Church* (1994), 2.B.1. See also 2.A.2, where the document critiques the tendency among some biblical scholars to "demythologize," which is to say, "de-miracle-ize"

the scriptures.
697 *The Interpretation of the Bible in the Church* (1994), 2.B.1.
698 *The Interpretation of the Bible in the Church* (1994), 2.B.3, 4.A.2.
699 See Phil. 2:12, Jas. 2:14–16.
700 See Christopher R. Seitz, ed. *Nicene Christianity: The Future for a New Ecumenism* (Grand Rapids, MI: Brazos Press, 2001), 191.
701 See endnote 181.
702 Seitz, 201.
703 See John 17, Eph. 4:1–6. See Seitz, 193.
704 See Papandrea, James L., *Trinity 101: Father, Son, Holy Spirit* (Liguori, MO: Liguori Publications, 2012), 88-90.
705 See 1 Pet. 2:4–5, 9–10, cf. Exod. 19:5–6.
706 See Heb. 10:24–25. See also Second Vatican Council's Decree on the Apostolate of Lay People, *Apostolicam Actuositatem*.
707 See Luke 22:19, 1 Cor. 11:24.
708 See Phil. 2:12–13.
709 Papandrea, James L., *Spiritual Blueprint: How We Live, Work, Love, Play, and Pray* (Liguori, MO: Liguori Publications, 2010), 78-90.
710 Seitz, 11.
711 When one engages in dialogue with other denominations, one quickly realizes that often our greatest divisions are not along denominational lines—that is, they are not between Catholics and Protestants, but between traditional Catholics and evangelical Protestants on the one hand, and those who would reject the seven essentials above on the other. Whether we label this liberalism or progressivism, the non-traditional position usually presents itself as open-minded, forward thinking, and modern. In reality, it is relativistic, and usually universalist, in the sense that sin is reduced to injustice, the need for salvation is minimized, and the role of Christ is reduced to a good teacher and example.
712 *Unitatis Redintegratio* 4.
713 See Rom. 8:8–10.
714 See 2 Cor. 5:17–18.
715 See John 1:11–13.
716 See 1 Cor. 11:26. Cf. also John 15:4–7.